D0123173

Knudsen®

Cooking for Compliments

Introduction
Let's get acquainted 2
Taking Care of Dairy Foods
Preserve quality and taste 4
Breakfast & Brunch
Start the day right 7
Appetizers, Dips & Spreads
Elegant and delicious! 23
Snacks & Beverages
With protein for health 40
Salads
Depart from the usual 46
Special Touches For Familiar Foods
Foods gain new zest! 69
Sour Cream Main Dishes & Vegetables
Around-the-world flavors 76
Cottage Cheese Main Dishes & Vegetables
More protein—fewer calories! 96

Breads & Butters
Bake-up some happy memories 110
Cheesecakes & Cheese Pies
Build your cookery reputation 124
Cakes & Frostings
Back to basic goodness! 133
Pies & Pastries
Every recipe holds a surprise 145
More Desserts
Irresistible treats 158
Nutrition & Dairy Foods
Why milk is so important 178
How Dairy Foods Are Made
Things you need to know 179
Easy Ways To Measure Dairy Foods 181
Equipment For Cooking With Dairy Foods . . . 181
Conversion To Metric Measure 182
Index 183

Publisher and Distributor: H.P. Books, PO Box 5367, Tucson, AZ 85703 602/888-2150
Co-Publisher: Knudsen Corporation, PO Box 2335, Terminal Annex, Los Angeles, California 90051

TO ENSURE PERFECTION:

These recipes were developed and tested by the Home Economics Staff of Knudsen Corporation, Los Angeles, California. Knudsen is famous for dairy products of superb quality. Knudsen products are recommended because they work perfectly with these recipes. If you live in an area not served by Knudsen, use the finest dairy products available in your locality and you will enjoy complete success and delicious results from these recipes.

Publisher: Helen Fisher; Editor-in-Chief: Carl Shipman; Editors: Carlene Tejada, Judi Ellingson; Recipe Development: Barbara Lane; Book Design: Josh Young; Typography: Mary Kaye Fisher, Cindy Coatsworth, Frances Ruiz; Food Stylist: Mable Hoffman; Photography: George de Gennaro Studios.

ISBN: Softcover, 0-912656-91-3; Hardcover, 0-912656-92-1
Library of Congress Catalog Card Number: 77-88223 © 1977, Knudsen Corporation. Printed in U.S.A.

Cover photo: Traditional Cheesecake With Apricot-Peach Glaze, see page 129.

Introduction

What does a kitchen counter crowded with groceries mean to you? Many things, I'm sure. But most of all, a promise of things to come. You could look at a grocery-filled counter and see only hours of preparation and cleanup. If that's the case, TV dinners should do the job. If your heart is in cooking, you carefully search through the assortment of cans, boxes and cartons to get the very best value and quality. You brave crowded supermarket aisles to find a new item. Or you drive miles out of your way to a specialty store. To an outsider, that pile of groceries may be mundane. To you, it's the promise of compliments to come!—The promise of appreciation that makes your efforts in the kitchen worthwhile.

This book is for the cook who likes to go the extra measure. Here are recipes, quick and not-so-quick, but all with a special touch. Somewhere in each recipe there's a dab or cupful of sour cream, cottage cheese or another dairy food to add extra flavor, richness or nutrition. If you haven't discovered the excitement that dairy foods bring to cooking, don't wait. Try a recipe tonight! Special Touches For Familiar Foods is a whole chapter full of quick and easy ideas for using dairy foods every day.

The recipes you'll find in this book are detailed enough for the new cook and concise enough for the experienced one. Many of the recipes are beautifully basic and come with several variations. All the recipes have been tested and retested with dairy products from the Knudsen Corporation, Los Angeles, California. You'll find a treasury of information on the how's and why's of cooking with dairy foods so you can create your own dishes.

This book includes three informative chapters. One of them tells you how and why you should take care of dairy foods. There's a chapter explaining what good nutrition is and why milk and milk foods are so important. And another on how dairy foods are made—to help answer your questions about which product to buy or whether you can substitute one dairy product for another.

Yes, you can expect more from this book than a collection of reliable recipes. These pages are an invitation to a new world of cooking and eating experiences. This book will be your guide as you turn those bags of newly purchased groceries into well-deserved compliments.

Taking Care of Dairy Foods

Enjoy dairy foods when they are at their very best—FRESH! Basically there are only two rules to remember: keep dairy foods cold, and keep them covered.

KEEP DAIRY FOODS COLD

The last items to be picked up on your market trip should be dairy products and frozen foods. Put them in your own refrigerator or freezer as soon as possible. Car trunks can be very warm! Keep your refrigerator at a constant temperature between 35°F (2°C) and 40°F (4°C). The colder your refrigerator the longer your dairy products will stay in peak condition. Don't open the door unnecessarily or leave it open. Turn it to a colder setting in warm weather to compensate for the warmer outside air and more frequent door openings. Temperatures above 40°F (4°C) encourage the growth of yeasts and molds. Acid flavors may develop in the cultured products and fluid milks may develop off-flavors. Don't set the dial as low as 32°F (0°C) or dairy products could freeze.

Do not let milk products sit out of the refrigerator unnecessarily. Once these products have warmed to near room temperatures, the flavors may change permanently. For this reason, don't put milk products from a serving bowl or pitcher back into the original carton with the fresh product. It is unlikely that harmful organisms will grow in dairy products at refrigeration temperature. But if a product is contaminated from the outside and allowed to warm for a period of time—it could develop undesirable characteristics.

KEEP DAIRY FOODS COVERED

The original dairy product carton is designed to protect its contents. Open it only when you are using the product and keep it closed and refrigerated whenever it's not being used. Here's why.

Air carries yeast and mold spores that are looking for a nourishing place to multiply.

Dairy products eagerly absorb other flavors like cantaloupe, onion or whatever. This is another reason for not mixing the product from the table with the fresh product in the original carton.

Uncovered foods dry out—even in the refrigerator. Cover open dishes with plastic wrap.

Light changes the flavor of milk products and destroys the riboflavin (vitamin B_2).

Use only clean metal utensils when spooning from the carton. Wooden spoons are porous and very difficult to clean thoroughly.

WHEN IS DAIRY FOOD FRESH?

Appearance, aroma and flavor are the homemaker's tests for freshness. If a dairy product looks and smells normal, the next test is to taste it. Milk products that have been kept cold and covered are safe to taste. If they taste fresh, use them as you normally would. It is normal for a layer of moisture (whey) to collect on yogurt, sour cream and cottage cheese—especially if the product has warmed up or if some of it has been spooned from the carton. Just stir it up for normal consistency. If the surface of the sour cream, yogurt or cottage cheese is leveled, this moisture does not collect so readily.

Cultured products like yogurt, sour cream and buttermilk are especially resistant to spoilage because of the lactic acid content. Bacteria that ordinarily cause spoilage do not grow well in cultured products.

Yeasts and molds will grow on the cultured dairy products. It is extremely unlikely that they would be harmful, but they are unappetizing. Most people just spoon them off and if the product smells and tastes normal, they use it as they usually would. This applies to cream cheese, too.

HOW LONG ARE DAIRY PRODUCTS FRESH?

If dairy products are kept cold and covered—as described in the previous paragraphs—it is possible to predict an approximate time span of their freshness. Under these conditions, cottage cheese, fluid milks and creams will normally be fresh for a week to ten days beyond the code date stamped on the carton. Hoop cheese (you may know it as baker's cheese or pot cheese), because it's unsalted, is more fragile and should be consumed within a few days. It is not unusual for sour cream to be in

perfect condition for over two weeks. Yogurt and cream cheese may last even longer. Any of these products may remain fresh for a greater period of time than estimated here. The temperature of the refrigerator plays a most important role in freshness. The closer to 35°F (2°C) that your refrigerator maintains, the longer your dairy products will last. As the temperature of the refrigerator rises above 40°C (4°C) the life of your dairy products, as well as other foods, will be shortened.

FREEZING DAIRY FOODS

If you find that you have overbought for a party or are leaving town unexpectedly, freezing is a simple, safe and good means of preserving dairy products for a limited time. The nutritional values are not changed and the cultures are not harmed. Because of texture changes, we do not recommend buying large quantities specifically for freezing. In most cases, freezing causes dairy products to become grainy. Because of this, most frozen dairy products find their way into cooked dishes.

Cottage cheese or hoop cheese (baker's cheese or pot cheese) that has been frozen is actually easier to use in casseroles, egg dishes and baking than fresh products. Freezing breaks down the curd so that it is easily blended into other ingredients. Sour cream, buttermilk and plain yogurt should be used in baking. Thawed cream cheese is fine for casseroles and some baking (not cheese pie). The fluid milks and creams should be used in baking if they are very "flaky." Otherwise they can be used in puddings and sauces or for drinking if they show practically no texture change. Whipping cream can be frozen in the carton, thawed and used in baking. See Fabulous Biscuits, page 113. Or, it can be whipped, frozen in dollops on a foil-lined cookie sheet and bagged in plastic for freezer storage. Serve the frozen dollops on pudding or pie. Don't try to whip cream that has been frozen. It becomes very heavy and grainy. Fruit-blended yogurt usually shows very little change after it is thawed and vigorously stirred. Use it in recipes or eat it right from the carton. For the least texture change and the longest storage life, dairy products should be frozen as quickly as possible at temperatures below 0°F (−18°C). Above 0°F (−18°C), such as in ice cube sections within refrigerators, the food will freeze, but it will have a much less desirable texture after thawing. An overcrowded freezer slows freezing.

In most cases the dairy carton is a perfect freezer container. It is moisture- and vapor-proof. Seal opened milk or cream cartons with freezer tape and overwrap cream cheese, hoop cheese (baker's cheese or pot cheese) and butter with foil. If there's a lot of air space in the cottage cheese, sour cream or yogurt carton because the contents are partly used, press a layer of plastic wrap against the surface of the product and cover. Or transfer the product to a clean glass jar, leaving air space at the top for expansion in freezing.

It is not possible to give an exact time limit for freezer storage of dairy products. The condition of the product when it is frozen, how well it is wrapped and the temperature of the freezer all affect the product. Up to one-month storage has been very satisfactory for all products except hoop cheese (baker's cheese or pot cheese), which should be limited to one or two weeks. Longer storage does not change the safety of the various products, it only exaggerates the texture changes. Butter can be frozen for up to six months.

Frozen dairy products can be thawed in the refrigerator, at room temperature or in warm water. Speed in thawing, as in freezing, helps minimize texture changes. Because the water, protein and fat portions freeze and thaw at different rates, it is important to thaw the fluid milks and creams completely before using any part of them. Vigorously shake or stir any of the dairy products after thawing and plan to use them soon.

STORING ICE CREAM AND SHERBETS

The ice cream you buy should be frozen solid and not softened. Ice cream that has thawed and been refrozen in market or home freezers has an icy texture.

Ice cream, ice milk and sherbets should be stored at 0°F (−18°C) or below. Like other fresh dairy products, for best texture and flavor they should be eaten fresh. For frozen desserts, that means within 3 to 4 weeks.

Freezers tend to draw moisture from foods. In long storage, ice creams may shrink and become sticky. For this reason you may want to overwrap ice cream packages in foil or freezer wrap, or place them in a plastic container for protection. For the same reason, if the package is only partially full, press a piece of plastic wrap against the surface of the sherbet or ice cream to retard dehydration or the formation of ice crystals.

Breakfast & Brunch

Few dishes smell as good or taste as good as those served at breakfast. No other meal is as simple to prepare or so basically low in calories.

All considered, breakfast-brunch entertaining is an ideal way to develop a quick reputation as a superb host or hostess. It takes a minimum of tableware, time and talent. Practice on your family and graduate to entertaining friends. A leisurely breakfast or brunch is a great way to start any day.

The difference between a weekday breakfast and a weekend brunch may be only the linens, the dinnerware, the garnishes and the hour. Brunch is served mid-morning. The basic menu is the same.

Fruit or Juice
A Breakfast Meat
An Egg Dish
Cereal—Pancakes—Coffeecake
Milk—Hot Chocolate—Coffee—Tea

Brunch menus would tend to be more fancy and might include creamed dishes, soufflés and perhaps potatoes or other mild-flavored hot vegetables.

These breakfast and brunch recipes need not be reserved just for the hours before noon. Midnight breakfasts and Sunday-supper breakfasts are great, too.

EGGS

Eggs and breakfast are almost synonymous. Although there are endless ways to prepare them, it's easy to get into a rut. When you have time to enjoy a leisurely breakfast, it's fun to vary the usual scrambled, fried, poached or soft-cooked eggs. Cottage cheese, cream cheese and sour cream are delicious companions for eggs. For special brunches or suppers try Cottage Cheese Soufflé, page 15, Cottage Quiche, page 11, or Hampshire Creamed Eggs, page 10.

SOUFFLÉS

Soufflés are not as difficult as you may think. A soufflé is simply a baked mixture of beaten egg whites and thick white sauce.

Because of their reputation, you can establish yourself as a *chef extraordinaire* by preparing one successfully. A few props are helpful: Most important—a straight-sided soufflé pot. The six-cup size is the most useful and can double for the popular molded dessert soufflés such as Lemon Cheese Soufflé, page 166. A large copper bowl and a balloon wire whip for beating egg whites will absolutely confirm your expertise.

The most important step for a soufflé is the serving. It must be served popping out of its casserole *as soon as it is baked.* Take it to the table, pierce it quickly and confidently with a big spoon and dish out a generous serving for each guest. Serve a cheese sauce or mushroom sauce over the soufflé or a creamed vegetable beside it. Fresh fruit is the ideal appetizer or dessert.

THE QUICHE

A quiche (pronounced *keesh*) is a savory, rather than sweet, custard pie. This is a great way to show off your pastry- or custard-baking ability.

Although the original quiche, which is supposed to have originated in the Lorraine province of France, was merely a cream-and-egg custard seasoned with salt and baked in a crust, the surrounding provinces have adapted it to their own tastes. We have taken the same liberty.

The one trick to baking a quiche is to remove it from the oven at exactly the right moment. An egg custard is done when a knife inserted in the center comes out clean. A milky residue indicates underbaking; a watery residue indicates overbaking.

Cottage Scrambled Eggs

These eggs look and taste better than plain scrambled eggs—fewer calories per serving, too.

3 eggs
1/4 cup cottage cheese

Salt and pepper to taste
Butter

Put eggs, cottage cheese, salt and pepper into blender jar; blend until smooth. Or, beat cottage cheese in mixing bowl to mash. Add eggs, salt and pepper; beat until well-blended. In a small fry pan, melt enough butter to coat bottom and sides. Heat gently until bubbly. Pour eggs into fry pan Without stirring, gently push cooked portion to center, continuing until eggs are fully cooked but not dry. Serve immediately. Makes 2 servings.

Variation

Iceberg Eggs: Fold about 1/3 cup finely shredded iceberg lettuce into eggs as they finish cooking. Serve topped with crumbled crisp bacon.

Creamy Scrambled Eggs

Delicious! For a special occasion.

1 (3-oz.) pkg. cream cheese
6 eggs
1/2 teaspoon seasoned salt

1 tablespoon fresh or frozen chives,
   if desired
2 tablespoons butter

Dice cream cheese with a piece of strong thread. Hold one end of thread tightly in each hand and slice through the cheese, first vertically, then horizontally. Beat eggs with seasoned salt and chives, if desired. Heat butter over low heat in large fry pan until bubbly. Add egg mixture and diced cream cheese. Cook over low heat, stirring occasionally, until cheese melts slightly and eggs are cooked. Serve immediately. Makes 3 or 4 servings.

Variation

Eggs Marvelous: Omit chives. Add 1/3 cup whipping cream or 1/4 cup dairy sour cream to beaten eggs. Sauté 1 tablespoon minced green onion in butter. Add 1 to 2 teaspoons minced green pepper, if desired. Proceed as above.

To make delicious scrambled eggs, add a rounded tablespoon of dairy sour cream to 2 eggs. Mix well and scramble as usual.

French Omelet For One

Don't expect your first omelet to be beautiful. But once you've mastered the technique, your omelets will look as good as they taste.

2 tablespoons omelet filling,
  see below
2 eggs
1 tablespoon water

1 to 2 tablespoons butter
Dairy sour cream
Salt to taste

Prepare selected omelet filling from below and set aside. Heat 7- or 8-inch fry pan or omelet pan over medium-high heat. Mix eggs and water lightly with fork. Add butter to hot fry pan—tilt pan to coat sides and bottom. When butter is bubbly but not browned, add eggs all at once. Shake pan and quickly stir eggs with fork, keeping tines flat against bottom of pan, until eggs are about half cooked. Let pan rest over heat a moment to cook the bottom. Quickly spread or sprinkle no more than 2 tablespoons filling over the eggs on the front half of pan. Lift and fold remaining half of eggs over filling, shaping omelet to a semicircle. Work quickly. A French omelet is served slightly under-cooked. It can be fully cooked over lower heat, if desired. Loosen omelet with spatula and turn on-to warmed plate by inverting fry pan over plate. Rub a little butter over omelet to glaze, if desired. Top with generous dollop of sour cream. Serve with salt to taste. Makes 1 serving.

Omelet Fillings

Fresh Fruit: Sugared fresh peach slices, orange sections, blueberries, raspberries or halved straw-berries.
Cottage: Plain, chive or pineapple cottage cheese.
Smoked Salmon: Chive cottage cheese and diced smoked salmon.
Roquefort: Cottage cheese and crumbled Roquefort or blue cheese.
A la Russe: Diced leftover baked, hashed brown or boiled potatoes and cottage cheese. Garnish with green onion.
Chili: Canned chili con carne and chopped green onions.
Cheese: Grated Cheddar or Swiss cheese.
Fines Herbes: Minced parsley, chives and tarragon.
Cold Cut: Cottage cheese and diced ham, wiener or luncheon meat.
Florentine: Creamed spinach.
Caviar: Cottage cheese and red or black caviar.
Taco: Chopped tomato, grated cheese, shredded lettuce and hot sauce.
Avocado: Cottage cheese, diced avocado and crumbled bacon.
Green Chili: Cottage cheese and chopped green chilies.
Mock Blintz: Cottage cheese. Garnish omelet with powdered sugar; top with fruit preserves.

Use a seasoned pan—one that is never detergent washed—to prevent omelets from sticking. Using Clarified Butter, page 111, helps, too.

Hampshire Creamed Eggs

Creamed eggs never tasted so good.

1 recipe Basic Sour Cream Sauce,
   page 72
1/4 teaspoon salt
6 to 8 hard-cooked eggs,
   peeled and sliced

Hot buttered toast, biscuits or
   Buttermilk Corn Bread,
   page 115

Prepare Basic Sour Cream Sauce, page 72. Fold in salt and most of the eggs; reserve a few egg slices for garnish. Spoon mixture onto hot buttered toast, biscuits or Buttermilk Corn Bread, page 115. Garnish with reserved egg or sieved hard-cooked egg yolk. For a special treat, serve shortcake-style over split layers of Buttermilk Corn Bread. Makes 4 to 6 servings.

Variations

Asparagus & Egg Luncheon Dish: Arrange hot asparagus spears on toast. Top with Hampshire Creamed Eggs. Garnish with paprika.

Hampshire Creamed Chipped Beef: Omit 1/4 teaspoon salt and eggs. Loosen contents of 1 (5-oz.) jar dried chipped beef and put in large strainer. Pour about 2 quarts boiling water over beef to blanch. Drain, shred and fold into sauce. Fresh chipped beef does not need blanching.

Hampshire Creamed Ham: Omit 1/4 teaspoon salt. Substitute 1 cup diced ham for all or part of the eggs.

Hampshire Creamed Tuna: Omit eggs. Drain and flake 2 (6-1/2-oz.) cans white tuna. Fold into sauce. Add instant minced onion, chopped pimiento and cooked peas, if desired. Salmon is excellent, too.

Chicken à la King: Omit eggs. Fold in 1 to 2 cups cubed, skinned and boned, cooked chicken, 2 tablespoons minced pimiento and 1/2 cup cooked peas.

Slice and fry leftover baked potatoes, top with dairy sour cream and serve beside ham and eggs.

Cottage Quiche

Our version of Quiche Lorraine with delicious variations.

1 unbaked Standard Pastry Crust,
  page 157
8 strips bacon, fried crisp and crumbled
1/2 cup grated Cheddar cheese
3 eggs
1 cup half-and-half

1 cup (1/2 pint) cottage cheese
1 tablespoon flour
1/2 teaspoon dill weed
1/2 teaspoon dry mustard
1/4 teaspoon salt
2 tablespoons Parmesan cheese

Preheat oven to 425°F (218°C). Prebake pastry crust for 10 minutes or until edges are lightly browned. Remove pastry and lower oven heat to 350°F (177°C). Spread bacon and Cheddar cheese over bottom of pastry crust. Put remaining ingredients except Parmesan cheese into blender jar and blend on low speed until smooth. Or, beat cottage cheese in mixing bowl to mash, add remaining ingredients except Parmesan cheese and beat until well-blended. Pour over bacon and cheese. Sprinkle with Parmesan cheese. Bake 35 to 45 minutes or until a knife inserted just off-center comes out clean. Serve immediately. Leftovers can be reheated later. Makes 6 servings.

Variations

Ham Cottage Quiche: Substitute 4 ounces julienned boiled or baked ham for the bacon.
Beef Cottage Quiche: Substitute 2 to 2-1/2 ounces shredded, blanched dried beef for the bacon.
Sausage Cottage Quiche: Substitute 5 cooked and sliced smoked link sausages for the bacon.
Tuna Cottage Quiche: Substitute 1 (2-3/4-oz.) can white tuna, drained and flaked, for the bacon.

Ham & Egg Casserole

An easy meal-in-a-dish breakfast with "planned-over" ham and boiled potatoes.

1 to 2 medium potatoes, cooked,
  peeled and thinly sliced
4 hard-cooked eggs,
  peeled and sliced
1 cup diced cooked ham

Salt and pepper to taste
1 egg
1 cup (1/2 pint) dairy sour cream
1/4 cup Buttered Breadcrumbs,
  page 120

Preheat oven to 350°F (177°C). Generously butter a 1-1/2-quart shallow baking dish. Layer potatoes, sliced eggs and ham in baking dish; season with salt and pepper. Bake 10 minutes. Beat egg in a medium bowl. Blend in sour cream. Pour over potatoes, sliced eggs and ham. Sprinkle with Buttered Breadcrumbs, page 120. Return to oven and bake 5 minutes or until heated through. Serve immediately. Makes 4 servings.

Buttermilk Pancakes

So light and tender, they melt in your mouth. Refrigerate or freeze leftover batter in an airtight container for another day.

1 cup sifted flour
1 tablespoon sugar
1/2 teaspoon salt
1/2 teaspoon baking soda

1 egg
1 cup buttermilk, more if desired
2 tablespoons butter, melted

Preheat a lightly oiled griddle or fry pan. Sift and measure flour; sift again with sugar, salt and baking soda. Beat egg in medium bowl. Blend in buttermilk. Add dry ingredients, beating until smooth; blend in melted butter. Add up to 1/4 cup more buttermilk for thinner cakes. Cook on lightly oiled griddle or fry pan. Turn pancakes when surface bubbles begin to break. Serve immediately. Makes 14 to 16 three-inch pancakes.

Variations

Blueberry Buttermilk Pancakes: Stir in 2/3 cup well-drained canned blueberries or 1 cup fresh or thawed frozen blueberries just before cooking. Serve with syrup, sweetened whipped cream or sour cream and additional blueberries.
Apple Buttermilk Pancakes: Fold 1 cup chopped apple into batter.
Strawberry Buttermilk Pancakes: Fold 1 cup thinly sliced berries into batter.
Pineapple Buttermilk Pancakes: Fold 1 (8-3/4-oz.) can well-drained crushed pineapple into batter.
Peanut Butter Pancakes: Blend 1/3 cup creamy-style peanut butter into batter.

Family Pancakes

They'll never know you used a mix to make these light moist pancakes.

2 eggs
1 cup (1/2 pint) dairy sour cream
2 cups milk

2-1/3 cups biscuit mix
2 tablespoons butter, melted

Preheat a lightly oiled griddle or fry pan. Beat eggs in a large bowl. Blend in sour cream. Stir in milk. Mix well. Add biscuit mix and beat until smooth. Stir in melted butter. Cook on lightly oiled griddle or fry pan. Turn pancakes when surface bubbles begin to break. Makes about 20 four-inch pancakes.

Buttermilk Pancakes with Peaches and Whipped Sour Cream Topping

Cottage Cheese Pancakes

Dieters can enjoy these with a clear conscience.

2 tablespoons butter, melted
4 eggs, separated
1 cup (1/2 pint) cottage cheese
1/2 cup sifted flour

1/4 teaspoon salt
Lowfat fruit yogurt or other
  low-calorie topping

Preheat a lightly oiled griddle or fry pan. Put all ingredients except egg whites and yogurt or topping in blender jar and blend on low speed until cottage cheese is smooth. Or, beat cottage cheese in mixing bowl to mash; add remaining ingredients except egg whites and yogurt or topping, and beat until thoroughly blended. Whip egg whites until stiff but not dry. Fold into cheese mixture. Drop by tablespoons onto lightly oiled griddle or fry pan. Shape into circles with back of spoon. Turn when underside is lightly browned. Serve with lowfat fruit yogurt or other low-calorie topping. Makes 16 to 20 three-inch pancakes.

Delightful Yogurt Pancakes

Yogurt gives marvelous flavor and texture. Refrigerate leftover batter for the next morning.

1 cup sifted flour
1 tablespoon sugar
3/4 teaspoon baking soda
1/2 teaspoon salt

4 eggs
1 (8-oz.) carton plain yogurt
1/4 cup water

Preheat lightly oiled griddle or fry pan. Sift and measure flour; sift again with sugar, baking soda and salt. In medium bowl, beat eggs until light and lemon colored. Blend in yogurt and water. Add dry ingredients and beat until well-blended. Cook small pancakes on lightly oiled griddle or fry pan. Turn when underside is lightly browned. Makes 24 three-inch pancakes.

Top ready-to-eat cereal with fruit-flavored yogurt. You won't need cream or sugar.

Cottage Cheese Soufflé

Delicious for any meal and full of protein, too.

1/4 cup (1/2 stick) butter
1/3 cup flour
1/2 cup milk or
   1/2 cup chicken broth
1 cup (1/2 pint) cottage cheese
1/4 teaspoon paprika
1/2 teaspoon dry mustard

1/2 teaspoon Worcestershire sauce
3 dashes Tabasco® sauce
6 eggs, separated
1 teaspoon salt
1/2 teaspoon cream of tartar,
   for better volume, if desired

Butter sides and bottom of a 1-1/2-quart soufflé dish or round casserole. Set aside. Prepare water bath by placing a large shallow pan of water in center of oven; preheat oven to 325°F (163°C). Water should be deep enough to come halfway up outside of soufflé dish or casserole. Melt butter in stainless steel or enamel saucepan. Stir in flour. Cook until mixture froths but does not brown. Stir in milk or broth, cottage cheese, paprika, dry mustard, Worcestershire sauce and Tabasco® sauce; mix well. Heat, stirring constantly, until cheese curd melts and sauce thickens. Whip egg whites with salt and cream of tartar, if desired, just until whites form short, distinct, moist-looking peaks. Overbeaten whites cause the soufflé to shrink. Beat egg yolks slightly in a large bowl. Slowly add hot cottage cheese sauce, stirring constantly. Fold 1/3 of the whites thoroughly into sauce. Gently fold in remaining whites. Pour into buttered soufflé dish or casserole. Run spatula through soufflé about 1-inch in from edge to assure well-formed "top hat." Place in hot water bath and bake 50 to 60 minutes, or until knife inserted in center comes out clean. Serve immediately. Makes 4 dinner servings or 6 brunch servings.

Variations

Cheese-Plus Soufflé: For a more pronounced cheese flavor, add 1/4 cup grated Parmesan cheese or 1/2 cup grated sharp Cheddar cheese with cottage cheese.

Crusty Cottage Cheese Soufflé: For a delicious crisp crust, sprinkle 2 tablespoons grated cheese over soufflé 10 minutes before end of baking time.

Meaty Cottage Cheese Soufflé: Fold into the cheese-yolk mixture any of the following: 1 cup diced cooked turkey or chicken; 1 (6-1/2-oz.) can tuna, well-drained and flaked; 1 cup well-drained chopped, cooked broccoli or asparagus; 1 (12-oz.) can well-drained whole kernel corn or Mexican-style corn.

Cottage Cheese Soufflé à la Mer: Fold into the cheese-yolk mixture, 1 (6-1/2-oz.) can crab meat, well-drained and flaked.

One-fourth cup of cottage cheese gives as much protein as 1 egg. And fewer calories!

Cheese Blintzes

Blintzes are related to crepes. Fruit jam and sour cream are essential toppings for cheese blintzes.

2 eggs
1 cup water
1/2 teaspoon salt
1 cup sifted flour
Cheese Filling, see below

1 tablespoon butter
Powdered sugar, if desired
Dairy sour cream
Jam or preserves

Cheese Filling:
2 cups (1 pint) cottage cheese or
   2 (8-oz.) pkgs. hoop or
   pot cheese plus 1/4 teaspoon salt

2 eggs
2 teaspoons vanilla
2 teaspoons sugar

Beat eggs in a medium bowl. Blend in water, salt and flour; beat until smooth. Or, combine all ingredients in blender jar; blend until smooth. Batter should be very thin. Refrigerate about 1 hour. Prepare Cheese Filling; set aside. Heat a lightly buttered, 6- to 8-inch fry pan over medium heat. Pour about 3 tablespoons batter into hot fry pan. Quickly swirl batter to form a very thin pancake covering bottom of pan. Return to heat. When bottom is browned and top is set, turn out onto cooling rack. Cook 1 side only. Spread about 2 tablespoons filling on center of browned side. Fold sides in and roll jelly-roll fashion. Melt butter in a large fry pan over medium-low heat. Place filled blintzes, seam-side down, in fry pan. Brown on both sides. Sift powdered sugar over blintzes, if desired. Serve with sour cream and jam or preserves. Makes 12 blintzes or 6 servings.

Cheese Filling:
Combine ingredients and blend thoroughly. Set aside until ready to cook blintzes.

Buttermilk Waffles

This batter is even better the next day.

2 cups sifted flour
2 teaspoons baking powder
3/4 teaspoon baking soda
1/2 teaspoon salt
1 tablespoon sugar

3 eggs
1-1/2 cups buttermilk
1/2 cup (1 stick) butter, melted, or
   1/2 cup cooking oil

Preheat waffle baker. Sift and measure flour; sift again with baking powder, baking soda, salt and sugar. In a large bowl, beat eggs until light and lemon colored. Mix in buttermilk. Add dry ingredients and blend well. Blend in melted butter or oil. Bake according to waffle baker instructions. Makes 8 six-inch square waffles.

Variation

Fluffy Buttermilk Waffles: Reduce butter to 1/4 cup (1/2 stick). Separate eggs. Whip whites until stiff but not dry. Beat yolks and add to dry ingredients with buttermilk. Fold whites into finished batter before baking.

Sour Cream Waffles

These are the most tender waffles in the world.

1-1/2 cups sifted flour
1 teaspoon sugar
3/4 teaspoon baking soda
1/2 teaspoon baking powder

1/2 teaspoon salt
3 eggs
2 cups (1 pint) dairy sour cream
1/4 cup (1/2 stick) butter, melted

Preheat waffle baker. Sift and measure flour; sift again with sugar, baking soda, baking powder and salt. In a large bowl, beat eggs until light and lemon colored. Blend in sour cream. Add dry ingredients and blend well. Blend in melted butter. Bake according to waffle baker instructions. Makes 6 six-inch square waffles.

Layered Buttermilk Crumb Cake

Don't think you have to eat it all at once! This cake stays fresh for several days if well-wrapped—or you can freeze it.

2-1/2 cups sifted flour
1-1/2 cups light-brown sugar,
  firmly packed
1/2 cup granulated sugar
1/2 teaspoon salt
1/2 teaspoon cinnamon
3/4 cup (1-1/2 sticks) butter,
  room temperature

1 cup chopped nuts
1/2 teaspoon cinnamon
1/4 teaspoon nutmeg
2 tablespoons granulated sugar
1 teaspoon baking soda
1 egg
1 cup buttermilk

Preheat oven to 350°F (177°C). Butter and flour a 13" x 9" x 2" baking dish. Sift and measure flour. In a large electric-mixer bowl combine flour, brown sugar, 1/2 cup granulated sugar, salt and 1/2 teaspoon cinnamon. With mixer on low speed, cut in soft butter until mixture is uniform and crumbly. Remove 1-1/2 cups crumb mixture and mix with nuts. Combine 1/4 cup crumb-nut mixture with 1/2 teaspoon cinnamon, nutmeg and 2 tablespoons sugar to make topping; set aside. Press remaining crumb-nut mixture onto bottom of baking dish. To remaining crumbs in mixer bowl, add baking soda, egg and buttermilk. Beat at medium speed for 1/2 minute. Pour batter over crumb layer in baking dish. Sprinkle with reserved crumb topping. Bake 40 to 45 minutes. Serve warm or cooled. Makes 15 to 20 servings.

Sour Cream Coffeecake Sublime

An elegant coffeecake, worth baking for the aroma alone.

Cinnamon-Nut Topping, see below
2-1/4 cups sifted flour
2 teaspoons baking powder
1/2 teaspoon baking soda
1/2 teaspoon salt
3/4 cup (1-1/2 sticks) butter,
   room temperature

1-1/2 cups sugar
2 eggs
1 teaspoon vanilla
1 cup (1/2 pint) dairy sour cream,
   room temperature

Cinnamon-Nut Topping:
1/2 cup chopped nuts
1 teaspoon cinnamon

2 tablespoons sugar

Preheat oven to 350°F (177°C). If using a glass baking dish, preheat oven to 325°F (163°C). Butter and flour a 9-inch tube pan or a 13" x 9" x 2" baking dish. Set aside. Prepare Cinnamon-Nut Topping. Set aside. Sift and measure flour; sift again with baking powder, soda and salt. Cream butter with sugar. Add eggs and vanilla, beating until light and fluffy. Add flour mixture in three portions alternating with sour cream, beating well after each addition. Spread half of batter in pan. Sprinkle with half of Cinnamon-Nut Topping. Spoon on remaining batter and sprinkle with remaining topping. Bake cake in tube pan 45 to 50 minutes. Bake oblong cake 40 minutes. Cake begins to pull away from sides of pan when done. Cool 20 minutes before removing from pan. Serve warm or cooled. Makes 12 to 16 servings.

Cinnamon-Nut Topping:
Mix all ingredients together and set aside until ready to use.

Variations

Fruit-Filled Sour Cream Coffeecake: Place fruit on top of first layer of batter; sprinkle with half the topping. Proceed as in basic recipe. Suggested fruits: 2/3 cup diced dried apricots, peaches, or dates; 1 cup well-drained canned apricots, peaches, pineapple tidbits or blueberries; 1 peeled, cored, thinly sliced, raw baking apple.

Lemon Sour Cream Coffeecake: Add 1 tablespoon each fresh lemon juice and grated lemon peel to finished batter. Swirl topping through batter with fork instead of layering. Bake as above.

Apple-Cream Custard Coffeecake

Makes a delicious dessert, too.

1-1/2 cups sifted flour
2/3 cup sugar
2 teaspoons baking powder
1/2 teaspoon salt
1 teaspoon cinnamon
1/8 teaspoon allspice
1/2 cup milk

1/4 cup (1/2 stick) butter,
   room temperature
1 egg
1 cup diced, pared tart apple
Sour Cream Topping, see below
1/3 cup sugar
1/2 cup finely chopped walnuts

Sour Cream Topping:
2 eggs
3/4 cup dairy sour cream

Preheat oven to 375°F (191°C). Butter an 11" x 7" x 2" baking dish. Sift and measure flour; sift again with 2/3 cup sugar, baking powder, salt, cinnamon and allspice into large bowl. Add milk, butter and egg. Beat until smooth. Fold in apple. Pour into baking dish. Prepare Sour Cream Topping. Spread evenly over cake batter; sprinkle with 1/3 cup sugar and nuts. Bake 30 minutes. Serve warm. Makes 8 servings.

Sour Cream Topping:
In a small bowl, beat eggs. Blend in sour cream.

Quick Cheese Danish

Something for a beginner—or anyone who feels like a quick treat.

1 cup (1/2 pint) cottage cheese
1 (3-oz.) pkg. cream cheese
1 egg yolk
3 tablespoons sugar
1/2 teaspoon vanilla

1/2 teaspoon grated orange peel
2 pkgs. refrigerated biscuits
   (20 biscuits)
Orange marmalade or other jam
Sifted powdered sugar

Preheat oven to 400°F (204°C). Butter cookie sheets. Beat cottage cheese and cream cheese in a medium bowl until cheese curd is partially broken. Blend in egg yolk, sugar, vanilla and orange peel. Refrigerate. On a lightly floured board, using a rolling pin or your hands, flatten each of the biscuits into a 3-inch circle. Put 1 tablespoon cheese mixture in center of each circle. Form rim around dough by moistening edge and pinching together at 3 or 4 points. Bake on buttered cookie sheets 15 minutes, or until lightly browned. Remove to cooling racks. Spoon orange marmalade onto each Cheese Danish. Garnish with sifted powdered sugar. Makes 20 pastries.

Fabulous Buttermilk Donuts

Donuts take some practice. Once you've perfected the process, no one will let you forget it.

1 egg
2 egg yolks, if desired
1 cup sugar
1 cup buttermilk
1 tablespoon butter, melted
1 teaspoon vanilla
3-1/2 cups sifted flour

2-1/2 teaspoons baking powder
1/2 teaspoon baking soda
1/2 teaspoon salt
1/2 teaspoon ginger
1 teaspoon nutmeg
1 to 2 qts. cooking oil
Sifted powdered sugar, if desired

In a medium bowl, beat egg and egg yolks, if desired, until light and foamy. The 2 egg yolks make an even lighter, more tender donut with almost no fat absorption. Beat in sugar. Blend in buttermilk, melted butter and vanilla. Sift and measure flour. Sift again with baking powder, baking soda, salt, ginger and nutmeg into buttermilk mixture. Mix with electric mixer on low speed just until combined—dough will be quite soft. Turn onto a well-floured board. Dust fingers generously with flour. Gently pat dough to 3/8-inch thickness. Cut donuts with floured cutter. If time allows, let cut donuts stand uncovered for 30 minutes before frying. This reduces fat absorption. Preheat cooking oil to 370°F to 375°F (187°C to 191°C). Cooking oil should be maintained at least 1-inch deep throughout cooking. Slide donuts into preheated oil with slotted pancake turner. Fry only a few donuts at one time. Make sure oil is hot before beginning each batch. Add oil as necessary. Turn as soon as they float to the surface. Turn again when one side is medium golden brown. Remove when both sides are equally browned. Drain on absorbent paper. When cool, sprinkle with sifted powdered sugar, if desired. Makes about 2-1/2 dozen donuts, using a 2-3/4-inch donut cutter.

Spread apple butter and cottage cheese over your morning toast. It's an old Pennsylvania Dutch treat.

Old-Fashioned Cinnamon Rolls

Good and gooey!

1 recipe Yeast Crescent dough,
  page 117
1/2 cup (1 stick) butter, melted
1 cup dark corn syrup

1/2 cup light-brown sugar,
  firmly packed
2/3 cup finely chopped pecans

Butter-Cinnamon Filling:
1/2 cup (1 stick) butter, melted
1 cup light-brown sugar,
  firmly packed

1 tablespoon cinnamon
1/3 to 1/2 cup raisins, if desired

Prepare Yeast Crescent dough, page 117. Refrigerate dough for 3 hours. Blend melted butter, corn syrup, brown sugar and pecans together. Spread in 2 nine-inch round or eight-inch square cake pans. Prepare Butter-Cinnamon Filling; set aside. On lightly floured board, roll half of dough to a 12" x 18" rectangle. Spread evenly with half of Butter-Cinnamon Filling. Roll, jelly-roll fashion, beginning with narrow end. Repeat with remaining half of dough and filling. Cut each roll into 12 slices and arrange slices in pans on top of corn syrup mixture. Place in a warm place. Let rise until doubled in size. Preheat oven to 350°F (177°C). Bake 25 to 30 minutes or until golden brown. Invert onto serving plate and serve warm. Makes 24 cinnamon rolls.

Butter-Cinnamon Filling:
Blend all filling ingredients together.

Top breakfast strawberries with a dollop of plain dairy sour cream or Whipped Sour Cream Topping, page 158, and a sprinkling of brown sugar.

Appetizers, Dips & Spreads

Give a do-it-yourself "catered" party! Almost all of the ideas presented here let you do most of the preparation days or weeks ahead of the big event.

Your appetizers should have a variety in flavors. The basic appetizer flavors are seafood, cheese, meats, poultry, eggs, fresh vegetables and fruits, onion or garlic and other herbs and spices. The soft textures and compatible flavors of sour cream and cream cheese allow stronger appetizer flavors to complement instead of clash.

The texture of the foods you select should vary. Some should be crunchy, some chewy, some soft. Serve some hot foods and some cold. Vary the shapes and sizes. Serve large things, small things, chunks, cubes, triangles, balls, crescents and sticks. Color is important. Choose red and green foods. Contrast dark and light foods.

It's possible for just three appetizers to include nearly all the forms of variety mentioned. Here is one party plan.

Hurry-Curry Appetizer Meatballs, page 26
Nutty Blue Cheese Spread in Cucumber Wedges, page 37
Crab & Water Chestnut Dip, page 34
Wheat Crackers and Potato Chips

HOT APPETIZERS

Here are several great recipes to serve from a warming tray or right out of the oven on a silver tray: Serve hot chunks of broiled ham or bologna with a dip of Mustard Sauce, page 73. Barbecue miniature kabobs of boned, skinned chicken marinated in a sweet oil-and-vinegar dressing. Serve with Orange Sauce, page 73. Try chunks of barbecued or deep-fried beef with Roquefort Dip, page 33, or Horseradish Sauce, page 74. Tiny cubes of Cottage Quiche, page 11, make very elegant hors d'oeuvres. The quiche can be made ahead and will hold up beautifully on a warming tray. Cubes of Herbed Tomato-Cheese Bread, page 118, served from a warming tray, are delicious topped with a pepperoni slice. Like little bites of pizza! Try tiny

Fabulous Biscuits, page 113, with thin-sliced ham or rare beef for hearty appetizer sandwiches.

COLD APPETIZERS

For a very special occasion, surround a Coeur à la Crème mold, page 167, with black or gray caviar and top with tiny slivers of lemon with peel intact. Serve with melba toast. This is perfect with champagne.

To make Beefy Cheese Balls, cut a 3-ounce package of cream cheese into 12 cubes. Flatten each cube in your fingers and shape around a cocktail onion or stuffed green olive. Roll in finely shredded dried chipped beef. Serve on toothpicks.

Try Dill Cheese Balls. Mix cream cheese and a little finely minced dill pickle. Roll into small balls and coat with a mixture of chopped hard-cooked egg and parsley.

If you're confused by some terms relating to appetizers, here are some helpful definitions:

Antipasto—Literally, from the Italian, "before the meal." An appetizer of spicy foods served as a first course at the table. Like the French "hors d'oeuvre."

Appetizer—A small portion of tasty food or drink served before or as the first course of a meal. Appetizers should not be too filling because they are meant to stimulate the appetite. This general term includes the Slavic "zakooska," the Italian "antipasto" and the French "hors d'oeuvre."

Canapé—From the French word meaning "couch." Small crackers or fresh, toasted or fried shapes of crustless bread, spread with spicy bits of meat, fish or cheese. They may be served hot or cold.

Hors d'oeuvre—Literally, from the French, "outside the main work." Hot or cold appetizers served at the table before the main part of the meal. Unlike canapés they are not served on a bread or cracker base.

Pâte—A pastry case filled with meat, fish, vegetables or fruit.

Zakooska or Zakuska—A wide selection of simple, spicy, appetizer tidbits served at a zakooska hour, which is the Russian equivalent of the American cocktail hour.

SOUR CREAM DIPS

Most dips improve if they are made and refrigerated a few hours before serving. This time allows the flavors to develop and blend. However, dry herb flavors may become too strong with long storage. Add more sour cream and a little more salt to correct this. Flavors like horseradish, lemon juice, sherry and other liquors become weaker. Add more of these ingredients as needed before serving. Most dips keep very well. A few exceptions would include such dips as avocado and seafood combinations.

Try dips made with sour cream and dry seasoning or sauce mixes. To 2 cups (1 pint) dairy sour cream, add one of these: taco seasoning mix, Sloppy Joe seasoning mix, Spanish rice seasoning mix, beef stew seasoning mix, spaghetti sauce mix, or chili seasoning mix.

You don't have to serve only chips and crackers with dips. Vegetable dippers are colorful, appetizing and delicious. Try some of these with the dip you serve tonight: cauliflower flowerets, celery fans or sticks, carrot slices or sticks, whole mushrooms, ripe olives, radishes, cherry tomatoes, cucumber slices, green onions, green pepper, broccoli flowerets, turnip or kohlrabi slices, or zucchini squash. Your calorie-counting guests will love you!

TEA SANDWICHES AND CANAPÉS TO FREEZE

Many tea sandwiches and canapés can be made in advance and frozen. Tiny sandwiches spread with butter or cream cheese spreads will freeze well for up to a month. Other items to complete them must be well-chosen for freezing or added closer to serving time.

Spread softened cream cheese or soft—not melted—butter over each bread shape to prevent fillings from soaking into the bread. Do not use mayonnaise as a spread because it will separate in freezing and make the bread soggy.

Soften cream cheese at room temperature and mix a little half-and-half with it. Blend in flavorings if desired, and top with freezable items to garnish. A few of the foods that freeze very well and can be used in the cream cheese spread or to garnish are:

Ham, ground or thinly sliced

Beef, cooked and ground or thinly sliced

Chicken or turkey, cooked and ground or thinly sliced

Cheddar cheese, grated or sliced

Egg yolks, hard-cooked (not the whites!)

Peanut butter

Pieces of crab, lobster or shrimp

Arrange the tea sandwiches on a foil-lined cookie sheet and freeze. When they are frozen solid, place them in airtight containers or wrap in heavy foil. Separate layers with plastic wrap or foil.

Allow 30 minutes to thaw tiny canapés or tea sandwiches. Add fragile or nonfreezable items and serve.

QUICK CANAPÉS

Canapés are a delicious and elegant way to stretch precious appetizer ingredients. Prepare them just before the guests arrive—or recruit some help during the party to help replenish.

Spread a layer of cream cheese softened with dairy sour cream over cracker or toast shapes or sauté crustless bread shapes in butter. Add flavorful tidbits and garnishes and serve immediately. Try these toppings, and vary them to suit your own whims:

A small piece of smoked salmon and a tiny piece of lemon with peel.

A dab of black caviar and a tiny piece of lemon with peel.

A shrimp or half shrimp and a tiny piece of lemon with peel.

One or two smoked oysters and a sprig of parsley.

A slice of cucumber, a dab of sour cream and a sprinkling of garlic salt.

A slice of cucumber, a dab of sour cream and a bit of caviar or a tiny shrimp.

A slice of avocado, a dab of sour cream and a sprinkling of garlic salt.

A slice of avocado, a sprinkling of crumbled Roquefort or blue cheese and a dab of sour cream.

A slice of avocado, a dab of sour cream and a tiny shrimp.

A thin slice of onion or red apple, a bit of marinated herring and a dab of sour cream.

Clockwise from top right: Petite Pâtes, Bacon-Stuffed Mushrooms, Hurry-Curry Appetizer Meatballs (variation of Open-Sesame Appetizer Meatballs), Miniature Cornucopias, Quick Canapés, Shrimp Stuffed With Nutty Blue Cheese Spread, Cherry-O-Crab Appetizers.

Open-Sesame Appetizer Meatballs

Ali Baba would love these!

2 tablespoons butter
2 tablespoons flour
1/4 teaspoon salt
Dash cayenne pepper
1/2 cup beef broth
1 teaspoon soy sauce
1 teaspoon Worcestershire sauce

2 tablespoons toasted
   sesame seeds, see tip, page 29
1 cup (1/2 pint) dairy sour cream,
   room temperature
1 recipe Tasty Appetizer
   Meatballs, see below

In a stainless steel, glass or enamel saucepan, melt butter over medium heat. Blend in flour, salt and cayenne pepper. Heat, stirring until bubbly. Add broth all at once and cook, stirring, until sauce thickens. Stir in soy sauce, Worcestershire sauce and sesame seeds. Empty sour cream into medium bowl; gradually add sauce, stirring constantly. Return sauce to pan. Fold in Tasty Appetizer Meatballs, below, and heat gently to serving temperature. Serve from chafing dish with toothpicks. Makes 60 to 64 appetizer meatballs.

Variation

Hurry-Curry Appetizer Meatballs: Omit soy sauce, Worcestershire sauce and sesame seeds. Cook 1 teaspoon curry powder in butter 1 minute. Proceed according to recipe directions. Before adding sour cream, fold in 1 tablespoon lemon juice and well-drained contents of 1 (8-1/2-oz.) can crushed pineapple.

Tasty Appetizer Meatballs

A great basic meatball! Use for Open-Sesame Appetizer Meatballs or your favorite sauce recipe.

1 lb. lean ground beef
2/3 cup minced onion
1/2 cup soft breadcrumbs
   (1 slice bread)
1 egg
1/4 cup milk
1/2 teaspoon salt
1/8 teaspoon pepper

1 tablespoon plus 1 teaspoon
   Worcestershire sauce
1 teaspoon MSG (monosodium glutamate),
   if desired
Cooking oil
1 cup beef broth, bouillon
   or consommé

Combine ground beef, onion, breadcrumbs, egg, milk, salt, pepper, Worcestershire sauce and MSG, if desired. Shape into small 1-inch meatballs. Fry in hot cooking oil, at least 3/4-inch deep, until lightly browned. The meatballs will hold their shape and brown without turning. Remove from oil and drain on paper towels. Simmer meatballs in broth about 10 minutes or until cooked through. Reserve broth for use in your favorite sauce. Meatballs may be made ahead and frozen after simmering for use later. Freeze loose on cookie sheets. When frozen solid, wrap for freezing. Remove as many as you need and thaw completely in chafing dish or 300°F (149°C) oven before adding to a sauce. Makes 60 to 64 appetizer meatballs.

Mushrooms In Sour Cream Sauce

Impressive, delicious and so easy to make!

1 lb. small whole mushrooms
1/4 cup (1/2 stick) butter
1 small clove garlic, crushed
2 tablespoons flour
1/2 cup beef broth
1/2 teaspoon salt

1/8 teaspoon pepper
1/2 teaspoon dill weed
1-1/2 teaspoons lemon juice
1 tablespoon dry sherry
1/2 cup dairy sour cream,
  room temperature

Sauté half the mushrooms in a third of the butter. Remove with slotted spoon to a plate. Repeat with remaining half of mushrooms and another third of butter. Reserve excess liquid. Melt remaining butter in a saucepan. Add garlic and sauté until golden but not browned. Stir in flour. Cook until bubbly. Add broth, salt, pepper, dill weed, lemon juice, sherry and excess liquid from cooking mushrooms. Cook, stirring, until sauce thickens. At this point the sauce and mushrooms can be refrigerated separately until an hour before serving. Reheat sauce before proceeding. Empty sour cream into a medium bowl. Gradually add heated sauce, stirring constantly. Return to pan and fold in mushrooms. Heat through and serve immediately from chafing dish. Makes about 50 appetizers.

Savory Clam Puffs

Freeze the batter until cooking time, or freeze the finished puffs.

1 (3-oz.) can minced clams
Water
1/4 cup (1/2 stick) butter
1 teaspoon salt
1 cup sifted flour
4 eggs
1 (3-oz.) pkg. cream cheese,
  room temperature

1/2 teaspoon paprika
1/2 teaspoon caraway seeds
1/2 teaspoon curry powder
1 to 2 cups cooking oil
Salt

Drain clams; reserve broth and add water to make 1 cup. Heat broth, butter and salt in saucepan. When butter melts and a full boil begins, add flour all at once. Stir rapidly until mixture separates from sides of saucepan to form a ball. Remove from heat. Beat in 2 eggs, one at a time. Mix well after each addition. Blend in half the cream cheese. Repeat with remaining eggs and cream cheese. Add clams, paprika, caraway seeds and curry powder. Blend thoroughly. Heat cooking oil, at least 1-inch deep, to 375°F (191°C). Drop batter by half-teaspoons into hot oil and brown delicately, turning once. Drain on paper-towel-lined baking sheet and keep warm in 200°F (93°C) oven until serving time. Salt lightly. Makes about 60 appetizer-size puffs.

Cream Cheese Tea Sandwiches

Tea sandwiches tend to be more bland and sweet than canapés.

1 (8-oz.) pkg. cream cheese,
  room temperature
1 tablespoon butter,
  room temperature
1 tablespoon dairy sour cream
2 teaspoons sugar
Dash salt

1 or more variation ingredients,
  see below
Food coloring, if desired
Sliced day-old or partially frozen
  white, rye, fruit, nut or
  other kind of bread
Garnishes, see below

Beat cream cheese until smooth. Blend in butter, sour cream, sugar, salt and 1 or more variation ingredients. Add appropriate food coloring to match party decor, if desired. Cut bread into interesting shapes with knife or cookie cutter. Try rounds, diamonds, sticks, squares, triangles, cloverleafs and hearts. Spread cheese mixture generously over bread shapes, covering completely. To freeze, arrange on a foil-lined cookie sheet. When sandwiches are frozen solid, store in freezer in airtight containers or wrapped in heavy foil. Allow 30 minutes to thaw. Just before serving, top with desired garnish.

Variations (suitable for freezing)

Minced crystallized ginger
Grated citrus peel
Candied fruit or peel
Dried fruit
Roquefort or blue cheese
  (omit sugar from recipe)
Chutney
Peanut butter
Frozen citrus juice concentrate
Chives or parsley
  (omit sugar from recipe)

Garnishes (do not freeze)

Drained, canned fruit chunks
Fresh grapes, berries, citrus sections
Toasted flaked coconut
Nuts, halved or chopped
Fruit preserves
Cranberry sauce
Candied fruit or peel
Maraschino cherries

For tender hard-cooked eggs without discolored yolks, start in cold water to cover. Bring to a boil, reduce heat to a low simmer and cook 12 to 15 minutes. Plunge into ice water immediately. Fast cooling keeps the yolks bright.

Petite Pâtes

Tiny elegant pastry turnovers will bring on the compliments.

1 recipe Cream Cheese Pastry,
  page 154
About 1-1/2 cups filling,
  see below

Topping, if desired,
  see below

Preheat oven to 425°F (218°C). Roll Cream Cheese Pastry, page 154, on generously floured board to about 1/16-inch thickness. Cut into 2-1/2-inch circles with cookie cutter. Place approximately 3/4 teaspoon filling on each pastry circle. Too much filling will cause pastry to burst during baking. Moisten edge of pastry with water. Fold in half, gently pressing edges together to seal. Place sealed pâte on cookie sheet. Crimp curved edge with fork tines. Pierce top with fork tines or knife tip. Inscribe various patterns to identify fillings, if desired. Sprinkle with topping, if desired. Bake 10 to 12 minutes or until golden. Makes 35 appetizers.

Suggested Fillings:

Cocktail franks, wieners or
  bologna, chopped
Sweet pickles, chopped
Stuffed olives, chopped or sliced
Deviled ham and horseradish or
  Dijon-type mustard
Liver spread and pickle relish
Smoked oysters
Chicken spread and chutney
Crushed pineapple and chopped
  Macadamia nuts
Refried beans and diced green chilies
Crumbled bacon and date halves

Suggested Toppings:

Finely chopped nuts
Shredded coconut
Sesame seeds
Caraway seeds
Parmesan cheese

To toast sesame seeds, sprinkle them on a cookie sheet and bake at 325°F (163°C) about 5 minutes or until golden. Toasting develops the character of the sesame seed flavor.

Bacon-Stuffed Mushrooms

Very, very elegant! Leftover Bacon-Stuffed Mushrooms can be rewarmed days later.

1 lb. small mushrooms
  (about 50)
4 slices bacon, diced
1 medium onion, minced
2 tablespoons minced green pepper
1 teaspoon salt
Dash pepper
1/8 teaspoon MSG
  (monosodium glutamate), if desired

1 (3-oz.) pkg. cream cheese,
  room temperature
1/2 cup Buttered Breadcrumbs,
  page 120
1/4 cup hot water
Parsley for garnish

Preheat oven to 375°F (191°C). Butter a 13" x 9" x 2" baking dish. Set aside. Wash and dry mushrooms. Remove stems; chop and reserve for stuffing. Sauté diced bacon, onion, green pepper, chopped mushroom stems, salt, pepper and MSG, if desired. Remove from heat when cooked through but not browned. Combine cream cheese with bacon mixture. Press firmly into mushroom caps, mounding slightly. Put Buttered Breadcrumbs, page 120, into a small bowl. Lightly press filling side of mushrooms into crumbs to coat. Place mushrooms in buttered baking dish, filling-side up. At this point mushrooms may be covered and refrigerated 1 to 2 days. Add 1/4 cup hot water to baking dish and bake uncovered 15 to 20 minutes. Garnish each with parsley sprig. Makes about 50 stuffed mushrooms.

Cherry-O-Crab Appetizers

These tiny tomatoes taste as good as they look!

30 cherry tomatoes
1 (3-oz.) pkg. cream cheese,
  room temperature
2 tablespoons dairy sour cream
2 teaspoons dry sherry
1/2 teaspoon salt

2 teaspoons capers
1/2 teaspoon poppy seeds
1 (6-1/2-oz.) can crab meat,
  drained and flaked
Parsley for garnish

Remove stems from washed tomatoes. Cut off tops to make small caps and scoop pulp from bottoms with a small spoon. In a medium bowl, blend cream cheese, sour cream and sherry. Stir in remaining ingredients except parsley. Fill tomatoes with crab mixture. Stick toothpicks into centers of caps and stick securely into filled tomatoes. Garnish with tiny sprigs of parsley and refrigerate until serving time. Will hold several hours. Makes 30 appetizers.

Variation

Crab Puffs: Prepare Appetizer Puff variation of Cream Puffs, page 154. Omit cherry tomatoes and prepare double recipe of filling. Fill cooled puffs.

How To Make Bacon-Stuffed Mushrooms

1. Remove the stems from clean and dry mushrooms. Chop the stems and reserve for the stuffing.

2. Press bacon mixture firmly into the mushrooms, making small mounds of stuffing.

3. After dipping the stuffed end of the mushrooms into Buttered Breadcrumbs, place mushrooms in a buttered baking dish. Add water and bake 15 to 20 minutes.

Miniature Cornucopias

Crunchy cornucopias will disappear in minutes.

20 slices white bread
1/4 cup (1/2 stick) butter, melted
1 recipe Deviled Ham Spread,
  page 38

Parsley for garnish
Paprika for garnish

Preheat oven to 350°F (177°C). With a 3-inch, round cookie cutter, cut circle from each bread slice. Flatten each circle with rolling pin, pressing firmly. Brush both sides with melted butter, roll to form cornucopia and fasten with toothpick. Insert small ball of crumpled foil. Bake on ungreased cookie sheet 12 minutes or until toasted. At serving time, fill with a spoonful of Deviled Ham Spread, page 38, and garnish with parsley sprig at fold of cornucopia. Sprinkle paprika over filling. Makes 20 miniature cornucopias.

Perky Dill Dip

This dip is flavored especially for serving with crunchy vegetable dippers.

1 (3-oz.) pkg. cream cheese,
  room temperature
1/2 teaspoon grated lemon peel
1 tablespoon lemon juice

1/4 teaspoon dill weed
1/2 teaspoon salt
1 cup (1/2 pint) dairy sour cream
Assorted vegetable dippers

Combine cream cheese, lemon peel, lemon juice, dill weed and salt; beat until fluffy. Blend in sour cream. Chill thoroughly and serve with vegetable dippers. Makes about 1-1/4 cups dip.

Devil's Dip

Something hot and tasty for appetizer adventurers.

1 cup (1/2 pint) dairy sour cream
1 (4-1/2-oz.) can deviled ham
5 teaspoons horseradish

1/8 teaspoon liquid smoke
1/4 teaspoon salt
Mild-flavored crackers or chips

Combine all ingredients except crackers or chips, and blend thoroughly. Serve with mild-flavored crackers or chips. Makes 1-1/2 cups dip.

Bean Olé Dip

Salud! A patio party wouldn't be complete without a little touch of Mexico.

1 (3-oz.) pkg. cream cheese,
   room temperature
1 (8-oz.) can refried beans
1/2 cup dairy sour cream
2 tablespoons minced green pepper
1 tablespoon minced onion

2 teaspoons diced green chilies
2 teaspoons chili sauce
1 teaspoon chili powder
1/2 teaspoon Worcestershire sauce
Tortilla chips

In a medium bowl, mash cream cheese with fork. Blend in refried beans. Add remaining ingredients, except tortilla chips, and blend thoroughly. Refrigerate at least 3 hours. Serve with tortilla chips. Makes about 2 cups dip.

Festive Avocado Dip

Sour cream makes this dip taste great and also slows darkening of the avocado.

1 large ripe avocado
1/2 cup dairy sour cream
1 tablespoon diced green chilies

1 teaspoon grated onion
1/2 teaspoon garlic salt
1/2 teaspoon lemon juice

Peel and chunk avocado. Combine all ingredients without completely mashing avocado. Serve immediately or spoon into airtight container. Lay plastic wrap over surface. Cover and refrigerate. Makes about 1-1/2 cups dip.

Roquefort Dip

Serve with assorted vegetable dippers to please your calorie-conscious guests.

2 tablespoons Roquefort or blue
   cheese, room temperature
2 cups (1 pint) dairy sour cream
1/2 teaspoon salt
1 teaspoon minced green onion
1/4 teaspoon Worcestershire sauce

1/2 teaspoon MSG
   (monosodium glutamate), if desired
1 clove garlic, crushed
Assorted vegetable dippers or
   mild-flavored crackers

In medium bowl, mash Roquefort or blue cheese with fork. Add remaining ingredients, except dippers or crackers, and blend thoroughly. Refrigerate 1 hour. Serve with vegetable dippers or mild-flavored crackers. Makes about 2 cups dip.

Cottage Cheese Dip

A spicy basic dip for the high-protein, low-calorie group!

1 cup (1/2 pint) small curd
  cottage cheese
1/4 cup dairy sour cream
1 teaspoon horseradish
1 teaspoon grated onion

1/4 teaspoon salt
1/4 teaspoon Worcestershire sauce
1/8 teaspoon celery seed
Corn chips

Blend thoroughly all ingredients except corn chips. Refrigerate 2 to 3 hours to blend flavors. Serve with corn chips. Makes about 1-1/4 cups dip.

Variations

Deviled Ham Cheese Dip: Add deviled ham to taste to basic dip.
Avocado Cheese Dip: Add mashed avocado to basic dip. Season with lemon juice, Worcestershire sauce, salt and pepper.
Roquefort Cottage Cheese Dip: Crumble Roquefort or blue cheese; add to taste to basic dip.

Crab & Water Chestnut Dip

Mystify your guests with the Oriental touches.

1 (6-1/2-oz.) can crab meat
1 (5-oz.) can water chestnuts
2 cups (1 pint) dairy sour cream

2 tablespoons soy sauce
2 tablespoons minced green onion
Mild-flavored chips or crackers

Drain and shred crab meat; remove tendons. Mince water chestnuts and drain on paper towels. Combine sour cream, soy sauce and onion. Blend. Refrigerate. Serve with mild-flavored chips or crackers. Makes 3 cups dip.

Creamy Guacamole Dip

A heavenly blend.

1 (6-oz.) can frozen guacamole
1/2 cup dairy sour cream

1/4 teaspoon salt

Thaw guacamole. Fold in sour cream and salt. Refrigerate until ready to serve. Makes about 3/4 cup dip.

Calcutta Dip

A bit of exotic India.

1 (2-1/4-oz.) can chicken spread
1 cup (1/2 pint) dairy sour cream

Minced chutney to taste
Curry powder to taste

Combine all ingredients and refrigerate until ready to serve. Makes a little more than 1 cup dip.

Dried Beef Dip

Here's a dip with a bite!

Dried beef, as desired
1 cup (1/2 pint) dairy sour cream

Horseradish to taste

With kitchen shears, snip slices of dried beef into sour cream. Mix well. Add horseradish. Refrigerate 2 hours to blend flavors. Makes a little more than 1 cup dip.

Green Chili Dip

A fire-and-ice blend.

Diced green chilies to taste
1 cup (1/2 pint) dairy sour cream

Salt to taste

Combine all ingredients. Mix well. Refrigerate until ready to serve. Makes about 1 cup dip.

Horseradish Dip

For strong palates!

Horseradish to taste
1 cup (1/2 pint) dairy sour cream

Salt to taste
Minced green onion for garnish

Combine horseradish, sour cream and salt. Mix well. Refrigerate until ready to serve. Garnish with minced green onion. Makes about 1 cup dip.

Liverwurst Dip

Easy and tasty.

1 (2-1/4-oz.) can liver spread
1 cup (1/2 pint) dairy sour cream

Salt to taste
Pickle relish to taste

Combine all ingredients and refrigerate until ready to serve. Makes a little more than 1 cup dip.

Olive Dip

For the many olive lovers among us.

1 (4-1/2-oz.) can chopped ripe olives
1 tablespoon instant minced onion

3/4 teaspoon salt
2 cups (1 pint) dairy sour cream

Combine all ingredients. Mix well. Refrigerate until ready to serve. Makes about 1-1/4 cups dip.

Quick Bean Dip

Delicious with crisp tortilla chips.

1 (10-1/2-oz.) can bean dip
1 cup (1/2 pint) dairy sour cream

2 teaspoons minced green onion
1/2 teaspoon salt

Combine all ingredients. Mix well. Refrigerate until ready to serve. Makes about 1-2/3 cups dip.

Red Caviar Dip

Far removed from the ordinary!

1 (8-oz.) pkg. cream cheese,
  room temperature
1/4 cup dairy sour cream

1/2 teaspoon lemon juice
1 (2-oz.) jar red caviar

Blend cream cheese and sour cream. Add lemon juice. Fold in red caviar. Refrigerate until ready to serve. Makes about 1 cup dip.

Nutty Blue Cheese Spread

Add new shapes to your appetizer assortment.

1 (8-oz.) pkg. cream cheese,
   room temperature
1 (3-oz.) pkg. blue or Roquefort
   cheese, room temperature
1/2 cup chopped walnuts
   (omit if mixture is to be frozen)

2 tablespoons minced parsley
1 tablespoon dry sherry
Dairy sour cream, if desired
Crackers

Blend cheeses; stir in walnuts, parsley and sherry. Thin with sour cream if softer mixture is desired. Serve with crackers. Makes about 1-1/2 cups spread.

Variations

Blue Cheese Nuggets: Increase walnuts to 1 cup. Combine all ingredients except walnuts and form into small balls. Roll in finely minced walnuts. Serve on toothpicks.
Stuffed Celery: Fill cavity of celery sticks with spread.
Stuffed Cucumber: Hollow out a peeled cucumber. Fill with Nutty Blue Cheese Spread. Cut in 1/2-inch slices; quarter each slice. Serve with toothpicks.
Roquefort Stuffed Shrimp: Omit walnuts and reserve parsley. Split shrimp halfway through on vein side. Fill with cheese mixture and roll backs in parsley. Serve with a squeeze of fresh lemon juice.
Roquefort Apple Slices: Spread unpeeled red apple slices with cheese spread. Serve as a dessert or an appetizer.

Sesame-Cheese Spread

Toasted sesame seeds give an interesting nut-like flavor.

1 (8-oz.) pkg. cream cheese,
   room temperature
1 cup grated sharp Cheddar cheese (4 oz.)
1 tablespoon dairy sour cream
1/2 teaspoon soy sauce

1/8 teaspoon salt
2 tablespoons toasted sesame seeds,
   see tip, page 29
Crackers

Blend cheeses; stir in remaining ingredients, except crackers. Add additional sour cream if softer mixture is desired. Serve with crackers. Makes about 1-1/2 cups spread.

Variations

Cheese Dip: Substitute 1-1/2 cups sour cream for cream cheese and increase salt to 1/2 teaspoon.
Cheddar Cheese Balls: Combine all ingredients except sesame seeds and crackers. Form into small balls and roll in sesame seeds. Use more seeds, if necessary.

Braunschweiger Spread

Liverwurst with a tasty twist.

1 (3-oz.) pkg. cream cheese,
  room temperature
1 (4-oz.) pkg. Braunschweiger or
  liverwurst
1 hard-cooked egg, chopped

1 teaspoon grated onion
1-1/2 to 2 teaspoons horseradish
1/4 teaspoon Worcestershire sauce
Pumpernickel bread or wheat crackers

Blend all ingredients except bread or crackers. Chill. Serve with pumpernickel bread or hearty wheat crackers. Makes 1 cup spread.

Deviled Ham Spread

"Deviled" or "Diable" refers to foods highly spiced with seasonings like peppers, Worcestershire sauce, mustard, horseradish and garlic. This recipe is just a little devilish.

1 (3-oz.) pkg. cream cheese,
  room temperature
1 (4-1/2-oz.) can deviled ham
3 tablespoons minced onion
1-1/2 teaspoons well-drained horseradish
1/8 teaspoon celery seed

Dash salt and pepper
Miniature Cornucopias, page 32,
  if desired
Crackers or bread for canapés,
  if desired

Blend thoroughly all ingredients except Cornucopias and crackers or bread. Use as filling for Miniature Cornucopias, page 32, or as spread for crackers or canapés. Freeze, if desired. Makes 1 cup spread.

Dilly Crab Spread

Try this refreshing spread for a summer gathering.

1 (3-oz.) pkg. cream cheese,
  room temperature
1 (7-1/2-oz.) can crab meat,
  well-drained and flaked
1/4 teaspoon salt

2 tablespoons fresh lime juice
1/4 teaspoon dill weed
Dairy sour cream, if desired
Mild-flavored crackers

Combine all ingredients except sour cream and crackers. Refrigerate 1 hour. Thin with sour cream if softer mixture is desired. Serve with mild-flavored crackers. Makes about 1-1/2 cups spread.

Variation

Crunchy Crab Spread: Omit lime juice and dill weed. Add 1 tablespoon minced green onion, 1 teaspoon Worcestershire sauce and 1/2 cup finely chopped almonds.

Corned Beef Spread

A little dairy magic and corned beef becomes a taste-tempting spread.

1 (3-oz.) pkg. cream cheese,
  room temperature
1 cup (1/2 pint) dairy sour cream
1 teaspoon soy sauce

1/3 cup minced dill pickle
1 (12-oz.) can corned beef
Wheat crackers
1/2 teaspoon paprika

Blend cream cheese until smooth. Gradually mix in sour cream and soy sauce. Stir in dill pickle. Flake corned beef into cream cheese mixture, removing excess fat. Mix well and chill. Serve on wheat crackers; garnish with paprika. Makes about 2-1/2 cups spread.

Variation

Tuna Spread: Omit corned beef. Drain and flake 1 (6-1/2-oz.) can white chunk tuna. Combine with remaining ingredients.

Cheese Apple

A classic. It improves with age.

1 (8-oz.) pkg. cream cheese
4 oz. blue cheese
4 oz. smoked processed sharp
  Cheddar cheese
2 tablespoons finely minced green pepper
2 tablespoons finely minced pimiento

1/4 teaspoon garlic salt
1 cup finely chopped almonds,
  tinted red
Red food coloring, diluted
Yellow food coloring, if desired
Crackers

Let cheeses warm to room temperature. Combine green pepper, pimiento and garlic salt. Blend thoroughly. Chill. To tint almonds, dilute several drops of red food coloring with a little water. For brighter red, add a drop or two of yellow food coloring. Add chopped almonds and toss until evenly colored. Spread on paper towels; dry completely. Keep leftover tinted almonds to "repair" Cheese Apple for serving another time. Shape cheese mixture into a round ball. Roll in dry tinted almonds. Garnish with stem and leaf from real apple or other fruit. Surround with crackers and serve with spreader. Makes 2 cups spread.

Variation

Cheese Holly Berry: Omit stem and leaf. Garnish with holly leaves for the holiday season.

To chop hard-cooked eggs quickly, use a pastry blender.

Adults, teenagers and children consume more and more food away from the family table. Their snacks take a significant bite out of the family food budget and total up to an even more noticeable figure on the calorie count. In spite of this, most snack foods are composed mostly of sugar, starch and fat and provide very few essential nutrients. In too many cases snack meals end up replacing regular meals or cutting the appetite for them. Because of this, it's important that between-meal snacks are as nourishing as regular family meals.

A well-balanced snack, like a well-balanced meal, should, as much as possible, include foods from the basic four food groups—fruits and vegetables, cereals, meat and milk. The essential nutrients provided by each of the food groups are more useful to the body when eaten together.

Marketing for snacks should focus on protein foods, such as lunch meats, eggs and cheeses, including cottage cheese. Milk, yogurt, buttermilk and ice cream also provide protein, calcium, other minerals and vitamins. Fresh fruits and vegetables are a source of vitamins A and C. Breads and crackers supply essential B vitamins.

There are many dairy foods that are great for snacking because they need no preparation:
Cottage Cheese—Complete, easy-to-digest protein, ready to eat right from the carton. It provides more protein for fewer calories than most of the common meat or meat substitute foods.
Yogurt—Yogurt provides all of the protein and calcium of milk and is delightfully filling. It comes in plain and fruit flavors, and some is lowfat.
Buttermilk—In spite of the rich-sounding name and the creamy texture, buttermilk has fewer calories and less fat than lowfat milk. It is famous as a refresher because of its thirst-quenching quality. Try it wth a little salt and maybe even some pepper.

Snack foods can be fun, appetizing, quick and nutritious. You'll find many suggestions in this section for using cottage cheese, yogurt, butter-milk and other dairy foods in snacks. Dips and cheese spreads, see Appetizers, Dips & Spreads, pages 23 to 39, can be served with vegetable dippers and wheat crackers. The nutritious and appetizing snacks you plan for your family will let you feel more comfortable when an occasional meal is skipped. And your family will be healthier and happier for it.

YOGURT IS:

A Quick Breakfast—A carton of fruit-flavored yogurt really improves a breakfast of toast and coffee.
A Bag Lunch—Carry a carton of frozen fruit-blended yogurt to school, the office or the beach. By noon it's thawed and ready to eat. Stir well.
An After-School Snack—A half carton of fruit-flavored yogurt provides real satisfaction and still leaves room for dinner. Serve it with a cookie.
A Bedtime Snack—A half carton of fruit-flavored yogurt keeps you from going to bed hungry. It's easy to digest and doesn't keep you awake.

ANYTIME SNACKS

These treats are special in the afternoon or evening, and just as delicious at mid-morning or midnight:

Spear bananas with wooden skewers or ice cream sticks and freeze. Coat with vanilla or fruit-blended yogurt; roll in coconut, chocolate shavings or chopped nuts, and freeze until solid.

Fill packaged taco shells with cottage cheese, lettuce, tomato, avocado and taco sauce. Or spread crisp tortillas, tostada fashion, with the same ingredients.

Mix cottage cheese and seasonings with hard-cooked egg yolk for deviled eggs.

Stuff celery or cucumbers with cottage cheese. Sprinkle with seasoned salt.

Spread plain cottage cheese or Cottage Cheese Dip, page 34, on wheat crackers or wheat toast.

Serve boysenberry or apple pie with a generous scoop of vanilla yogurt. Pie à la yogurt!

Make individual pizzas by spreading cottage cheese on English muffin halves. Top with pizza topping and pepperoni slices. Warm under broiler.

Layer fruit-flavored gelatin with cottage cheese and fruit in a parfait glass.

Serve chunks and spears of fresh fruit with fruit-blended yogurt as a dip.

Apple slices with cottage cheese are crisp and appetizing.

Spread cottage cheese on graham crackers—top with jelly.

To make yogurt popsicles, spoon fruit-blended yogurt into paper cups. Spear with a plastic spoon and freeze.

COTTAGE CHEESE SANDWICH IDEAS

A well-planned sandwich is a small, balanced meal in itself. It includes bread, a protein food, lettuce and perhaps tomato. A glass of milk, or one of the snack drinks in this section completes the nutritional picture.

B.L.T.C.C. Sandwich—Add cottage cheese to your next bacon-lettuce-tomato sandwich. Top with avocado slices for a glamor touch.

Peanut Sandwich—Mix chopped peanuts with cottage cheese for a delicious sandwich spread. It doesn't stick to the roof of your mouth!

Open-Face Cottage-Avocado Sandwich—Mash ripe avocado with garlic salt and pepper; blend with cottage cheese. Spread on a toasted English muffin, sourdough bread or French bread. Cottage cheese enhances the flavor of avocado.

Egg, Tuna or Ham Salad Sandwiches—Mix cottage cheese with egg, tuna or ham salad sandwich fillings. Add seasonings to taste. Because cottage cheese adds low-calorie protein and moistness, it cuts the need for high-calorie salad dressings.

Avocado and Bacon Sandwich—Give a protein boost to an avocado sandwich with a thick layer of cottage cheese. It complements the avocado and bacon—and holds it together at the same time.

Cottage Cheese Salad Sandwich—Mix chopped vegetables with cottage cheese. Vegetables to try include cucumber, radish, green onion, carrot, celery and ripe or green olives. Spread on toasted wheat bread.

BUTTERMILK COOLERS

A buttermilk cooler is a combination of buttermilk and fruit or vegetable juice. It's a great way to drink buttermilk whether you're a fan or a first-timer.

Combine 1 quart of buttermilk with 1 (6-oz.) can frozen concentrated orange or pineapple juice, lemonade, limeade or punch. Stir well. This makes 4 or 5 tall drinks. How about a Garden Cooler? Blend equal parts ice-cold buttermilk and tomato juice or vegetable juice cocktail. Season with Tabasco® sauce, Worcestershire sauce, salt, pepper and lemon juice. To make a Fruit Cooler, mix equal parts buttermilk and apple, orange, pineapple or apricot juices.

HOT CHOCOLATE

Hot chocolate is a treat for a frosty winter breakfast, a rainy day lunchbox or an after-the-game snack, and there are many easy recipes available.

The one step always involved in making hot chocolate is heating milk—a simple but sometimes annoying process. The skin that forms on hot milk and causes it to boil over is composed primarily of milk protein. When it's discarded, up to 13% of the milk nutrients are wasted. This loss can be eliminated by keeping a lid on the milk while it's heating or by whipping it to a froth and keeping it frothy while heating. In either case, heat gently and stay nearby. You will have no boilovers or unappetizing skin formation.

To keep punches cold without diluting, add scoops of ice cream or sherbet or frozen juice cubes. Or line a large bowl with crushed ice and place the smaller punch bowl inside.

Lemon-Buttermilk Frost

Try our version. Then take off on your own.

1 pint vanilla ice cream
1 qt. buttermilk
1 (6-oz.) can frozen lemonade concentrate
   or 1/2 cup lemon juice, 1/2 cup sugar and
   1/4 teaspoon grated lemon peel

In a large bowl, beat ice cream to soften. Add buttermilk and lemonade concentrate or lemon-juice mixture. Beat until frothy and serve immediately. Makes about 2 quarts.

Variations

Raspberry Buttermilk Frost: Substitute 1 pint raspberry sherbet for ice cream. Add 1/4 cup sugar.
Sunshine Buttermilk Frost: Omit lemonade concentrate and add 1 cup orange juice, 1-1/3 cups prune juice, 2 tablespoons lemon juice, 1/3 cup sugar and 1/8 teaspoon salt.

Chocolate Malt

Rich and creamy! You can't buy a malt this good.

1 pint vanilla ice cream or
  ice milk
1/4 cup milk
1 to 2 tablespoons chocolate syrup

1 teaspoon instant malted milk powder
Sweetened whipped cream,
  if desired

Chill 2 tall glasses. Combine all ingredients except sweetened whipped cream in blender jar or electric-mixer bowl. Blend or beat until thickened and smooth. For thinner malt, increase milk to 1/2 cup. Pour into chilled glasses and top with dollop of sweetened whipped cream, if desired. Makes 2 servings.

Variations

Vanilla Malt: Omit chocolate syrup.
Strawberry Malt: Substitute strawberry ice cream for vanilla and strawberry topping for chocolate syrup.
Chocolate Shake: Omit instant malted milk powder.

Lemon-Orange Freeze

Taste-tingling refreshment!

1/2 cup orange juice
1 (8-oz.) carton orange or lemon
    fruit-blended yogurt

1 cup (1/2 pint) lemon sherbet

Put ingredients in blender jar in order listed and blend until smooth. Serve immediately. Makes 2 or 3 tall drinks.

Variation

Boysenberry Freeze: Substitute cranberry juice and boysenberry fruit-blended yogurt for orange juice and orange yogurt.

Yogurt Delight

Create your own blend with your favorite carbonated beverage and fruit-flavored yogurt.

1 (8-oz.) carton lime fruit-blended yogurt
1 (12-oz.) bottle ginger ale

Divide yogurt into 3 tall glasses. Add a little ginger ale and stir until smooth. Fill glasses with remaining ginger ale. Stir and serve. Makes 3 tall drinks.

Variations

Figure 8 Soda: Substitute 1 (12-oz.) bottle lemon-lime dietetic soda for ginger ale.
Miscellaneous Yogurt Delights: Substitute boysenberry, orange, cherry, lemon or strawberry fruit-blended yogurt for lime yogurt with various carbonated beverages.

Berry Buttermilk Nog

Eating on the run? Try a buttermilk nog.

2 cups buttermilk
1 (10-oz.) pkg. frozen strawberries,
    partially thawed

3 eggs
2 teaspoons lemon juice
Dash salt

Combine ingredients in blender jar and blend until smooth. Makes 3 servings, 241 calories each.

Orange Buttermilk Nog

Breakfast in a glass!

2 cups buttermilk
1/2 can (6-oz. size) frozen
   orange-juice concentrate
2 eggs

2 teaspoons sugar or honey
Dash salt
1/2 teaspoon lemon juice, if desired

Combine ingredients in blender jar and blend until smooth. Makes 2 servings, 289 calories each.

Islander Buttermilk Nog

Exotic island flavors blend in another version of the buttermilk nog.

1 cup buttermilk
1/2 cup papaya or guava nectar
1 banana
2 eggs

1 teaspoon sugar
1 teaspoon lemon juice
Dash salt

Combine ingredients in blender jar and blend until smooth. Makes 2 servings, 275 calories each.

Tropical-Delight Punch

No one will guess the ingredients in this one. It's a beautiful blending of flavors!

1-1/2 cups guava nectar
1 small banana
2 (8-oz.) cartons pineapple
  fruit-blended yogurt

1 (1-qt.) bottle lemon-lime soda

Have all ingredients well-chilled. Blend guava nectar and banana until smooth in blender jar or electric-mixer bowl. Empty yogurt into punch bowl or large pitcher. Blend in banana mixture. Just before serving, stir in soda. Makes 2 quarts.

Variation

Tropical Lime Refresher: Substitute pineapple juice for guava nectar and lime fruit-blended yogurt for pineapple yogurt. Add crushed pineapple, if desired.

Salads

Defining "salad" in five easy words is a difficult task. Webster says it's "a dish of lettuce or other vegetables, herbs, or meat or fowl, fish, eggs, fruit, etc., prepared with various seasonings or dressings and usually served cold. Herbs or plants used in salads are usually eaten raw." A salad can be served as an appetizer, a side dish, a main dish or a dessert, depending on its ingredients. We have complicated the issue further by adding another variation—chilled soups or liquid salads. Even with this almost limitless definition we tend to slip into the tossed salad rut. Variety in salad dressings is the first step out of the rut. Here you'll find many dressings made of sour cream, yogurt and cottage cheese. The creamy compatible flavors of dairy foods enhance delicate fresh fruit and vegetable flavors. For a flavor treat that's simple and exotic at the same time, coat chunks of fresh banana in dairy sour cream and roll in shredded coconut. Arrange on lettuce-lined salad plates with pineapple spears and papaya or cantaloupe wedges. A beautiful and delicious salad. If you want to dress up jellied consommé, arrange a crab leg or shrimp on top. Mix dairy sour cream with lemon juice and salt to taste. Dollop over consommé and garnish with fresh dill sprig or minced chives.

Broadening the salad ingredients is the next step. The wide selection of fruits and vegetables in the marketplace opens up new salad experiences. Familiar ingredients used in new ways are just as good. Add a scoop of cottage cheese for a protein boost. It's compatible with fruit, vegetables, seafood and potatoes. Garnish a beautifully arranged salad with Ginger Cheese Balls, page 52.

Varying the form of the salad is another way out of the rut. Instead of tossing ingredients together, try arranging them, molding them, freezing them or liquefying them. Adding cottage cheese, sour cream, yogurt or buttermilk to a gelled salad as part of the liquid completely changes the look and the taste. Cut pieces into interesting shapes. Use your imagination.

SALAD DRESSINGS

There are multitudes of ready-made salad dressings in the supermarket but none can match the flavor of a fresh dressing "whipped up" just for the occasion. Sour cream, yogurt or cottage cheese can be the beginnings of a great dressing that's low in calories, too.

Caloric Values of Common Salad Dressings:

	Calories per 2 tablespoons
Lowfat plain yogurt	18
Plain yogurt	22
Dairy sour cream	60
Salad dressing (mayonnaise type)	113
French, commercial	118
Homemade oil and vinegar	172
Mayonnaise	184

SALAD DRESSINGS FROM DRY MIXES

Many salad dressing mixes give directions for mixing with sour cream. The results are not only delicious but significantly lower in calories. The mixes made up with sour cream will cut the calories to 1/3 or even 1/4 of the original oil-and-vinegar or mayonnaise versions. To cut calories and fat even lower, try them with plain yogurt instead of sour cream. Try mixes for Caesar dressing, French dressing or bacon dressing.

SOME GREEN SALAD COMBINATIONS

Westerners usually serve the green salad as an appetizer—to heighten the appetite for the courses to follow. The Frenchman serves it after the entrée—to clear the taste buds for the desserts and wines to come. For many of us it is eaten with the main dish, "family style."

Whenever it's served, the difference between an ordinary green salad and a superb one depends on the choice and application of the dressing. Above all, serve green salads well chilled.

Salade Italiano—Assorted greens, salami triangles, marinated garbanzo beans, Bermuda onion rings and garlic version of Basic Sour Cream Dressing, page 48, or a French dressing mix with dairy sour cream.

Mushroom Green Salad—Butter lettuce, sliced fresh mushrooms, chopped green onions, chopped parsley and Basic Sour Cream Dressing, page 48.

Avocado-Cucumber Green Salad—Romaine lettuce, sliced cucumber, chopped green onion, sliced avocado, crumbled crisp bacon and the garlic version of Basic Sour Cream Dressing, page 48.

Caesar Salad—Romaine lettuce, croutons, Parmesan cheese and packaged Caesar dressing mix with dairy sour cream.

Spinach Salad—Fresh spinach, shoestring beets, chopped hard-cooked eggs, crumbled bacon and packaged bacon dressing mix with dairy sour cream.

Family Tossed Salad—Assorted greens, tomatoes, chopped celery, cucumber, onion, green pepper, sliced radishes, shredded red and green cabbage, grated carrot and Thousand Island Dressing, page 49, or Roquefort Cheese Dressing, page 48.

Citrus Green Salad—Assorted mild greens, tangerine or orange wedges, Bermuda onion rings and French dressing mix made with dairy sour cream.

MOLDED SALADS

A molded salad can be very simple or it can be a work of art. Either way, it's a do-ahead salad that can be ready to serve hours before you bring it to the table. If you enjoy using your artistic talents, the shape of the mold, the ingredients, their arrangement and colors, are things you can vary endlessly.

There is only one caution: *Do not use either fresh pineapple or fresh papaya* in a molded salad. They contain enzymes that destroy the ability of gelatin to gel.

HOW TO MOLD AND UNMOLD GELATIN SALADS

One 3-ounce package of flavored gelatin or 1 envelope of plain gelatin will gel 2 cups of liquid. The first cup must be water or liquid that can be boiled such as fruit or vegetable juice, carbonated drink, canned fruit syrup or broth. If the liquid is too sweet the gelatin will be very soft. If a recipe calls for more than two 3-ounce packages of gelatin, allow only 1-3/4 cups liquid per package instead of the usual 2 cups. Large molds require a firmer gel.

Thoroughly dissolve the flavored gelatin in 1 cup of boiling liquid. This is important! Part or all of the second cup of liquid can be one or more of these dairy products. All dairy products should be added to liquid that is *cool* but not set.

1 cup of:	Replaces:
Cottage Cheese	1/2 cup liquid
Dairy sour cream	1/2 cup liquid
Plain yogurt	3/4 cup liquid
Fruit-blended yogurt	2/3 cup liquid
Milk, buttermilk or cream	1 cup liquid

Before adding other ingredients, let gelatin thicken to consistency of unbeaten egg white. Otherwise the ingredients tend to float or sink.

Add up to 2 cups of other well-drained ingredients, such as fruit, nuts, vegetables, eggs or meat, per 3-ounce package of gelatin. Pieces should be small or salad will be fragile and difficult to serve.

Oil the inside of the mold or spray it with a non-stick compound for easier unmolding. Pour gelatin and added ingredients into mold and refrigerate several hours or until firm.

To unmold, pull edges of gelatin away from mold with fingers or dip a small pointed knife in warm water and run it around edge to loosen. Moisten top of mold as well as surface of chilled serving plate. Gently shake gel to loosen from mold. If the mold has not been oiled or treated, dip it to the rim in warm water for about 5 seconds. Hot water will melt the gel. Place moistened plate over mold and invert.

CHILLED SOUPS OR "LIQUID SALADS"

The idea of serving cold soup is still a new one for most people. In spite of that, converts are not difficult to recruit. Iced soups are appetizing and refreshing, for example Iced Middle East Cucumber Soup, page 64. Serve them in chilled mugs in the living room or in elegant icers at the table and don't forget that final dollop of sour cream.

MAIN DISH SALADS

When the weather is warm—and the kitchen is, too—nothing sounds more appealing or perks up sluggish appetites faster than a cool refreshing salad.

Main dish salads tend to be low in calories, fats and carbohydrates. They are usually uncomplicated and can be prepared and garnished long before serving. It is protein that makes a main dish salad different from an appetizer or accompaniment salad. A main dish salad may contain cottage cheese, meat, seafood or eggs.

Basic Sour Cream Dressing

These creamy dressings have only 1/3 the calories of mayonnaise or oil-and-vinegar dressing.

1 cup (1/2 pint) dairy sour cream
1/2 teaspoon salt
1/8 teaspoon pepper

1 to 2 tablespoons lemon juice
1 teaspoon sugar, if desired

Blend all ingredients and refrigerate 1 to 2 hours to blend flavors. Makes about 1 cup.

Variations

Herbed Sour Cream Dressing: Add 1/4 to 1/2 teaspoon of 1 or more of the following dry herbs or 3/4 to 1-1/2 teaspoons fresh: tarragon, marjoram, beau monde seasoning, savory, chervil, dill weed (for cucumbers or coleslaw), basil (for tomatoes), oregano (for tomatoes), or thyme (for tomatoes or beets).
Creamy Horseradish Dressing: Add about 1 teaspoon horseradish.
Creamy Garlic Dressing: Add 1 crushed garlic clove.
Olive Dressing: Add 1/4 cup chopped ripe or stuffed olives.
Sour Cream French Dressing: Stir in 1/4 cup French dressing.
Cheese & Cream Dressing: Add 1/4 cup Parmesan or Cheddar cheese.

Roquefort Cheese Dressing

A creamy version of an all-time favorite.

1 (3-oz.) pkg. cream cheese,
   room temperature
1 teaspoon fresh lemon juice
1/2 teaspoon garlic salt

3 tablespoons Roquefort or blue cheese
   (1-1/2-oz.), room temperature
1 cup (1/2 pint) dairy sour cream

Blend cream cheese with lemon juice, garlic salt and Roquefort or blue cheese. Gradually blend in sour cream and refrigerate 2 hours to blend flavors. Makes about 1-1/2 cups.

Creamy Roquefort Dressing

Double or triple this to serve a crowd.

2 tablespoons Roquefort cheese (1 oz.)
1/2 cup mayonnaise
1/2 cup dairy sour cream
1/3 cup buttermilk

1 teaspoon lemon juice
1/4 teaspoon onion salt
1/4 teaspoon garlic salt
Freshly ground pepper

In small bowl, crumble Roquefort cheese with fork. Blend in mayonnaise, sour cream and remaining ingredients. Refrigerate 3 to 4 hours to blend flavors. Makes about 1-1/2 cups.

Green Goddess Dressing

This tangy San Francisco creation is a Western favorite.

2 tablespoons tarragon vinegar or
   2 tablespoons white vinegar and
   1/8 teaspoon tarragon
1 small clove garlic
4 small green onions with fresh tops
   (about 1/4 cup chopped)
1 tablespoon anchovy paste

1/4 cup coarsely chopped parsley,
   packed
1/8 teaspoon tarragon
1/8 teaspoon salt
1/2 cup mayonnaise
1 cup (1/2 pint) dairy sour cream

Combine all ingredients except mayonnaise and sour cream in blender jar. Blend until nearly smooth. Fold blended mixture into mayonnaise and sour cream. Refrigerate several hours to blend flavors. Makes 2 cups.

Thousand Island Dressing

For quick Thousand Island Dressing, you can mix chili sauce and sour cream. But this recipe is the real thing.

1/4 cup chili sauce
1-1/2 teaspoons minced pimiento
1 tablespoon minced green pepper
1 tablespoon minced onion

1 hard-cooked egg,
   finely chopped or grated
1 cup (1/2 pint) dairy sour cream
Salt and pepper to taste

Blend all ingredients and refrigerate several hours to blend flavors. Makes about 1-1/2 cups.

Cottage Dressing

A spicy dressing for dieters—only 21 calories per tablespoon.

1 cup (1/2 pint) small curd cottage cheese
2/3 cup dairy sour cream
1/2 medium clove garlic, crushed
2 teaspoons tarragon vinegar
1 teaspoon dry mustard

1/4 to 1/2 teaspoon salt
1/4 teaspoon pepper
1/4 teaspoon paprika
1/4 teaspoon sugar
1/2 teaspoon Worcestershire sauce

Combine all ingredients in blender jar or electric-mixer bowl. Blend or beat until smooth. Refrigerate to blend flavors. Makes about 1-2/3 cups.

Combination Fruit Salad

A year-round fruit salad prepared in minutes. Wonderful for a buffet with ham or chicken.

2 cups (1 pint) dairy sour cream
2 cups miniature marshmallows,
   plain or fruit-flavored
1 (3-1/2-oz.) can flaked coconut

5 to 6 cups well-drained chunked fruit,
   from suggested fruits, below
(select 2 or more)

Combine sour cream, marshmallows and coconut. Fold in well-drained *canned* fruit. Do not add dark bleeding fruit like Bing cherries until fresh fruits are added later. Fresh pineapple or papaya should not be used in this salad. Refrigerate several hours or overnight to soften marshmallows and blend flavors. At serving time, fold in *fresh* fruits and any other dark canned fruits. Make certain apples, bananas and other fruits that darken are well-coated with dressing. Makes 8 to 10 servings.

Suggested Fruits:

Canned pineapple chunks
Canned or fresh apricots
Canned or fresh mandarin orange segments
Canned or fresh pears
Canned Bing cherries (rinsed and well-drained)
Canned or fresh peaches or nectarines
Canned fruit cocktail or fruits for salad
Canned or fresh seedless grapes
Fresh apples
Fresh bananas
Fresh cantaloupe
Fresh strawberries or blueberries
Chopped dates

2 (1-lb. 13-oz.) cans equal about 5 cups chunked, drained fruit.

Basic Dressing For Fruit Salad

Fruit flavors come alive with sour cream.

2 tablespoons fresh lemon or
   lime juice
2 tablespoons sugar or honey

Dash salt
1 cup (1/2 pint) dairy sour cream

Blend juice, sugar or honey and salt. Gradually blend in sour cream. Refrigerate several hours to blend flavors. Only 28 calories per tablespoon. Makes about 1-1/4 cups.

Variation

Tangy Yogurt Dressing: Substitute 1 (8-oz.) carton plain yogurt for sour cream. Only 12 calories per tablespoon.

Waldorf Salad

Waldorf Salad made with sour cream. Mm-m-m.

1 cup (1/2 pint) dairy sour cream
1 tablespoon sugar
1/2 teaspoon salt
1 tablespoon lemon juice

2 medium-large red apples
  (about 3 cups diced)
1 cup chopped celery
1/2 cup chopped walnuts

Combine sour cream, sugar, salt and lemon juice. Refrigerate. Core and dice unpeeled apples; fold immediately into dressing. Fold in celery and walnuts. Serve immediately. Makes 6 servings.

Variations

Tropical Waldorf Salad: Substitute 1 cup diced banana or well-drained canned pineapple tidbits for 1 cup of apple.
California Waldorf Salad: Add a few raisins or chopped dates.
Party Waldorf Salad: Substitute 1 cup miniature marshmallows for sugar.

Ginger Cheese Balls

Here's a fruit salad garnish with spicy flavor!

1 (8-oz.) pkg. cream cheese
1 tablespoon plus 1 teaspoon
  minced crystallized ginger

1/4 teaspoon salt
Whipping cream, if desired
1/4 cup finely chopped walnuts

Combine cream cheese, ginger and salt. Soften with whipping cream, if desired. Form into balls and roll in finely chopped walnuts. Makes about 8 cheese balls for garnish.

Danish Cheese Balls

Try these as a delectable fruit salad garnish.

1 (4-oz.) pkg. blue cheese
1 (8-oz.) pkg. cream cheese

Lemon juice, if desired
1/4 cup finely chopped walnuts

Blend blue cheese with cream cheese. Soften with lemon juice, if desired. Form into balls and roll in finely chopped walnuts. Makes about 12 cheese balls for garnish.

Frozen Fruit Delight

Enjoy this salad with a warm-weather dinner or a winter-holiday feast.

1 (1-lb.) can apricot halves
1 (1-lb.) can pineapple tidbits
1 (11-oz.) can mandarin orange segments
1-1/2 teaspoons unflavored gelatin
1 (3-oz.) pkg. cream cheese,
   room temperature

1 cup (1/2 pint) dairy sour cream
1/3 cup sugar
1 cup (1/2 pint) whipping cream,
   whipped
2/3 cup diced pecans, if desired

Turn freezer to coldest setting. Drain canned fruits; reserve syrup. Dice apricot halves. Soften gelatin in 1/4 cup reserved syrup in a heat-proof cup. Place cup in a pan of simmering water until gelatin is dissolved. Beat cream cheese until smooth. Gradually blend in sour cream, sugar, dissolved gelatin and additional 1/4 cup syrup. Fold in whipped cream, drained fruits and pecans, if desired. If the salad is to be frozen for more than 2 days, omit the pecans. Spoon into a 9-inch square baking dish. Cover tightly with foil and freeze. Move salad from freezer to refrigerator 1 hour before serving. Makes 12 servings.

Variation

Frozen Yogurt Delight: Omit sugar. Substitute 1 (8-oz.) carton pineapple fruit-blended yogurt for sour cream. Substitute 1 (3-1/2-oz.) can flaked coconut for pecans.

Carrot & Raisin Salad

This nutritious and crunchy year-round salad keeps for days in the refrigerator.

Orange-Nutmeg Dressing, chilled,
   see below
4 cups grated carrots
   (about 5 medium)

1 (8-3/4-oz.) can crushed pineapple,
   well-drained
1/2 cup raisins, packed

Orange-Nutmeg Dressing:

1/2 teaspoon salt
2 tablespoons sugar
1/4 to 1/2 teaspoon nutmeg

1 to 2 teaspoons grated orange peel
1 tablespoon plus 1 teaspoon lemon juice
1 cup (1/2 pint) dairy sour cream

Prepare Orange-Nutmeg Dressing; refrigerate. Fold carrots, pineapple and raisins into dressing. The dressing will become light and bubbly. Makes 8 servings.

Orange-Nutmeg Dressing:
Combine dressing ingredients; refrigerate to blend flavors.

Hampshire Cole Slaw

Keep this favorite in your cooking repertoire.

Sour Cream Dressing, chilled,
  see below
1 small head cabbage
  (5 to 6 cups shredded)

1/4 cup chopped parsley, packed
3 tablespoons chopped green onion
Paprika for garnish

Sour Cream Dressing:
2 tablespoons lemon juice
1 teaspoon salt
2 tablespoons sugar
1/4 teaspoon pepper
1/4 to 1/2 teaspoon celery seed

1/4 teaspoon paprika
1 pimiento, minced
  (about 2 tablespoons)
1 cup (1/2 pint) dairy sour cream

Prepare Sour Cream Dressing; refrigerate. Shred or chop cabbage and add to dressing with parsley and onion. Mix and refrigerate. Just before serving, toss lightly and sprinkle with paprika. Makes 6 servings.

Sour Cream Dressing:
In large bowl, blend dressing ingredients; refrigerate until ready to serve.

Farmer's Chop Suey

A cold, crunchy and delicious side dish or luncheon salad.

1 large firm cucumber,
  peeled and cubed
1 medium green pepper,
  cut in chunks
1 cup sliced radishes
6 green onions with tops, sliced

3 medium tomatoes
1/2 teaspoon salt
1/8 teaspoon pepper
1 cup (1/2 pint) cottage cheese
1-1/2 cups dairy sour cream
1 teaspoon lemon juice

Combine cucumber, green pepper, radishes and green onion in a large bowl; refrigerate until ready to serve. Just before serving, seed and chop tomatoes. Add with remaining ingredients to vegetables. Mix well and serve. Makes 6 servings.

Most vegetable salads improve if the dressings are added several hours before serving. Leafy green salads, of course, must be dressed at the last minute.

Fresh Mushroom Salad

Here's an experience you'll want to repeat.

Lemon-Sugar Dressing, see below
1/4 lb. very fresh mushrooms
2 green onions

1 small head iceberg lettuce
2 hard-cooked eggs, grated

Lemon-Sugar Dressing:
1 cup (1/2 pint) dairy sour cream
1 tablespoon lemon juice

1 teaspoon salt
1 teaspoon sugar

Prepare Lemon-Sugar Dressing; refrigerate. Wash and thinly slice mushrooms and green onions; refrigerate. Cut lettuce in quarters and arrange on 4 salad plates. Just before serving, fold mushrooms and onion into dressing. Spoon over lettuce and sprinkle generously with grated eggs. Makes 4 servings.

Lemon-Sugar Dressing:
Blend dressing ingredients and refrigerate until ready to serve.

Cucumbers In Sour Cream

Cucumber slices in a refreshing dressing.

2 tablespoons lemon juice
1/2 teaspoon salt
1/8 teaspoon pepper
1/2 teaspoon paprika
1/2 small onion, minced

1 small clove garlic, crushed
1 cup (1/2 pint) dairy sour cream
2 medium cucumbers,
    peeled and sliced

Combine all ingredients in large bowl. Mix and refrigerate. Toss lightly before serving. Makes 4 to 6 servings.

Variations

Cucumbers & Apple in Sour Cream: Substitute 1/2 apple, chopped, for onion.
Cucumbers in Yogurt: Substitute plain yogurt for sour cream; omit paprika and add 1 teaspoon dried mint.

Potato, macaroni and bean salads are traditionally made with mayonnaise. Enjoy fresh new flavor and lower calories by dressing these salads with half dairy sour cream and half mayonnaise.

Cooked Zucchini-Mushroom Salad

You won't be sorry you tried this great make-ahead salad.

Spicy Dressing, see below
1 lb. zucchini,
   cut in 1/2-in. slices
1 tablespoon diced pimiento
1/2 cup bottled Italian dressing

1/2 lb. fresh mushrooms, sliced
2 tablespoons minced onion
1/2 clove garlic, crushed
Shredded Parmesan cheese

Spicy Dressing:
1/3 cup dairy sour cream
1 teaspoon lemon juice
1/4 teaspoon marjoram

1/8 teaspoon Tabasco® Sauce
1/4 teaspoon salt
Dash pepper

Prepare Spicy Dressing; refrigerate until ready to serve. Cook zucchini in boiling salted water 3 to 5 minutes or until just tender; drain. Marinate zucchini and pimiento in Italian dressing about 1 hour, tossing often. Drain dressing into a large fry pan. Boil dressing until only oily portion remains. Add mushrooms, onion and garlic; sauté until tender. Drain and add to zucchini; refrigerate. At serving time, toss Spicy Dressing with zucchini mixture. Serve and garnish with Parmesan cheese. Makes 4 to 5 servings.

Spicy Dressing:
Blend dressing ingredients and refrigerate to blend flavors.

Molded Pineapple-Chutney Salad

A spicy condiment for a roast or curried dish.

1 (11-oz.) can mandarin orange segments
1 (8-3/4-oz.) can crushed pineapple
Water
2 (3-oz.) pkgs. orange-pineapple gelatin
1/2 (10-oz.) jar mango chutney

2 (3-oz.) pkg. cream cheese,
   room temperature
1/2 cup dairy sour cream
1 (3-1/2-oz.) can flaked coconut
Crisp lettuce leaves

Drain orange segments and crushed pineapple well; reserve syrup and add water to make 2 cups. Heat syrup mixture in a medium saucepan. Sprinkle gelatin over surface and stir just until gelatin is dissolved. Remove 1/2 cup dissolved gelatin and let stand at room temperature. Chill remaining gelatin to consistency of unbeaten egg white. Mince chutney. Fold with well-drained fruit into thickened gelatin; pour into a 1-1/2-quart mold and chill until *almost set*. Meanwhile, beat cream cheese until smooth; gradually blend in reserved gelatin and sour cream. Fold in coconut. Spoon onto *almost-set* gelatin. Refrigerate until firm. Unmold on lettuce-lined plate and serve. Makes 12 servings.

Lemon-Lime Ring Mold

One of our most requested recipes.

Chilled Dressing, see below
1 (3-oz.) pkg. lime gelatin
1 (3-oz.) pkg. lemon gelatin
2 cups boiling water
1 (8-3/4-oz.) can crushed pineapple

1 cup (1/2 pint) cottage cheese
1 cup (1/2 pint) dairy sour cream
1/2 cup finely chopped walnuts
Crisp lettuce leaves

Chilled Dressing:
1 cup (1/2 pint) dairy sour cream
2 teaspoons horseradish, if desired

Salt to taste

Prepared Chilled Dressing; refrigerate. Dissolve gelatins in boiling water. Add entire can of crushed pineapple and chill to consistency of unbeaten egg white. Fold cottage cheese, sour cream and walnuts into thickened gelatin. Pour into a 9-inch ring mold or a 1-1/2-quart mold and chill until set. Unmold onto lettuce-lined plate and serve with Chilled Dressing. Makes 8 to 10 servings.

Chilled Dressing:
Combine dressing ingredients; refrigerate until ready to serve.

Layered Perfection Salad

The dressing is built right into this salad.

1 (3-oz.) pkg. lemon gelatin
1 cup boiling water
1 teaspoon beef stock base
1 cup cold water
1 tablespoon white vinegar

1/4 teaspoon salt
1/2 cup finely shredded cabbage
1/2 cup minced celery
2 tablespoons minced green pepper
2 tablespoons minced pimiento

Dressing Layer:
1-1/2 teaspoons unflavored gelatin
1/4 cup cold water
3/4 cup boiling water
1 tablespoon white vinegar

1 teaspoon sugar
Pinch salt
1 cup (1/2 pint) dairy sour cream

Dissolve gelatin in boiling water. Stir in beef-stock base until dissolved. Add cold water, vinegar and salt. Chill to consistency of unbeaten egg white. Fold in vegetables and pimiento. Pour into a 9-inch square baking dish. Chill until *almost set.* Prepare Dressing Layer. Pour cooled dressing on *almost-set* salad. Chill until firm. Cut in squares and serve. Makes 6 servings.

Dressing Layer:
Soften gelatin in cold water. Add boiling water and stir until dissolved. Add vinegar, sugar and salt. Cool to room temperature and blend in sour cream.

Lemon-Lime Ring Mold and Iced Middle East Cucumber Soup, on following pages

Fruit Ring Mold With Dressing

A most attractive buffet fruit ring.

1 (11-oz.) can mandarin orange segments
1 (1-lb.) can pineapple chunks
2 (3-oz.) pkgs. orange gelatin
1 cup boiling water
1-3/4 cups ginger ale

2 (3-oz.) pkgs. cream cheese
1/2 cup minced walnuts
12 maraschino cherries
1 recipe Basic Dressing For Fruit Salad
    made with honey, page 50

Drain orange segments and pineapple chunks; reserve 1 cup syrup. In a large bowl, dissolve gelatin in boiling water. Add reserved syrup and ginger ale. Chill until slightly thickened. Form cream cheese into 24 small balls; roll in walnuts and chill. Drain cherries on paper towels. Arrange cheese balls and cherries in bottom of a 1-1/2-quart ring mold. Spoon over just enough thickened gelatin to hold in place, refrigerate. Fold well-drained fruit into remaining gelatin; let stand at room temperature. When galatin in mold is *almost set,* fill with remaining gelatin-fruit mixture; chill until set. Serve Basic Dressing For Fruit Salad, page 50, from small bowl in center of unmolded Fruit Ring Mold. Makes 8 servings.

Snow-Capped Cranberry Mold

This sweet and spicy gelatin mold isn't only for the holidays. Serve it anytime with pork, game or poultry.

2 envelopes unflavored gelatin
1 cup water
2 (1-lb.) cans whole cranberry sauce
2 teaspoons grated orange peel

1/4 teaspoon salt
1/2 cup diced walnuts
Orange-Cinnamon Topping, see below
Twist of orange peel

Orange-Cinnamon Topping:
2 teaspoons unflavored gelatin
1/4 cup water
2 cups (1 pint) dairy sour cream

1/4 cup orange marmalade
1/4 teaspoon cinnamon
Dash salt

Soften gelatin for salad in 1/2 cup water. In a small saucepan, blend remaining 1/2 cup water with cranberry sauce and bring to boiling. Add softened gelatin, orange peel and salt, stirring until gelatin is dissolved. Chill to consistency of unbeaten egg white. Fold in walnuts and pour into a 9-inch square baking dish. Refrigerate until *almost set.* Prepare Orange-Cinnamon Topping. Pour topping over *almost-set* cranberry gelatin. Refrigerate until set. Cut in squares and serve garnished with twist of orange peel. Makes 9 servings.

Orange-Cinnamon Topping:
Soften gelatin in water in a heat-proof cup. Place cup in a pan of simmering water until gelatin is dissolved. Combine sour cream, marmalade, cinnamon and salt. Gradually blend in dissolved gelatin.

1. Form cream cheese into 24 balls. Roll in minced walnuts and chill.

2. Drain cherries on paper towels and arrange with cream cheese balls in the bottom of the ring mold.

How To Make Fruit Ring Mold With Dressing

3. Surround with just enough of the thickened gelatin mixture to hold in place. Refrigerate until gelatin is *almost set*.

4. Pour remaining room temperature gelatin-fruit mixture over the *almost-set* gelatin. Chill until completely set and serve with Basic Dressing For Fruit Salad made with honey.

Molded Citrus-Crunch Salad

Buttermilk gives the surprise tang.

1 (1-lb.) can grapefruit sections
Water
1 (3-oz.) pkg. lemon gelatin
1 cup buttermilk
1/2 cup minced celery

1/4 cup diced walnuts
1 (11-oz.) can mandarin orange segments
  well-drained
Dairy sour cream
Grated citrus peel for garnish

Drain grapefruit; reserve syrup and add water to make 1 cup. Heat syrup in a medium saucepan. Add gelatin, stirring until dissolved. Cool to room temperature. Blend buttermilk into cooled gelatin and chill to consistency of unbeaten egg white. Fold celery, walnuts and drained grapefruit and orange segments into thickened gelatin. Spoon into a 1-quart mold and chill until set. Unmold. Serve with sour cream and grated citrus peel for garnish. Makes 4 to 6 servings.

California Fruit-Yogurt Mold

Summer's bounty makes a colorful salad.

3/4 cup orange juice
1 (3-oz.) pkg. orange gelatin
1/4 teaspoon salt
1 (8-oz.) carton orange fruit-blended yogurt
1 tablespoon lemon juice
1 avocado, peeled and diced
1 (11-oz.) can mandarin orange segments,
  drained

1 (1-lb.) can grapefruit sections,
  drained
2 tablespoons chopped pistachio nuts, if desired
Crisp lettuce leaves
Dairy sour cream
Salt to taste
Grated orange peel for garnish

Heat orange juice in a glass, enamel or stainless steel saucepan. Add gelatin and salt, stirring until dissolved. Cool to room temperature. Blend in yogurt and lemon juice. Chill to consistency of unbeaten egg white. Fold in avocado, orange segments, grapefruit sections and pistachio nuts, if desired. Spoon into a 1-1/2-quart mold or 6 individual molds. Refrigerate until set. Unmold on lettuce-lined plate and serve with sour cream, salted to taste. Garnish with grated orange peel. Makes 6 servings.

The short period between cutting and serving fruit is long enough to cause some fruits to darken. Avocados, pears, bananas, peaches, apples, nectarines, apricots and plums are common offenders. To inhibit darkening, dip the cut fruit in citrus juice, honey or sour cream. Or use one of the ascorbic acid products on the market.

"Chili" Tomato Soup

Tomato soup never tasted like this before! And it's easy, too.

1 slice onion, about 1/8-inch thick
2 tablespoons sherry
1 teaspoon horseradish
1/4 teaspoon salt
1/4 teaspoon chili powder

1/4 teaspoon Worcestershire sauce
1 (10-1/2-oz.) can tomato soup
3/4 cup water
1 cup (1/2 pint) dairy sour cream

Put all ingredients, except sour cream, in a blender jar; blend until onion is puréed. Add sour cream and blend on low speed just until well-mixed. Refrigerate 3 to 4 hours to blend flavors. Makes 4 or 5 half-cup servings.

Borsch à la Crème

Exquisite flavor and delightful color.

1 (8-oz.) can diced beets
1 tablespoon lemon juice
3 tablespoons minced onion
1/4 teaspoon dill weed

1/2 teaspoon salt
1 cup (1/2 pint) dairy sour cream
Dairy sour cream for garnish
Minced chives for garnish

Put beets, lemon juice, minced onion, dill weed and salt in blender jar; blend until smooth. Empty sour cream into a medium bowl. Gradually blend in beet mixture. Refrigerate several hours to blend flavors. Serve in well-chilled cups or bowls. Garnish with sour cream and minced chives. Makes 4 half-cup servings.

Crème Vichyssoise Glacé

You won't find vichyssoise in a French cookbook. It was created in New York City to celebrate the opening of the Ritz-Carlton Hotel's Roof Garden in 1910.

1-1/2 cups diced raw Russet potato
   (about 1-1/2 medium)
1 small onion, chopped
1/2 teaspoon salt
1/8 teaspoon dill weed
Dash white pepper

1-1/2 cups chicken broth
1 cup half-and-half
1 tablespoon fresh minced parsley
1 cup (1/2 pint) dairy sour cream
Dairy sour cream for garnish
Minced chives for garnish

Cook potato, onion, salt, dill and pepper in broth until potato is tender and breaks when pierced with a fork. Add half-and-half and parsley and blend in blender or put through a food mill. Chill. Just before serving, blend in sour cream. Serve in chilled cups or bowls. Top each serving with a dollop of sour cream and sprinkle with minced chives. Makes 4 three-quarter-cup servings.

Iced Middle East Cucumber Soup

Great on a warm summer evening!

1 medium cucumber
1 cup chicken broth
1 (1/2-in.) slice medium onion
3/4 teaspoon salt
1/4 to 1/2 teaspoon dry mint leaves
Dash garlic powder

1/2 teaspoon lemon juice
1 cup (1/2 pint) dairy sour cream
1 (8-oz.) carton plain yogurt
Chopped onion or cucumber slices
    for garnish

Peel cucumber and remove seeds; cut into thick slices. Put in blender jar with broth, onion, salt, mint, garlic powder and lemon juice. Blend until cucumber is finely grated but not liquefied. If blender is not available, put cucumber and onion through a food grinder and mix in other ingredients. Combine sour cream and yogurt in bowl. Gradually stir in cucumber mixture. Blend well and refrigerate 1 hour to blend flavors. Serve in chilled cups or bowls. Garnish with chopped onion or cucumber slices. Makes 4 to 6 servings.

Stuffed Iceberg Lettuce

Here's a different look for lettuce salad.

1 head iceberg lettuce
1 (3-oz.) pkg. cream cheese,
    room temperature
3 tablespoons dairy sour cream
1/4 teaspoon Worcestershire sauce
1 teaspoon lemon juice
1/2 teaspoon salt

3 tablespoons minced,
    peeled and seeded tomato
2 tablespoons grated carrot
1 tablespoon minced green pepper
1 tablespoon minced green onion
1 tablespoon minced celery
2 teaspoons minced parsley

Core and hollow out center of lettuce; drain on paper towels. Blend cream cheese, sour cream, Worcestershire sauce, lemon juice and salt. Mix in remaining vegetables. Stuff lettuce with vegetable-cream cheese filling. Wrap in plastic wrap. Refrigerate 5 or 6 hours. Slice in wedges and serve. Makes 6 servings.

Kidney Bean Salad

A delicious old-fashioned salad.

3 (15-oz.) cans kidney beans,
   rinsed and drained
1 cup sweet pickle relish, drained
1/2 cup chopped celery
4 hard-cooked eggs, minced
1/3 cup minced green onion
1/2 cup chopped cucumber
1 tablespoon minced pimiento

1/2 cup dairy sour cream
1/2 cup mayonnaise
1 tablespoon prepared mustard
1 teaspoon champagne vinegar or
   distilled vinegar
1 teaspoon salt
Chopped green onion or
   red onion rings for garnish

Combine all ingredients except onion for garnish. Mix well and refrigerate 1 to 2 hours. Just before serving, toss lightly and garnish with additional chopped green onion or red onion rings. Makes about 8 cups or 12 to 16 servings.

Baja Shrimp Salad

You'll love this served on a sea shell with refried beans and tortillas, or in Cream Puffs, page 154.

1/2 cup dairy sour cream
2 tablespoons mayonnaise
1 cup diced cucumber
1/4 cup minced celery
2 tablespoons minced green onion
2 tablespoons lemon or lime juice
2 teaspoons sweet pickle relish
1/2 teaspoon salt
1/4 teaspoon oregano

1/4 teaspoon tarragon
3/4 lb. freshly cooked medium shrimp or
   2 (6-1/2- or 7-oz.) cans medium, deveined
   shrimp, well-drained
1 large avocado, peeled and diced
Crisp lettuce leaves
Lime twists or whole shrimp
   for garnish

Blend sour cream, mayonnaise, cucumber, celery, onion, lemon or lime juice, relish, salt, oregano and tarragon. Refrigerate 1 to 2 hours. Just before serving, fold in shrimp and avocado. Spoon onto lettuce-lined plates and garnish with twists of lime or whole shrimp. Makes 4 servings.

Three-Way Potato Salad

Make this salad with macaroni, mashed potatoes or boiled potatoes. It's delicious all three ways.

1-1/4 lbs. boiling potatoes
Boiling water
1 teaspoon salt
1/2 cup sweet pickle juice
Tangy Dressing, see below
1/3 cup diced celery

1/4 to 1/3 cup minced green onion
2 tablespoons minced pimiento
2 tablespoons minced sweet pickle
2 tablespoons sliced ripe olives,
   well-drained
2 hard-cooked eggs, chopped

Tangy Dressing:
1/4 cup dairy sour cream
1/4 cup mayonnaise
1/2 teaspoon prepared mustard
1/2 teaspoon champagne vinegar or
   distilled vinegar

1 teaspoon salt
Dash white pepper

Cook whole potatoes in boiling salted water until tender when pierced with a fork. Peel and cube into pickle juice. Marinate 1 hour. Prepare Tangy Dressing. Drain potatoes. Mix in remaining salad ingredients and dressing. If this salad seems dry, add more dressing. Refrigerate until well-chilled. Makes 4 cups or 4 to 5 servings.

Tangy Dressing:
Combine dressing ingredients; refrigerate to blend flavors.

Variations

Mashed Potato Salad: Substitute 3 cups prepared instant mashed potatoes for 1-1/4 pounds potatoes, and use the 1/2 cup sweet pickle juice instead of 1/2 cup of the water in the package directions. Marinate 1 hour and continue as directed.
Smörgasbord Potato Salad: Substitute dill pickle juice for sweet pickle juice and dill pickle for sweet pickle. Add 3 tablespoons minced parsley. In the dressing, substitute 2 teaspoons horseradish for prepared mustard.
Macaroni Salad: Substitute 4 ounces salad macaroni, cooked and drained, for 1-1/4 pounds potatoes.

Confetti Egg Salad

A very economical main dish!

1 envelope unflavored gelatin
1/2 cup cold water
1 tablespoon champagne vinegar or
   distilled vinegar
1/2 teaspoon salt
3/4 cup dairy sour cream
1/4 cup sandwich spread
2 teaspoons prepared mustard

4 hard-cooked eggs, finely chopped
1 cup minced celery
1/4 cup minced green pepper
2 tablespoons sliced ripe olives,
   well-drained
2 tablespoons radish slices, halved
2 teaspoons minced green onion
Crisp lettuce leaves

Soften gelatin in water in a heat-proof cup. Place cup in a pan of simmering water until gelatin is dissolved. Add vinegar and salt to dissolved gelatin. Cool to room temperature. Blend sour cream, sandwich spread and mustard into cooled gelatin. Fold in remaining ingredients, except lettuce, and pour into a 3-cup mold. Chill until firm. Unmold onto lettuce-lined plate. Makes 4 servings.

Salmon Mousse

If you have a fish-shaped copper mold, this is the time to use it.

1 envelope unflavored gelatin
1/4 cup water
1 (1-lb.) can red salmon
1 cup (1/2 pint) dairy sour cream
1/4 cup chili sauce
1/2 cup minced celery
2 tablespoons grated onion

2 tablespoons sweet pickle relish
1 tablespoon prepared mustard
1 tablespoon lemon juice
1/2 teaspoon salt
Creamy Dressing, see below
Crisp lettuce leaves

Creamy Dressing:
1/4 cup dairy sour cream
1/4 cup mayonnaise

Salt to taste

Soften gelatin in water in a heat-proof cup. Place cup in a pan of simmering water until gelatin is dissolved. Remove skin and bones from salmon. Combine with sour cream, chili sauce, celery, onion, relish, mustard, lemon juice and salt in a large bowl; blend in dissolved gelatin. Pour into a 1-quart mold and chill until firm. Prepare Creamy Dressing. Unmold salad onto lettuce-lined plate. Serve with dressing. Makes 4 to 6 servings.

Creamy Dressing:
Blend sour cream and mayonnaise. Add salt to taste. Refrigerate until ready to serve.

New England Corned Beef Mold

Don't scratch this idea until you've tried it.

2 envelopes unflavored gelatin
1/2 cup cold water
1 tablespoon beef stock base
2 cups boiling water
1 cup (1/2 pint) dairy sour cream
2 tablespoons horseradish
1 teaspoon prepared mustard
1/2 teaspoon seasoned salt

1 (12-oz.) can corned beef
3 cups finely shredded cabbage
1/2 cup sliced, stuffed olives
1/4 to 1/3 cup minced green onion
1/4 cup diced green pepper
Parsley for garnish
Dairy sour cream
Salt to taste

Soften gelatin in cold water. Add stock base and boiling water, stirring until gelatin dissolves; cool. Blend sour cream, horseradish, mustard and seasoned salt into cooled gelatin. Chill to consistency of unbeaten egg white. Dice corned beef and add with cabbage, olives, onion and green pepper mixture. Fold until blended. Pour into a 9" x 5 x 2-3/4" loaf pan and chill until firm. Unmold and garnish with parsley. Serve with sour cream, salted to taste. Makes 8 servings.

Singapore Chicken Salad

A unique salad for a special luncheon.

Curry Dressing, see below
2 cups chunked, skinned and
 boned, cooked chicken
1 (1-lb. 4-oz.) can pineapple chunks,
 well-drained

1-1/2 cups diagonally sliced celery
1/2 cup toasted slivered almonds
Crisp lettuce leaves
Peeled cantaloupe wedges, if desired

Curry Dressing:
3/4 cup dairy sour cream
1/2 teaspoon salt
1/2 teaspoon curry powder

1 teaspoon lemon juice
1 tablespoon minced mango chutney
 with syrup

Prepare Curry Dressing and refrigerate. Combine chicken, pineapple, celery and almonds; refrigerate. Before serving, mix dressing with chicken mixture. Spoon onto lettuce-lined plate. For a special touch, surround with peeled cantaloupe wedges. Makes 4 to 6 servings.

Curry Dressing:
Combine dressing ingredients; refrigerate to blend flavors.

Special Touches For Familiar Foods

The joy of discovery can come from very simple things. Ever think of a carton of sour cream or cottage cheese—or even leftover sour cream dip—as a source of new interest to everyday cooking and eating? See what happens to familiar foods when you combine them in unexpected ways with a little sour cream or cottage cheese. The simple addition of a spoonful of sour cream to hamburgers, for instance, gives them a gourmet glow—whether it's mixed into the meat or spooned on top of the cooked pattie.

Discover the magic that a few spoonfuls of sour cream or cottage cheese will work in many packaged, takeout or frozen convenience foods. They immediately lose their mass-produced look and take on fresh new flavor. These little touches will bring back that I-did-it-myself pride.

Think of sour cream as a condiment or a garnish that you use to make simple foods more attractive. Foods will not only look better but will taste better, too. From soup to dessert, every course in the meal can benefit from your special touch. And you get this flavor and glamor with only 30 calories per level tablespoon.

Once you get into the swing of dressing up familiar foods with special touches, you'll be ready to explore the classic recipes throughout this book. Here are a few ideas to help you get started.

FIRST COURSES

Discover the newness that sour cream can add to familiar soups and salads. For only 1/3 the calories of mayonnaise!

Canned or Frozen Soup—Top individual servings of canned or frozen soups with a dollop of dairy sour cream. Especially good with tomato, potato, green pea, cream of shrimp or clam chowder. Choose a garnish of crushed herbs, grated Parmesan cheese, croutons, minced chives or crumbled bacon.

If serving soup from a tureen, put a heaping spoonful of dairy sour cream in the bottom of the tureen—stir while adding the hot soup. Good for almost all soups, cream or otherwise.

Buttermilk adds a tang to canned cream soups. Blend 1 soup can of buttermilk into the concentrated soup and heat just to serving temperature. Do not boil. Try cream of tomato, celery, chicken or potato soups. Buttermilk has all the protein and calcium of whole milk and only half the fat.

MAIN DISHES

Hamburgers—Top with leftover Roquefort Dip. Or make Roquefort Sauce, page 73, especially for hamburgers.

Steak or Roast Beef—Garnish with leftover horseradish dip or make Horseradish Sauce, page 74, especially for roast beef.

Disguise for Fried Liver—The next time you fry liver, stir a little sour cream or leftover onion dip into the pan brownings. It makes a delicious gravy you'll really appreciate. Particularly if you're only eating liver for your health.

Meat Loaf—Ground beef, meat loaf mixture and veal loaf will have a special flavor, be more moist and have more protein if made with cottage cheese instead of milk. Substitute cottage cheese, measure for measure, for milk in your favorite recipe or start by trying Cottage Meat Loaf, page 97.

A Can of Tuna or Salmon—Try our Tuna-Noodle Favorite, page 99. Or, if you have an au gratin potato mix, try the All-In-One Dinner, page 106.

Canned Chili—Try our Chilimex Casserole, page 100. So easy the teenagers can fix it themselves.

Casseroles—The most ordinary casserole takes on a party flavor when sour cream is added. Try it with some of your favorites. Add about 1/2 cup dairy sour cream and 2 teaspoons flour for 4 servings. See How to Prevent Curdling, page 76.

Canned or Frozen Beef Stew—Makes Instant Hungarian Goulash with dairy sour cream and a generous dash of paprika. Or start from scratch with Caraway Goulash, page 86.

Enchiladas—To make a heartier main dish out of frozen enchiladas, heat according to directions on the package. Serve on a heated plate. Top each serving with a layer of hot green chili salsa, if desired, then a layer of cottage cheese, a layer of diced avocado, a sprinkling of chopped green onion. Top with dairy sour cream. Scrumptious!

Other Mexican Treats—A glass of buttermilk with any hot Mexican food will cool tender palates. It's a great flavor blend. A dollop of dairy sour cream will do the same on a bowl of chili or in a taco.

Meat Marinades—Sour cream and buttermilk have been used by game hunters for years to tenderize meat and to mellow flavors. Marinate meat or fowl overnight. Try sour cream with pheasant.

SOUR CREAM SAUCES ON VEGETABLES

Any compatible vegetable can be served with a sour cream sauce at the table—but not all vegetables are at their best cooked with sour cream. The color of the vegetable decides.

White Vegetables—Cauliflower, turnips, onions and parsnips stay white when they are cooked or served in a sour cream sauce. They taste great, too.

Yellow and Orange Vegetables—Carrots, corn, crookneck squash and winter squash can be in a sour cream sauce or sauced at serving time. Either way they keep their beautiful color and taste great, too.

Green Vegetables—These are the most sensitive of vegetables. Long cooking causes them to gray. The presence of acid ingredients speeds this reaction. In most cases, it is best to add a sour cream sauce to green vegetables at serving time. In the case of casseroles using canned vegetables, there is no problem because the canning process has already changed their color. Popular green vegetables are artichokes, asparagus, green beans, broccoli, Brussels sprouts, green cabbage, peas, celery and zucchini.

Red Vegetables—Beets look and taste wonderful with sour cream. If they get together too soon it is the sour cream that changes color. Sour cream belongs *on* tomatoes, not *with* them. It takes a great deal of care to mix tomatoes with sour cream without curdling.

VEGETABLES & POTATOES

When a strikingly plain entrée heads the menu, plan to serve a sauce on the potato, noodle or vegetable.

Baked Potato—Any leftover dip? Top a baked potato with it for a nice change. Onion, blue cheese, horseradish and avocado are particularly good. Or try any of the toppings especially for baked potatoes, page 92.

Broiled Tomatoes—Give a lift to broiled tomatoes by topping them with dairy sour cream and a few minced chives.

Green Vegetables—Leftover Cheddar cheese dips are fabulous on broccoli, asparagus and Brussels sprouts. Leftover blue cheese or onion dips are good with vegetables.

Leftover Frozen or Canned Vegetables—Make them into a meatless main dish—Vegetable Bake, page 108.

Cook-Outs—Barbecue vegetable kabobs of mushrooms, cherry tomatoes, chunked green peppers, quartered onions and zucchini slices. Baste with oil-and-vinegar dressing and serve with Herb Sauce: Mix 1 cup (1/2 pint) dairy sour cream with 1/2 teaspoon each dill weed, tarragon and salt.

Corn on the Cob—Next time try sour cream instead of butter on corn-on-the-cob. It doesn't run off—it clings! Tastes great, too!

Instant Sauce for Dieter's Vegetables—Heat cottage cheese in a saucepan over low heat. Stir until the curd melts slightly and forms a sauce. Serve immediately over hot vegetables. Broccoli, asparagus, potatoes, cauliflower, and Brussels sprouts are especially good. Less than 30 calories per 2 tablespoons. And a bonus of 4 grams protein!

DESSERTS

Instant Pudding Mix—Make Mock Tapioca. Prepare a 3-1/4-ounce package of instant coconut-cream pudding according to package directions. Fold in up to 1 cup (1/2 pint) small curd cottage cheese and serve. Or, why not Instant Cheese Pie, page 125?

Simple Fruit Dessert—Spoon dairy sour cream right from the carton onto any fresh, canned or frozen fruits. Or go one more step by making one of the easy sour cream toppings on page 168.

New Twist on Shortcake—Spoon sugared cut strawberries or peaches over sponge cakes or split biscuits. Top with Whipped Creme Fraîche, page 168. It's even better than whipped cream.

Thompson Seedless Grapes—Make Grapes à la Suisse. Sweeten sour cream with brown sugar. Serve over seedless grapes. Next try Strawberries à la Suisse.

Buttermilk Fried Chicken

Chicken marinated in buttermilk with a spicy flavor twist.

1 (2-1/2- to 4-lb.) frying chicken,
   cut in pieces
2 to 3 cups buttermilk
1 cup flour
1 teaspoon curry powder
1 teaspoon salt

1 teaspoon paprika
1/2 teaspoon white pepper
1/4 cup (1/2 stick) butter
1/4 cup cooking oil
1 clove garlic, crushed

Place chicken pieces in a deep casserole and add buttermilk to cover. Refrigerate 1 to 4 hours. Preheat oven to 350°F (177°C). Combine flour, curry powder, salt, paprika and pepper in a small paper bag. Combine butter and oil in a medium fry pan over medium heat. Add garlic and sauté until golden. Toss lightly drained chicken in flour mixture and brown slowly in hot butter and oil a few pieces at a time. Place browned chicken, skin-side up, on a baking sheet. Bake uncovered 30 minutes or until tender. Makes 4 to 6 servings.

Cottage Hollandaise Sauce

A fail-proof hollandaise that's kind to weight-watchers.

1/4 cup (1/2 stick) butter
1 cup (1/2 pint) cottage cheese
2 eggs

1 tablespoon lemon juice
1/4 teaspoon dry mustard
1/4 teaspoon salt

Melt butter in a saucepan on low heat. Add cottage cheese and heat, stirring until curd melts slightly and mixture is warmed through. Place eggs, lemon juice, mustard and salt in blender jar and blend on low speed for 5 seconds. Gradually add heated cottage cheese mixture to egg mixture while blender is still on low speed. Blend just until completely smooth. Put blender jar in pan of hot water until serving time to keep sauce warm. Stir occasionally. Blend briefly before serving. Makes about 1-1/2 cups.

Instant White Sauce Mix

Make your own mix to keep on hand for instant sauce.

1/2 cup (1 stick) butter
1/2 cup flour

Cook butter over low heat until watery portion boils off. Stir in flour. Cook until frothy. Do not brown. Divide evenly into 4 small paper cups. Refrigerate until firm. Wrap in foil. This instant mix will keep several weeks in the refrigerator or months in the freezer. Makes 4 one-quarter cup portions.

Instant White Sauce

With your own mix, it's quick homemade sauce.

1 cup milk
1 recipe Instant White Sauce Mix, page 71

Salt to taste
Cayenne pepper to taste

Scald milk. Add Instant White Sauce Mix, page 71. Cook, stirring until thick and smooth. Add salt and cayenne pepper to taste. Makes about 1-1/4 cups sauce.

Basic Sour Cream Sauce

You can make or reheat this sauce and it won't curdle.

2 tablespoons (1/4 stick) butter
2 tablespoons flour
1 cup milk or 1 cup chicken broth
1/2 teaspoon salt

Dash cayenne pepper
1 cup (1/2 pint) dairy sour cream,
   room temperature

On medium heat, melt butter in a stainless steel, enamel or glass saucepan. Stir in flour and cook until bubbly. Add milk or broth all at once and cook, stirring until thickened and smooth. Stir in salt and cayenne pepper. Omit salt if broth is used. Empty sour cream into a medium bowl. Gradually add heated sauce, stirring constantly. Return to pan and heat gently to serving temperature. Season to taste. Makes 2 cups sauce.

Variations

Piquant: For tuna loaf and fish. Blend 1/8 teaspoon pepper, 2 tablespoons lemon juice, 1 teaspoon grated lemon peel and 2 teaspoons prepared mustard into sauce before adding to sour cream. Fold in 2 chopped hard-cooked eggs, if desired.
Horseradish: For roast beef, ground meat patties and ham. Add 1 teaspoon minced onion and 1 tablespoon prepared horseradish to sauce before adding to sour cream.
Cheese: For potatoes, cauliflower and broccoli. Blend 1 teaspoon Worcestershire sauce and 1 to 2 cups grated Cheddar cheese into sauce before adding to sour cream.

Can Opener Sour Cream Sauce

A delectable gourmet sauce in minutes.

1 (10-1/2-oz.) can white sauce or
   cream of mushroom soup
1/4 teaspoon salt

1 cup (1/2 pint) dairy sour cream,
   room temperature

Combine white sauce or soup with salt in a saucepan and heat. Empty sour cream into a medium bowl. Gradually add heated sauce, stirring constantly. Return to pan and heat gently to serving temperature. Makes about 2-1/4 cups sauce.

Mustard Sauce

Serve this tangy sauce with barbecued, baked, fried or broiled ham.

1 cup (1/2 pint) dairy sour cream
2 teaspoons prepared mustard

1 teaspoon horseradish
1/4 teaspoon salt

Blend ingredients and refrigerate. Makes 1 cup sauce.

Roquefort Sauce

Try this on broiled or barbecued steaks or hamburger patties.

1 cup (1/2 pint) dairy sour cream
1/4 cup (1-1/2-oz.) crumbled blue or
    Roquefort cheese

1/4 teaspoon salt

Blend ingredients and refrigerate. Makes 1-1/4 cups sauce.

Orange Sauce

Serve baked or broiled chicken à l'orange with this simple sauce.

1 cup (1/2 pint) dairy sour cream
1/4 cup orange marmalade

1/4 teaspoon salt

Blend ingredients in a glass, enamel or stainless steel saucepan. Warm slightly over very low heat. Makes 1-1/4 cups sauce.

You can substitute plain yogurt or buttermilk for sour cream in most sour cream sauces. Make an exact substitution and add 2 tablespoons of flour for each cup of plain yogurt or buttermilk. The additional flour will thicken the sauce and also protect the yogurt version from curdling.

Horseradish Sauce

The perfect accompaniment for roast beef!

1 cup (1/2 pint) dairy sour cream
1 tablespoon horseradish

1/4 teaspoon salt

Blend ingredients and refrigerate. Makes 1 cup sauce.

Pecan Dressing

Make this elegant dressing or stuffing for Cornish game hens or pork chops.

1/4 cup minced onion
1 tablespoon butter
1 egg
1-1/2 cups soft breadcrumbs
   (3 slices bread)
3/4 cup chopped pecans
1/2 cup finely chopped celery

1 cup (1/2 pint) cottage cheese
1/2 teaspoon salt
1/4 teaspoon thyme
1/8 to 1/4 teaspoon rosemary
1/8 teaspoon garlic salt
Buttered Breadcrumbs, page 120,
   if desired

Preheat oven to 325°F (163°C). Butter a 3-cup casserole. Sauté onion in butter until golden but not browned. Beat egg in a medium bowl. Blend in onion and remaining ingredients except Buttered Breadcrumbs. Spoon into casserole. Sprinkle with Buttered Breadcrumbs, page 120, if desired. Bake for 45 minutes. Makes about 2-1/2 cups dressing.

Quick Sour Cream Scalloped Potatoes

Improve on packaged scalloped and au gratin potatoes with a fresh flavor.

1 (6-1/2-oz.) pkg. scalloped potato mix
Boiling water
2/3 cup milk
2 tablespoons butter or margarine

2 teaspoons flour
1/2 cup dairy sour cream,
   room temperature
Buttered Breadcrumbs, page 120

In a 1-1/2 quart baking dish, prepare scalloped potatoes with boiling water, milk and butter or margarine according to package directions *except* mix flour with dry sauce mix and blend into sour cream before adding to potatoes and water. Sprinkle with Buttered Breadcrumbs, page 120. Bake according to package directions. Makes 4 to 6 servings.

Variation

Quick Sour Cream Au Gratin Potatoes: Substitute 1 (6-1/4 or 6-1/2-oz.) package au gratin potato mix for scalloped potato mix.

Rare Roast Beef with Horseradish Sauce

Sour Cream Main Dishes & Vegetables

To explore any of the great cuisines of the world you have to taste some delectable sauces. In France and China, for example, where cooking has reached a fine art, the sauce is probably the most treasured expression. It's the sauce that carries subtle spice and broth flavors and these flavors are eager to escape and tantalize your tastebuds. Actually, the enjoyment of a sauce begins before it touches the tongue. Visually it gives a moistness and softness to a dish. And the delicate flavors escape as teasing aromas to suggest the experience to come. No meal is at its best without a sauce.

The sour cream sauce is the foundation of the cookery of many peoples. What would Hungarian cookery be without a goulash? Russian cookery without Stroganoff? Sour cream sauces are basic throughout the Middle East, the Balkan countries and into Austria and Switzerland. They are enjoyed as far north as Scandinavia and as far east as India. And deservedly so! What more harmonious companion could meats, pastas and vegetables have? The mild tartness of the sour cream enhances subtle flavors and tempers strong ones at the same time. In this section you'll find recipes with roots reaching from all over the globe.

Before you begin your cooking adventure, take time to read on and find out how to treat sour cream sauces. They are precious and deserve a little special attention. Then—welcome to the world of saucery!

HOW TO PREVENT CURDLING IN SOUR CREAM SAUCES

The satisfaction of serving a Stroganoff, a goulash or a chicken paprika that hasn't curdled—and won't curdle when it's reheated a few days later—is tremendous. By being aware of a few rules—it can happen to you. First it's necessary to understand when and why the sensitive proteins in dairy products will curdle.

There is normally more than one cause for curdling—usually too much heat in combination with one of the other possibilities. Here are the factors that can cause milk, or in this case, sour cream, to curdle.

1. Heat—too much, too fast or too long.

2. Acid—from foods such as tomatoes, citrus juices, vinegar, pickles.

3. Salt—too much or all in one spot.

4. Alcohol—from wines or liquors used.

Most sour cream recipes can be made successfully by simply adjusting the procedure. Here are some rules to follow. The time taken to understand these rules will be well worth it because they apply to all milk sauces, cream soups, scalloped potatoes and such eating delights as Chicken Paprikash, page 84, and Caraway Goulash, page 86.

1. Bring the sour cream from the refrigerator before you start preparing the dish so that it will be at room temperature when combined with hot ingredients.

2. Have all acid, spice, salt and alcohol ingredients added to the meat sauce or white sauce before it is combined with the sour cream.

3. Salt lightly. Ham and dried beef are sources of salt.

4. After adding wine or liquor, boil the sauce a while to evaporate the alcohol before combining it with the sour cream.

5. The addition of flour guards against curdling. Add 2 tablespoons per cup of sour cream. It should be blended with fat or cold water and fully cooked in the sauce before combining with sour cream. Or it can be added directly to the sour cream. Egg yolk also inhibits curdling somewhat.

6. *Most importantly: Remove the white sauce or meat sauce from the heat and gradually add it to the room temperature sour cream—not the reverse.* This way, if there is excessive salt, alcohol or acid in the gravy it will not overwhelm the sour cream. *Do not add cold sour cream directly to a bubbling hot sauce!*

7. Add the heated sauce to the sour cream just before serving and warm gently. Always use *low heat when warming or holding a milk or sour cream sauce.*

8. Do not cover the pan once the sour cream is added. The heat and steam held under the lid can encourage curdling.

9. A false curdling may occur if there is free fat in the gravy. Avoid this by pouring excess fat from the meat or skimming it from the sauce before adding it to the sour cream. If there is still some fat floating on the surface and if the sauce is quite thick, add a little water and both problems will be solved.

10. Observing all of these rules will not absolutely guarantee a perfect sauce, but it is very good insurance. Foods are natural products and therefore vary in subtle ways from day to day, season to season. These changes affect the very delicate balance of a sour cream sauce. There will even be days when you can break many of these guides and still have a smooth sour cream sauce.

CURRY

A savory curry on fluffy rice with an assortment of condiments makes one of the most exotic and yet simple meals you can serve. It's truly a one dish meal. Curry can be made with sour cream, yogurt, plain milk or coconut milk. The acid of the sour cream or yogurt enhances the curry flavor. Curry is actually a blend of spices, the variety and amounts varying with the locale and the cook. Turmeric, fenugreek, cumin seed, coriander and peppers are basic.

The Condiments—Chutney is the essential condiment. Molded Pineapple-Chutney Salad, page 56, would replace the chutney and coconut condiments and is very attractive. Select additional condiments to complement the meat in the curry. Choose from this list or add your own: chopped peanuts, cashews or almonds, raisins, shredded coconut, chopped hard-cooked eggs, crumbled crisp fried bacon, chopped and seeded peeled tomato, chopped green pepper, chopped green onion or chives, chopped banana tossed in lemon juice.

To create your own sour cream casserole, start with one of the curdle-proof sour cream sauces, quick or regular, pages 72 to 74. Add leftover cooked meat, poultry, fish, eggs, rice, potatoes and vegetables. Mix in cheeses, breadcrumbs, dressings, herbs, spices, condiments and other non-liquid ingredients. Top with Buttered Breadcrumbs, page 120, and bake until heated through.

Beef Stroganoff

If you make this ahead and freeze it, leave out the sour cream. Add it just before serving.

1/4 cup (1/2 stick) butter
1/2 lb. fresh mushrooms
3/4 cup finely chopped onion
1/4 cup flour
3/4 teaspoon salt
1-1/2 lbs. beef sirloin tip,
   cut in strips 1/2-in. thick,
   2-in. long
Cooking oil as necessary
1 (10-1/2-oz.) can or
   1-1/3 cups beef bouillon

1 teaspoon Worcestershire sauce
3 tablespoons tomato paste,
   if desired
1/2 teaspoon MSG (monosodium glutamate),
   if desired
Water, if necessary
1 cup (1/2 pint) dairy sour cream,
   room temperature
Hot cooked noodles
Chopped parsley for garnish

Melt butter in a fry pan. Wash, drain and slice mushrooms. Sauté mushrooms until golden. Using slotted spoon, remove to a plate. Sauté onion until golden. Remove to a plate with slotted spoon. Combine flour and salt in a paper bag. Add beef strips and shake to dredge. Brown beef strips, a few at a time, in butter remaining in fry pan, adding oil as necessary. Remove to plate as soon as browned on both sides. Pour off excess oil. Return beef and onions to fry pan. Add bouillon, Worcestershire sauce, tomato paste and MSG, if desired; blend. Cover and simmer gently until meat is tender, 30 to 45 minutes. Stir occasionally to prevent sticking. Add water, if necessary, to make about 1 cup sauce. Before serving, add mushrooms to beef-sauce mixture and remove from heat. Empty sour cream into a medium bowl. Gradually add beef-sauce mixture, stirring constantly. Return to fry pan and heat gently to serving temperature. Serve over hot noodles. Garnish with chopped parsley. Makes 4 to 6 servings.

Variations

Original Beef Stroganoff: Omit mushrooms and tomato paste. Use beef tenderloin and cook just until sauce thickens. Add 1/2 teaspoon mustard, if desired.

Hamburger Stroganoff: Substitute about 1-1/2 pounds ground beef for sirloin. Reduce flour to 3 tablespoons and add to hamburger after draining excess fat. Add bouillon and cook just until thickened.

Quick Turkey Stroganoff: Omit beef. Add 2 tablespoons sherry with bouillon and heat to boiling. Add 2 cups chunked leftover turkey with sour cream.

Calorie-Conscious Stroganoff: Stir 2 tablespoons flour into beef after draining excess oil. Substitute 1 cup buttermilk or 1 cup plain yogurt for sour cream. Trims about 75 calories from each serving. Yogurt version is tangy.

The most ordinary casserole takes on a party flavor when sour cream is added. Try it in some of your own favorites. Follow the rules for preventing curdling on page 76.

How To Make
Beef Stroganoff

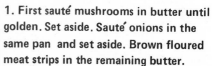

1. First sauté mushrooms in butter until golden. Set aside. Sauté onions in the same pan and set aside. Brown floured meat strips in the remaining butter.

2. After meat and onions have simmered in the sauce for 30 to 45 minutes, add mushrooms and remove from heat. Add a little of the sauce to the room temperature sour cream before adding sour cream to the meat sauce mixture. Serve over hot noodles.

Quick Hamburger Stroganoff

This quick family version is sturdy enough to withstand boiling and warming.

1 medium onion, chopped
2 tablespoons cooking oil
1 lb. lean ground beef
1 (10-1/2-oz.) can cream of mushroom soup
2 tablespoons catsup or chili sauce
1 small can sliced mushrooms, drained,
   if desired

1 cup (1/2 pint) dairy sour cream,
   room temperature
Salt to taste
Hot cooked noodles or rice

Sauté onion in oil until transparent. Add beef and cook until browned. Drain excess fat. Blend in soup, catsup or chili sauce and sliced mushrooms, if desired. Heat through. Remove from heat. Add sour cream all at once and blend well. Heat gently to serving temperature. Add salt to taste. Serve over hot noodles or rice. Makes 4 servings.

Veal Strips In Herbed Sauce

Flavorful herbs blend with sour cream.

1/3 cup flour
1-1/2 teaspoons salt
1/4 teaspoon pepper
2 lbs. thin veal cutlets,
   cut in strips
1/4 cup (1/2 stick) butter
1/2 cup chicken broth or
   1/2 cup dry white wine

2 teaspoons minced parsley
1/2 teaspoon basil
1-1/2 cups dairy sour cream,
   room temperature
Hot cooked noodles or rice
Minced parsley for garnish

Combine flour, salt and pepper in a paper bag. Add veal strips and shake to dredge. In a large fry pan, brown veal in butter. Add a little more butter, if necessary to complete browning. Add broth or wine, parsley and basil. Cook, stirring until thickened. Cover and simmer very slowly about 30 minutes or until veal is tender. Empty sour cream into a large bowl. Gradually add sauce, stirring constantly. Return mixture to fry pan and heat gently to serving temperature. Serve over hot noodles or rice. Garnish with minced parsley. Makes 6 to 8 servings.

Variation

Substitute 6 to 8 shoulder lamb or pork chops, cut in strips, for veal cutlets.

Lobster Newburg

Wonderful aroma! Delightful flavor! And not at all difficult to make.

2 (9-oz.) pkgs. frozen lobster tails
3 tablespoons butter
2 tablespoons flour
1 cup milk
1/4 cup dry sherry
1/2 teaspoon salt

2 teaspoons lemon juice
2 egg yolks
1 cup (1/2 pint) dairy sour cream,
   room temperature
Cooked rice, or pastry shells

Thaw lobster according to package directions. Remove from shell; cut into bite-size pieces. On medium heat, melt butter in a stainless steel or enamel saucepan. Sauté lobster briefly in butter. Remove to a plate with slotted spoon. Stir flour into remaining butter and cook until bubbly. Add milk all at once and cook, stirring until thickened. Slowly add sherry, salt and lemon juice to sauce. Cook 2 minutes. Beat egg yolks in a small bowl and blend in sour cream. Gradually add heated sauce, stirring constantly. Return to fry pan and cook gently 2 minutes. Do *not* boil! Fold in lobster. Heat gently to serving temperature. Serve over fluffy rice or in puff pastry shells. Makes 4 servings.

Chicken Divan

Sour cream adds a special touch to an already special dish.

4 frying chicken breasts, halved
Water, lightly salted
2 (10-oz.) pkgs. frozen broccoli spears or
   2 to 3 lbs. fresh broccoli
2 tablespoons butter
2 tablespoons flour
1 cup chicken broth

1 teaspoon Worcestershire sauce
1-1/4 cups grated mild Cheddar cheese
1 cup (1/2 pint) dairy sour cream,
   room temperature
Salt to taste
Paprika

Simmer chicken in lightly salted water to cover for 25 minutes or just until cooked through. Skin and bone cooked chicken. Cook broccoli and drain. Preheat oven to 325°F (163°C). Over medium heat, melt butter in a stainless steel, glass or enamel saucepan. Stir in flour and cook until bubbly. Add broth and Worcestershire sauce. Cook, stirring until thickened. Reduce heat. Stir in 1 cup of the cheese, heating gently until melted. Empty sour cream into 1 medium bowl. Gradually add cheese sauce, stirring constantly. Add salt to taste. Arrange broccoli in 8 portions in a 13" x 9" x 2" baking dish. Top each portion with half a chicken breast. Pour sauce over all. Sprinkle with remaining cheese and paprika. Bake 20 minutes or until heated through. Brown under broiler, if desired. Makes 8 servings.

Garlic Fried Chicken

This is home-fried chicken at its best.

Saucy Marinade, see below
1 (2-1/2- to 3-lb.) frying chicken

Flour for dredging
Cooking oil

Saucy Marinade:
1 cup (1/2 pint) dairy sour cream
2 cloves garlic, crushed
1 tablespoon lemon juice

1 teaspoon Worcestershire sauce
1-1/2 teaspoons seasoned salt
1/4 teaspoon pepper

Prepare Saucy Marinade. Cut chicken in serving pieces. Dip in marinade to coat. Put in shallow dish; spoon on remaining marinade. Cover and refrigerate overnight. Dredge marinated chicken in flour. Fry in hot cooking oil, 1-inch deep, until browned and crisp on both sides. Reduce heat and fry slowly until tender, about 40 minutes. Do not crowd chicken in pan and do not cover. Makes 4 servings.

Saucy Marinade:
Blend marinade ingredients together in a medium bowl.

Chicken Curry

A delicious curry with condiments already in the sauce.

1/4 cup blanched, slivered almonds
1/4 cup (1/2 stick) butter
1/2 cup chopped onion
1/2 cup chopped celery
1 tablespoon curry powder
1/2 teaspoon salt
1/4 teaspoon pepper
1/4 cup flour
1 cup chicken broth

1/2 cup seedless raisins
1 (8-oz.) can tomato sauce
1 teaspoon Worcestershire sauce
1 cup (1/2 pint) dairy sour cream, room temperature
3 to 4 cups chunked, skinned and boned, cooked chicken
Hot cooked rice
Condiments, if desired

On medium heat, sauté almonds in butter until golden. Add onion and celery. Cook until onion is transparent. Add curry powder, salt and pepper. Cook 1 minute. Stir in flour and cook 1 minute. Add broth and cook, stirring until sauce thickens. Mix in raisins, tomato sauce and Worcestershire sauce. Combine sour cream and chicken in a large bowl. Gradually add sauce, stirring constantly. Return to pan and heat gently to serving temperature. Serve with hot rice and an assortment of condiments, if desired. Makes 4 to 6 servings.

Swedish Meatballs

Meatballs with this subtle spice flavor will disappear in minutes.

1 lb. ground beef
1 egg
1 cup soft breadcrumbs
  (2 slices bread)
1 teaspoon brown sugar
1/2 teaspoon salt
1/4 teaspoon pepper
1/4 teaspoon ginger

1/4 teaspoon ground cloves
1/4 teaspoon nutmeg
1/4 teaspoon cinnamon
1/2 cup milk
Cooking oil
Sour Cream Sauce, see below
Boiled potatoes or hot cooked noodles
Minced parsley for garnish

Sour Cream Sauce:
2 tablespoons butter
2 tablespoons flour
1 cup beef broth
1/2 teaspoon salt

Dash cayenne pepper
1/2 teaspoon Worcestershire sauce
1 cup (1/2 pint) dairy sour cream,
  room temperature

Blend ground beef, egg and breadcrumbs thoroughly with brown sugar, salt, pepper, ginger, ground cloves, nutmeg, cinnamon and milk. Form into 12 meatballs. Fry in hot oil, about 1-inch deep, until fully cooked, turning only once. Drain on paper towels. Prepare Sour Cream Sauce. Fold meatballs into sauce. Spoon into a chafing dish, stainless steel or enamel pan. Heat gently to serving temperature. Serve with boiled potatoes or hot noodles. Garnish with minced parsley. Makes 4 servings.

Sour Cream Sauce:
Pour all excess oil from fry pan. Add butter to brownings. Stir in flour and cook until bubbly. Add broth, salt, cayenne pepper and Worcestershire sauce; cook, stirring until thickened and bubbly. Empty sour cream into a large bowl. Gradually add sauce, stirring constantly.

Variation

Swedish Appetizer Meatballs: Form 50 one-inch-diameter meatballs and fry. Serve in sauce from a chafing dish.

To bake potatoes in half the time, stick an aluminum nail through each potato from end to end. These nails can be purchased from housewares departments or novelty mail order houses.

Fillet Of Sole Gourmet

Handsome fish roll-ups add sophistication to a buffet supper.

1 (6-oz.) pkg. white and wild rice mix
1 (10-oz.) pkg. frozen asparagus spears or
   1-1/2 lbs. fresh asparagus
1 cup finely chopped celery
3 tablespoons butter
3 tablespoons flour
1 cup milk
1/2 teaspoon salt
1 teaspoon Worcestershire sauce

1 tablespoon fresh lemon juice
1 cup (1/2 pint) dairy sour cream,
   room temperature
6 sole fillets (1-1/2 to 2 lbs.)
1/2 fresh lemon
Salt to taste
2 tablespoons Parmesan cheese
2 tablespoons sliced almonds,
   lightly toasted

Butter an 11" x 7" x 2" baking dish. Cook rice according to package directions. Spoon into buttered baking dish. Cook asparagus according to package directions; drain. Preheat oven to 350°F (177°C). Sauté celery in butter. Stir in flour and cook 1 minute. Add milk all at once and cook, stirring until sauce thickens. Add salt, Worcestershire sauce and lemon juice. Empty sour cream into a medium bowl. Gradually add sauce, stirring constantly. Sprinkle fillets lightly with juice of half a lemon. Add salt to taste. Roll each fish fillet around 2 or 3 cooked asparagus spears. Arrange roll-ups on top of cooked rice, seam-side down. Spoon sour cream sauce over fish. Sprinkle with cheese and almonds. Bake 25 minutes or just until fish becomes milky white and flakes easily. Makes 6 servings.

Chicken Paprikash

Sweet pepper, or paprika, and sour cream are used generously in Hungarian cooking.

2 tablespoons flour
1 teaspoon salt
1 (2-1/2- to 3-lb.) frying chicken,
   cut in pieces
2 to 3 tablespoons butter
1 medium onion, finely chopped
1/2 medium green pepper,
   finely chopped
1 small clove garlic, crushed

1 tablespoon flour
1 tablespoon paprika
1/4 teaspoon salt
3/4 cup chicken broth
1 cup (1/2 pint) dairy sour cream,
   room temperature
Hot noodles or rice
Parsley for garnish

Combine 2 tablespoons flour and 1 teaspoon salt in paper bag. Add chicken pieces and shake to dredge. In a large stainless steel, enamel or teflon-lined fry pan, brown chicken in butter. Remove to a plate. In the same fry pan, sauté onion, green pepper and garlic until tender. Stir in 1 tablespoon flour, paprika and 1/4 teaspoon salt. Cook 1 minute. Add chicken broth and cook, stirring until thickened. Return chicken to pan and simmer, covered, about 45 minutes or until tender. Remove chicken and arrange in an 11" x 7" x 2" baking dish. Empty sour cream into a medium bowl. Gradually add paprika sauce, stirring constantly. Spoon sauce over chicken. Place chicken under broiler a few minutes or until sauce begins to bubble. Serve with hot noodles or rice. Garnish with parsley. Makes 4 servings.

Caraway Goulash

Paprika and sour cream give flavor to this popular beef dish.

2 lbs. stewing beef
1 tablespoon cooking oil
6 tablespoons (3/4 stick) butter
3 medium onions, chopped
1 clove garlic, crushed
6 tablespoons flour
4 teaspoons paprika
1 teaspoon salt

1 cup beef broth
1/2 teaspoon caraway seed
1/2 teaspoon marjoram
1 cup (1/2 pint) dairy sour cream,
    room temperature
Hot cooked noodles or rice
Minced parsley for garnish

Cut beef into 1-inch cubes. Brown in oil in a large saucepan. Remove to a plate. In the same pan, add butter. Sauté onion and garlic until tender. Stir in flour, paprika and salt. Cook 1 minute. Add broth, caraway seed and marjoram. Cook, stirring until thickened. Return meat to pan. Cover and simmer *very slowly* 1 hour. Remove cover and simmer 2 hours longer or until meat is tender. Empty sour cream into a large bowl. Gradually add meat sauce, stirring constantly. Return to pan and heat gently to serving temperature. Serve over hot noodles or rice. Garnish with minced parsley. Makes 8 servings.

Easy Hamburger Wellington

Meat loaf goes incognito—and elegant!

1 egg
2 lbs. lean ground beef
1 cup (1/2 pint) dairy sour cream
1/2 cup dry breadcrumbs
1/4 cup hamburger relish
1/4 cup finely chopped onion

1-1/2 teaspoons salt
1/8 teaspoon pepper
1 teaspoon Worcestershire sauce
1 recipe Fabulous Biscuit dough,
    page 113
Parsley for garnish

Preheat oven to 425°F (218°C). Beat egg slightly in a large bowl. Mix in ground beef, sour cream, breadcrumbs, relish, onion, salt, pepper and Worcestershire sauce. Shape into a loaf about 12-inches long. Prepare fabulous Biscuit dough, page 113. On well-floured board, roll out to a 12-inch square. Center meat loaf on dough and wrap dough around. Moisten overlapping edges to seal. Place loaf, overlapped-edge down, on a baking sheet. Cut several small vents on top. Bake 10 minutes. Reduce heat to 325°F (163°C) and continue baking 1 hour. Serve whole on a platter. Garnish with parsley. Makes 8 servings.

California Shrimp Curry

It's out of this world!

3/4 lb. fresh or frozen shrimp
1 large tomato
1 ripe avocado
2 tablespoons fresh lime juice
3 tablespoons butter
1-1/2 teaspoons curry powder
1/2 teaspoon salt

1 medium onion, chopped
3 tablespoons flour
1/2 cup chicken broth
1 cup (1/2 pint) dairy sour cream,
    room temperature
Hot cooked rice

Cook and clean shrimp; cut into bite-size pieces. Peel, seed and chop tomato. Peel and chunk avocado, toss gently with lime juice. Set all aside. Melt butter with curry powder and salt over medium heat. Add onion; sauté until transparent. Stir in flour. Cook 1 minute. Add broth and cook, stirring until sauce thickens. Empty sour cream into a medium bowl. Gradually add sauce, stirring constantly; return to pan. Just before serving, fold in tomato and shrimp. Heat *just* to serving temperature. Overheating toughens shrimp and thins the sauce. Fold in avocado and lime juice. Serve *immediately* over hot rice. Makes 4 servings.

Hearty Beef & Corn Casserole

Sour cream adds quality to this potluck casserole.

8 oz. extra-wide egg noodles
Water, lightly salted
1 tablespoon butter or oil
1 cup Buttered Breadcrumbs,
    page 120
1 lb. lean ground beef
1 medium onion, chopped
1/2 teaspoon basil
1/2 teaspoon MSG (monosodium glutamate),
    if desired

3/4 teaspoon salt
1/2 teaspoon pepper
1 (12-oz.) can whole kernel corn,
    well-drained
1 (10-1/2-oz.) can cream of mushroom soup
1 cup (1/2 pint) dairy sour cream,
    room temperature
1/4 cup chopped pimiento

Preheat oven to 375°F (191°C). Cook noodles in lightly salted water according to package directions, adding 1 tablespoon butter or oil to water; drain. Prepare Buttered Breadcrumbs, page 120. Brown beef with onion and basil in a 4-quart pot; drain excess fat. Fold in noodles and remaining ingredients. Pour into a 13" x 9" baking dish. Sprinkle with Buttered Breadcrumbs. Bake 30 minutes or until bubbly. Let stand 10 minutes before serving. Makes 6 servings.

Tortilla Chip Casserole

The younger set loves these flavors.

1 medium onion, finely chopped
2 tablespoons butter
2 (8-oz.) cans tomato sauce
1 (4-oz.) can diced green chilies
2 teaspoons leaf oregano
1 teaspoon salt
1 (8-oz.) pkg. tortilla chips

1/2 lb. Monterey Jack cheese,
  cut in 1/2-in. cubes
2 to 3 cups chunked, skinned and
  boned, cooked chicken
1 cup (1/2 pint) dairy sour cream,
  room temperature
1/3 cup grated Cheddar cheese

Preheat oven to 325°F (163°C). Butter a 2-1/2- or 3-quart casserole. Sauté onion in butter until transparent. Add tomato sauce, chilies, oregano and salt. Simmer sauce, uncovered, for 10 minutes; remove from heat. Layer in the buttered casserole, in order, half the following: tortilla chips, Monterey Jack cheese, chicken and sauce. Repeat with the other half of each. Bake 20 minutes. Remove from oven and spread sour cream over top; wreath with grated cheese. Broil just until cheese melts. Serve immediately. Makes 6 to 8 servings.

Mellow Macaroni Cheese Bake

Macaroni and cheese fit for a king—and maybe even the boss and his wife.

8 oz. elbow macaroni
Water, lightly salted
1 small onion, finely chopped
1/4 cup (1/2 stick) butter
1/4 cup flour
1 cup milk
1/2 teaspoon salt

1 teaspoon Worcestershire sauce
1-1/2 cups grated sharp
  Cheddar cheese (6 oz.)
1 cup (1/2 pint) dairy sour cream,
  room temperature
1/2 lb. bacon, crisp fried and crumbled,
  if desired

Preheat oven to 375°F (191°C) Butter a 2-quart casserole. Cook macaroni in lightly salted water according to package directions; drain. In a stainless steel, glass or enamel saucepan, sauté onion in butter until transparent. Stir in flour. Cook 1 minute. Add milk. Cook, stirring until sauce thickens. Add salt, Worcestershire sauce and cheese. Heat, stirring until cheese melts. Empty sour cream into a large bowl. Gradually add sauce, stirring constantly. Fold in macaroni. Pour into casserole and sprinkle with bacon, if desired. Bake 25 to 30 minutes or until bubbly. Makes 6 servings.

Variation

Substitute 1/4 cup Buttered Breadcrumbs, page 120, or 1/2 cup grated Cheddar cheese, for crumbled bacon, if desired.

Tuna-Noodle Casserole

New look for an old favorite.

1/2 cup Buttered Breadcrumbs,
   page 120
8 oz. egg noodles or
   elbow macaroni
Water, lightly salted
1 tablespoon butter or oil
1 cup (1/2 pint) dairy sour cream,
   room temperature
3 tablespoons butter
3 tablespoons flour

1/2 teaspoon salt
1/8 teaspoon pepper
1 (10-1/2-oz.) can
   cream of mushroom soup
1/8 teaspoon tarragon or basil
1/4 cup chopped pimiento
2 (6-1/2-oz.) cans white chunk tuna,
   well-drained
Chopped parsley for garnish

Preheat oven to 350°F (177°C). Butter a 3-quart casserole. Prepare Buttered Breadcrumbs, page 120. Cook noodles or macaroni in lightly salted water according to package directions. adding 1 tablespoon butter or oil to water; drain. Empty sour cream into a large bowl. Fold in noodles or macaroni. Melt 3 tablespoons butter in a saucepan. Stir in flour, salt and pepper; cook until bubbly. Add soup and tarragon or basil. Cook, stirring until mixture thickens. Gradually add sauce to noodles and sour cream, folding continuously. Fold in pimiento and tuna. Pour into buttered casserole and sprinkle with Buttered Breadcrumbs. Bake about 20 minutes or until piping hot. Garnish with chopped parsley and serve. Makes 6 servings.

Stuffed Baked Potatoes

A do-ahead recipe that's great for serving a crowd.

2 large baking potatoes
1 cup (1/2 pint) dairy sour cream
2 tablespoons butter
1/2 teaspoon salt
Freshly ground pepper

2 tablespoons minced green onion,
   if desired
Salt
Grated Cheddar cheese

Bake potatoes according to directions on page 92. Reduce oven heat to 375°F (191°C). Slice potatoes in half lengthwise. With a potholder protecting your palm, cup a potato half in your hand. Gently scoop insides of potato into a bowl, leaving just enough pulp next to potato skin to keep it from breaking. Repeat with remaining potato halves. Set aside potato skins. To scooped-out potato add sour cream, butter 1/2 teaspoon salt, pepper and green onion, if desired. Blend with fork until well-mixed but not necessarily smooth. Add salt as desired. Fill shells to heaping with potato mixture. Place on baking sheet and sprinkle with grated cheese. Potatoes may be refrigerated at this point for up to 24 hours. Bake 10 to 15 minutes, or longer if refrigerated. Brown cheese under broiler, if desired. Makes 4 servings.

Artichokes California-Style

Serve artichokes hot or cold with a quick and easy dip.

4 artichokes
Boiling water, lightly salted
4 (1/2-in.) lemon slices
4 tablespoons oil

4 cloves garlic, if desired
Melted butter or dip,
   see below

Trim artichokes by cutting 1 inch from top and all but 1 inch from stem. Snip off tips of all exposed leaves, if desired. Drop into boiling salted water. Add lemon, oil and garlic, if desired. Cook 20 to 45 minutes or until stem can be pierced easily with fork. Drain upside down. Cut off remaining stem to serve in upright position. Serve hot or cold with melted butter or dip, see below. Makes 4 servings.

Dips

Sour Cream Dip: Sour cream, salt and pepper to taste.
Lemon Dip: 1/2 cup sour cream, 2 tablespoons lemon juice, salt and pepper to taste, 1 teaspoon prepared mustard, if desired.
Calorie-Counters' Mayonnaise: Equal parts sour cream and mayonnaise, lemon juice and salt to taste.
Miscellaneous Dips: Dip or salad dressing mix made according to package directions with sour cream.

Sour Cream Scalloped Potatoes

Delicious scalloped potatoes—and they don't curdle.

1 cup Buttered Breadcrumbs,
   page 120
2 lbs. boiling potatoes, pared and
   thinly sliced
1 medium onion, chopped

Water, lightly salted
1 recipe Basic Sour Cream Sauce,
   page 72
1/8 teaspoon paprika

Preheat oven to 350°F (177°C). Butter an 11" x 7" x 2" baking dish. Prepare Buttered Breadcrumbs, page 120. Gently parboil potatoes and onion in salted water to cover just until tender, about 5 to 10 minutes. Drain. Prepare Basic Sour Cream Sauce, page 72, and add paprika. Layer half the potato-onion mixture and half the sauce in buttered baking dish. Repeat with remaining halves. Sprinkle with Buttered Breadcrumbs. Bake, uncovered, 30 minutes or until potatoes are very tender and sauce is bubbling. Makes 6 to 8 servings.

Variation

Sour Cream Au Gratin Potatoes: Substitute Basic Sour Cream Sauce with Cheese variation, page 72, for Basic Sour Cream Sauce.

Baked Potato With Sour Cream

The easiest and most nutritious method can be the most glamorous.

4 medium baking potatoes
Butter, shortening, oil or bacon fat
Salt and pepper to taste

Topping, see below
Garnish, see below

Select mature baking potatoes of uniform size and regular shape. Idaho Russets are the classic choice; large red potatoes are also good. Preheat oven to 425°F (218°C). Wash, dry and rub potatoes with butter, shortening, oil or bacon fat. A potato baked in foil is not as fluffy because foil holds in moisture. Pierce each potato with a fork so steam can escape. Place on a baking sheet. Bake 40 to 60 minutes. Potatoes are done when they yield easily to squeezing. To serve, roll potato under hand, slash top lengthwise and, using both hands, press ends toward center until potato pops open. Fluff with a fork. Sprinkle salt and pepper into potato. Serve with your choice of toppings and garnishes listed below. Makes 4 servings.

Toppings

(one cup of topping makes about 4 servings)
Sour cream
Leftover sour cream dips
Cottage cheese
A mixture of cottage cheese and
   sour cream
Thousand Island Dressing, page 49
Plain yogurt, herbed and seasoned
Basic Sour Cream Sauce With Cheese
   variation, page 72

Garnishes

Chopped chives or green onions
Crumbled crisp fried bacon
Crumbled blue cheese
Grated Cheddar cheese
Chopped parsley
Chopped green pepper
Minced pimiento
Dry or fresh herbs
Poppy, caraway or toasted sesame seeds

Mashed Potatoes

For mashed potatoes that melt in your mouth, whip them with sour cream.

1-1/2 lbs. Russet potatoes
   (about 3 medium)
Water, lightly salted

3/4 cup dairy sour cream
2 tablespoons butter
Salt to taste

Peel and quarter potatoes. Cook in boiling salted water until potatoes break apart when pierced with fork. Drain liquid from potatoes; reserve to make gravy, if desired. Return potatoes to low heat to dry any remaining moisture. Add sour cream and butter to potatoes. Heat slightly. Whip potatoes with electric mixer until smooth and fluffy. Salt to taste. Makes 4 to 6 servings.

Variation

Buttermilk Mashed Potatoes: Substitute 1/2 cup buttermilk for sour cream.

Emerald & White Vegetable Delight

It tastes as good as it looks.

1 small head cauliflower
Boiling water
1/2 teaspoon salt
1 teaspoon vinegar
1 recipe Basic Sour Cream Sauce
   made with chicken broth,
   page 72

1 or 2 (10-oz.) pkgs. frozen peas
Water, lightly salted
Paprika for garnish
Chopped pimiento for garnish

Wash cauliflower; remove green outer leaves and leave whole. Cook, covered, in 1 inch of boiling water to which 1/2 teaspoon salt and 1 teaspoon vinegar have been added. Vinegar added to cooking water keeps cauliflower white and firm textured. Cook just until tender when tested with fork, about 20 to 30 minutes. Prepare Basic Sour Cream Sauce, page 72. Cook peas in lightly salted water according to package directions; drain. Center cauliflower on serving platter. Surround with peas and top with sauce. Garnish with paprika and chopped pimiento. Serve with remaining sauce. Makes 4 to 6 servings.

Spinach à la Crème

The nicest way to serve cooked spinach.

1 (10-oz.) pkg. frozen chopped spinach
Water, lightly salted
1/4 cup minced onion
1 small clove garlic, crushed
2 tablespoons butter
1 tablespoon flour

1/4 teaspoon salt
1/2 cup dairy sour cream,
   room temperature
1 or 2 slices bacon, crisp fried
   and crumbled, if desired

Cook spinach in lightly salted water according to package directions. Drain thoroughly in strainer. Sauté onion and garlic in butter until tender. Stir in flour and cook 1 minute. Add drained spinach and salt. Cook, stirring over low heat until very thick. Remove from heat. Add sour cream all at once and blend. Fold in crumbled bacon, if desired. Heat gently to serving temperature. Makes 3 to 4 servings.

Variations

Buttermilk Creamed Spinach: Substitute 1/2 cup buttermilk for sour cream.
Special Spinach à la Crème: Substitute 1/2 cup whipping cream for sour cream.

Broccoli en Casserole

A green vegetable with a difference.

1 bunch fresh broccoli (about 1-1/2 lbs.) or
  2 (10-oz.) pkgs. frozen broccoli spears
Boiling water, lightly salted
1/2 recipe Basic Sour Cream Sauce,
  page 72

1 teaspoon instant minced onion
2 to 4 tablespoons Buttered Breadcrumbs,
  page 120
Lemon wedges or lemon juice

Preheat oven to 350°F (177°C). Butter an 11" x 7" x 2" baking dish. Cook broccoli in boiling salted water until tender. Drain and arrange in buttered baking dish. Prepare Basic Sour Cream Sauce, page 72; add instant minced onion. Pour sauce over broccoli. Prepare Buttered Breadcrumbs, page 120. Sprinkle over sauce. Bake 15 minutes. Serve with a squeeze of fresh lemon juice or lemon wedges. Makes 4 to 6 servings.

Very Special Creamed Carrots

Carrots are wonderful for a meal with unpredictable timing. They always keep their color.

1 lb. carrots
Boiling water, lightly salted
1/2 recipe Basic Sour Cream Sauce,
  page 72
2 tablespoons chopped parsley

1 teaspoon instant minced onion
Pepper to taste
2 to 4 tablespoons Buttered Breadcrumbs,
  page 120

Preheat oven to 350°F (177°C). Butter a 1-quart casserole. Peel carrots; slice on diagonal. Cook in small amount of boiling salted water until tender. Drain. Prepare Basic Sour Cream Sauce, page 72, fold in carrots, parsley, onion and pepper. Turn into buttered casserole. Prepare Buttered Breadcrumbs, page 120. Sprinkle over casserole. Bake 15 minutes. Makes 3 to 4 servings.

Zucchini With Sour Cream Topping

What a tasty way to serve zucchini!

8 small zucchini
Boiling water, lightly salted
2 tablespoons butter, melted
Salt and pepper to taste

1 cup (1/2 pint) dairy sour cream,
   room temperature
1/2 cup shredded sharp Cheddar cheese

Wash and trim ends from zucchini. In enough boiling salted water to cover, cook whole zucchini until tender, about 10 minutes. Brush zucchini with melted butter and place in an 11" x 7" x 2" baking dish. Blend salt and pepper into sour cream and spread over zucchini. Sprinkle with cheese. Broil just until cheese melts and begins to brown. Serve immediately. Makes 4 to 6 servings.

Spirited Sprouts

A savory, saucy vegetable for any time of year.

2 (10-oz.) pkgs. frozen Brussels sprouts or
  2 lbs. fresh Brussels sprouts
Water, lightly salted
6 strips bacon
1/2 cup minced onion

1 teaspoon salt
1/4 teaspoon Tabasco® sauce
1 cup (1/2 pint) dairy sour cream,
   room temperature
Paprika for garnish

Cook Brussels sprouts in lightly salted water according to package directions. Drain and keep warm. Fry bacon until crisp. Remove and drain on paper towels. Sauté onion in bacon fat until tender. Drain all excess fat. Crumble bacon and mix with onion and remaining ingredients. Fold into Brussels sprouts. Heat gently just to serving temperature. Serve garnished with paprika. Makes 6 servings.

Add a little butter or oil to the cooking water to prevent vegetables, macaroni or rice from boiling over.

Cottage Cheese Main Dishes & Vegetables

The Chilimex Casserole, page 100, contains an invisible ingredient that makes it more moist, more flavorful and more nutritious. It's cottage cheese. You may not think of cottage cheese as a main dish ingredient, but when you discover what advantages it brings, and how versatile it is, you will quickly accept its new role.

When you plan a meal, you almost automatically select a main dish that is a generous source of protein—like meat, fish, fowl, eggs or cheese. This happens whether you think of it in terms of nutrition or not. Cottage cheese, as an excellent source of complete body-building protein, fits right into this company. It also provides more protein for fewer calories than most common "diet" foods. Compare these figures. And the costs, too.

Protein And Calorie Contents Of Common Low-Calorie Main Dishes

	Grams Protein	Calories
3/4 cup cottage cheese	21	180
3/4 cup lowfat cottage cheese	24	150
1/4 broiler chicken, fried	22.4	232
1 broiled hamburger patty (1/4 pound raw)	21.8	224
3 hard-cooked eggs, large size	20.7	240
2 broiled lamb rib chops, fat trimmed (1/2 pound raw)	21.0	238

Add cottage cheese to a meatless casserole to make it more hearty. Use it with a potato or pasta dish to add flavor and replace some of the starch with protein. Cottage cheese will even give your meatballs and meat loaf extra moisture and flavor. However you plan to use it, you should know that when cottage cheese is heated it becomes a liquid. For this reason it must be measured as carefully as any liquid ingredient. See page 181 for instructions on measuring dairy foods accurately. Hot dishes, like the ones presented in this section, are wonderful for using any cottage cheese that you have in the freezer. Thawed cottage cheese blends into casseroles and batters easily and gives all the benefits of fresh cottage cheese.

You'll find recipes here that are wonderful for calorie counters, budget watchers, protein boosters, vegetarians and all others who enjoy good cooking. Discover this new world of cottage cheese cookery and enjoy the raves you'll get.

When you are preparing a waterbath in an aluminum pan, put a tablespoon of vinegar in the water to prevent darkening of the metal.

Cottage Meat Loaf

Meat loaf takes on new moistness and flavor.

1/4 cup catsup
2 teaspoons brown sugar
2 teaspoons prepared mustard
1 egg
1 lb. lean ground beef
1/2 cup cottage cheese
1/2 medium onion, minced
1/2 cup cracker crumbs

1/4 cup minced celery
1/4 cup minced green pepper
2 tablespoons toasted sesame seeds
1/2 clove garlic, crushed
1 tablespoon Worcestershire sauce
1/2 teaspoon salt
1/4 teaspoon basil
1/8 teaspoon pepper

Preheat oven to 350°F (177°C). Blend catsup, brown sugar, and mustard together. Set aside for topping. Beat egg slightly in a large bowl. Add remaining ingredients and mix thoroughly. Shape into loaf; place in a 9" x 5" x 2-3/4" loaf pan. Spread topping over loaf. Bake 1 hour or until done. Let stand 10 minutes before slicing. Makes 4 to 6 servings.

Hamburger Noodle Bake

A potluck supper favorite. Cut the recipe in half for a smaller group.

1 (8-oz.) pkg. medium or
   wide egg noodles
Water, lightly salted
1 tablespoon butter or oil
1 lb. lean ground beef
2 (8-oz.) cans tomato sauce

1 (8-oz.) pkg. cream cheese,
   room temperature
1 cup (1/2 pint) cottage cheese
1/4 cup dairy sour cream
1/3 cup minced green onion
1 tablespoon minced green pepper

Preheat oven to 350°F (177°C). Butter a 13" x 9" x 2" baking dish. Cook noodles in lightly salted water according to package directions, adding 1 tablespoon butter or oil to water; drain. Brown ground beef in a large fry pan, breaking into small pieces. Drain excess fat. Stir in tomato sauce and remove from heat. Blend cream cheese to smooth. Blend in cottage cheese, sour cream, onion and green pepper. Spread half of noodles over bottom of buttered baking dish. Cover with cheese mixture and then remaining noodles. Top with meat sauce. Bake 20 to 25 minutes. Makes 6 to 8 servings.

Variation

Hamburger Noodles Italiano: Sauté 1 clove crushed garlic with ground beef. Add 1 teaspoon chili powder, 1/2 teaspoon basil, 1/2 teaspoon leaf oregano and a pinch ground cloves to meat sauce. Proceed as above. Serve with shredded Parmesan cheese.

Meal-In-A-Pot

A delicious thin stew or hearty soup. Perfect with cole slaw and French bread.

2 teaspoons salt
1/2 teaspoon pepper
1 teaspoon paprika
2 medium potatoes
1 cup chopped celery
4 medium carrots

1 large green pepper
3 medium onions
2 lbs. ground beef
1-1/2 cups cottage cheese
1 (1-lb.) can stewed tomatoes,
   undrained

Preheat oven to 350°F (177°C). Butter a 4-quart Dutch oven. Combine salt, pepper and paprika; set aside. Peel and thinly slice potatoes; chop celery and carrots; mince green pepper; chop or slice and ring onions. Set all aside. Break up ground beef in fry pan and brown. Drain excess fat and blend in cottage cheese. In the buttered Dutch oven, layer the following in order, sprinkling combined seasonings over each: potatoes, celery and carrots, ground beef mixture, green pepper and onion. Top with tomatoes. Cover and bake 1-1/2 hours. Uncover for last half hour. Serve in individual casseroles or soup bowls. Makes 8 to 10 servings.

Tuna Casserole

One of our most requested recipes.

1 recipe Buttered Breadcrumbs, page 120
2 eggs
2 cups (1 pint) cottage cheese
1 (6-1/2-oz.) can white chunk tuna,
   drained and flaked

1/8 teaspoon pepper
1/2 teaspoon Worcestershire sauce
1/4 cup soft breadcrumbs

Butter a 1-quart casserole. Set aside. Prepare water bath by placing a large shallow pan of water in center of oven; preheat oven to 375°F (191°C). Water should be deep enough to come halfway up side of casserole. Prepare Buttered Breadcrumbs, page 120. Beat eggs in a large bowl. Blend in cottage cheese, tuna and remaining ingredients. Pour into casserole and sprinkle with Buttered Breadcrumbs. Set in water bath and bake 35 minutes or until just set. Makes 4 to 6 servings.

Variation

Substitute crushed potato chips for Buttered Breadcrumbs.

Tuna-Noodle Favorite

The kind of dish you get a craving for.

4 oz. egg noodles
Water, lightly salted
1 tablespoon butter or oil
1 (1-3/8- or 1-1/2-oz.) pkg.
  cheese sauce mix
1/2 cup milk

1 cup (1/2 pint) cottage cheese
1/2 (10-oz.) pkg. frozen peas
1 (6-1/2-oz.) can white chunk tuna,
  drained and flaked
Crushed cheese or garlic croutons

Cook noodles in lightly salted water according to package directions, adding 1 tablespoon butter or oil to water; drain. In a large saucepan, blend cheese sauce mix and milk until smooth. Add cottage cheese and cook, stirring often until sauce boils. Break up peas; add to sauce. Cook until peas are tender and sauce is smooth and thick. Fold in tuna and noodles. Heat to serving temperature. Turn into serving dish; sprinkle with crushed croutons. Serve immediately. Makes 4 servings.

Crab Meat Casserole

Everyone likes this low-calorie crab and cottage cheese custard.

1 recipe Buttered Breadcrumbs,
  page 120
3 eggs, separated
2 teaspoons flour
1/2 teaspoon salt

2 tablespoons finely minced onion
1-1/2 cups cottage cheese
1 (7-oz.) can crab meat, drained
Paprika

Butter a 1-1/2-quart casserole. Set aside. Prepare waterbath by placing a large shallow pan of water in center of oven; preheat oven to 325°F (163°C). Water should come up 1 inch on outside of casserole. Prepare Buttered Breadcrumbs, page 120. Mix egg yolks, flour, salt and onion. Fold in cottage cheese. Reserve several large chunks of crab meat. Flake remainder and fold into cheese mixture. Beat egg whites until stiff but not dry. Fold into crab cheese mixture. Pour into casserole and sprinkle with Buttered Breadcrumbs. Arrange reserved crab meat chunks on top and dust lightly with paprika. Place casserole in waterbath and bake 45 minutes or until set. Makes 4 to 6 servings.

Variations

Individual Crab Meat Casseroles: Bake in buttered individual shells as directed above from 20 to 30 minutes or until set.
Tuna-Cheese Casserole: Substitute 1 (6-1/2-oz.) can white chunk tuna, drained, for crab meat.

Chilimex Casserole

Let your teen-agers cook their own supper. They'll love this.

1 cup corn bread mix
1 cup (1/2 pint) cottage cheese
1/3 cup water

2 (15-oz.) cans chili con carne with beans
1 (12-oz.) can Mexican-style corn
Pimiento strips, if desired

Preheat oven to 425°F (218°C). In a medium bowl, blend corn bread mix, cottage cheese and water. Set aside. Blend chili con carne with beans and corn in an 11" x 7" x 2" baking dish. If chili is thin, drain the corn before adding to baking dish. Drop corn bread mix by spoonfuls onto chili. Garnish with pimiento strips, if desired. Bake 30 minutes or until browned and bubbling. Makes 4 to 6 servings.

South-Of-The-Border Chili Casserole

Mexican flavors with convenience foods.

1 (3-oz.) pkg. cream cheese,
   room temperature
3/4 cup cottage cheese
1/2 cup dairy sour cream
3 tablespoons minced green onion
2 tablespoons diced green chilies

1/4 teaspoon salt
1 cup (8-oz. can) chili and beans
1 (2-1/4-oz.) can sliced ripe olives
2 cups whole corn chips
1/2 cup crushed corn chips
1/2 cup grated sharp Cheddar cheese

Preheat oven to 350°F (177°C). Butter a 1-1/2-quart casserole; set aside. Blend cream cheese until smooth. Add cottage cheese, sour cream, onion, green chilies and salt; mix well. Combine chili and beans with olives. Layer in buttered casserole, in order: 1 cup whole corn chips, cheese mixture, 1 cup whole corn chips and chili-olive mixture. Sprinkle with crushed corn chips. Bake 25 minutes. Remove from oven; sprinkle with cheese. Bake 5 to 8 minutes longer or until cheese is melted. Makes 4 servings.

Salmon-Cheese Casserole

The delicate flavor of salmon enhances "planned-over" rice and cottage cheese.

1 recipe Buttered Breadcrumbs,
    page 120
1 (7-3/4-oz.) can salmon
2 eggs
2 tablespoons butter, melted
2 cups cooked rice
1 cup (1/2 pint) cottage cheese
2 tablespoons minced onion

2 tablespoons minced green pepper
2 tablespoons minced pimiento,
    if desired
1 tablespoon lemon juice
2 teaspoons prepared mustard
1/4 teaspoon salt
1/8 teaspoon pepper
1/8 teaspoon rosemary, crushed

Preheat oven to 350°F (177°C). Butter a 1-1/2-quart casserole. Prepare Buttered Breadcrumbs, page 120; set aside. Drain salmon and flake, removing bones and skin. In a medium bowl, beat eggs until fluffy. Fold in salmon, melted butter and remaining ingredients. Pour into buttered casserole; sprinkle with Buttered Breadcrumbs. Bake 30 minutes or until set. Makes 4 servings.

Cottage Enchiladas

So tasty no one will know it's meatless. Serve with guacamole and Spanish rice or refried beans.

1 cup (1/2 pint) dairy sour cream
1-1/2 cups cottage cheese
1/2 teaspoon salt
1/8 teaspoon pepper
1 (7-oz.) can green chilies
10 corn tortillas

1/4 cup (1/2 stick) butter
3/4 lb. Monterey Jack cheese,
    cut in strips
2 (7-oz.) cans green chili salsa or
    1-3/4 cups enchilada sauce,
    prepared from mix

Preheat oven to 350°F (177°C). Blend sour cream, cottage cheese, salt and pepper. Remove seeds from chilies, cut in strips. Sauté tortillas in butter a few seconds on each side to soften; drain on paper towels. Top each tortilla with about 2 spoonfuls cottage cheese mixture; reserve excess for topping. Reserve 1/3 of the Jack cheese and chili strips for garnish. Divide remaining Jack cheese and chili strips among tortillas. Spread half of chili salsa or enchilada sauce evenly over bottom of a 13" x 9" x 2" baking dish. Roll filled tortillas and arrange in baking dish. Pour remaining chili salsa or enchilada sauce over all. Cover baking dish with foil and bake 30 minutes or until very hot. Just before serving, spoon reserved cottage cheese mixture over top and garnish with reserved cheese and chili strips. Broil until cheese is bubbly. Makes 5 servings.

Lasagne

This delicious Italian dish tastes even better assembled and refrigerated a day or two before baking.

1-1/2 cups Thick Spaghetti Sauce,
   see below
4 oz. lasagne noodles
Water, lightly salted
1 tablespoon butter or oil
1/2 lb. ground beef
2 eggs

1 cup (1/2 pint) cottage cheese
3 tablespoons minced green onion
1 tablespoon minced parsley
3/4 teaspoon salt
1/2 lb. mozzarella cheese,
   thinly sliced
1/4 cup shredded Parmesan cheese

Thick Spaghetti Sauce:
1-1/2 cloves garlic, minced
2 tablespoons olive oil or butter
1 (1-lb.) can tomato purée
1 (6-oz.) can tomato paste
2-1/4 cups water

1/2 teaspoon brown sugar
1/2 teaspoon salt
1/2 teaspoon basil
1/4 teaspoon oregano
1/8 teaspoon tarragon

Prepare Thick Spagetti Sauce. Cook noodles in lightly salted water according to package directions, adding 1 tablespoon butter or oil to water; drain. Preheat oven to 350°F (177°C). Brown ground beef, breaking into pieces; drain excess fat. Cover bottom of an 11" x 7" x 2" baking dish with a thin layer of sauce; add beef to remaining sauce. Beat eggs in a medium bowl. Blend in cottage cheese, green onion, parsley and salt. In the baking dish, layer in order half the following: noodles, cottage cheese mixture, mozzarella slices and sauce. Repeat layers. Top with Parmesan cheese. At this point, lasagne may be baked or covered and refrigerated for 1 to 2 days. Bake 30 to 35 minutes, slightly longer if refrigerated, or until bubbly. Let stand 10 minutes before cutting. Makes 4 to 6 servings.

Thick Spaghetti Sauce:

Sauté garlic in olive oil or butter until lightly browned. Add remaining ingredients. Simmer gently, uncovered, about 1-1/2 hours. Makes about 3 cups of sauce.

Variations

Meatless Lasagne: Omit ground beef.
Tuna Lasagne: Omit ground beef. Add to sauce 1 (6-1/2-oz.) can white tuna, drained and flaked.
Shrimp Lasagne: Omit ground beef. Cook and drain 1 (12-oz.) package frozen shrimp. Cut into pieces and add to sauce.
Italian Sausage Lasagne: Omit ground beef. Add to sauce 3/4-pound fresh Italian sausage, cooked and chopped.
Lasagne Florentine: Cook 1 (10-oz.) package frozen chopped spinach according to package directions. Drain thoroughly and add to cottage cheese mixture.

Manicotti

Delicious! The compliments will really flow.

2-1/2 cups Thick Spaghetti Sauce,
   page 103
1 (5-oz.) pkg. manicotti (12 pieces)
Boiling water, lightly salted
1 (8-oz.) pkg. cream cheese,
   room temperature
1 cup (1/2 pint) cottage cheese
1/4 lb. mozzarella cheese, diced
2 eggs

1 tablespoon chopped parsley
1/2 teaspoon salt
1/8 teaspoon pepper
1/8 teaspoon nutmeg
1/2 cup sauterne wine
1 (3-oz.) can sliced mushrooms,
   drained, for garnish
Grated Parmesan cheese

Prepare Thick Spaghetti Sauce, page 103. Cook manicotti, 4 at a time, in boiling salted water 5 to 6 minutes or until just done but still firm; drain. Preheat oven to 350°F (177°C). Blend cream cheese with fork until smooth. Mix in cottage cheese. Stir in mozzarella cheese, eggs, chopped parsley, salt, pepper and nutmeg. Combine wine and spaghetti sauce. Pour half into a 13" x 9" x 2" baking dish. Using a knife, fill each manicotti with about 1/4 cup cheese mixture; arrange in baking dish. Pour remaining sauce over all. Garnish with mushroom slices. Bake 20 to 25 minutes or until bubbly. Serve with Parmesan cheese. Makes 6 servings.

Simple Sirloin Dish

A dinner party casserole from the freezer.

1 (14-oz.) pkg. frozen mushroom sauce
   with sirloin tips
4 oz. medium egg noodles
Water, lightly salted
1 tablespoon butter or oil
1/4 cup Buttered Breadcrumbs,
   page 120

1 (3-oz.) pkg. cream cheese,
   room temperature
1 cup (1/2 pint) cottage cheese
1/4 teaspoon thyme
1/4 to 1/2 teaspoon tarragon
1/2 teaspoon salt
Dash pepper

Thaw or heat mushroom sauce with sirloin tips to separate meat. Preheat oven to 400°F (204°C). Butter a 1-1/2-quart casserole; set aside. Cook noodles in lightly salted water according to package directions, adding 1 tablespoon butter or oil to water; drain. Prepare Buttered Breadcrumbs, page 120, set aside. In a medium bowl, blend cream cheese to smooth. Blend in remaining ingredients. Fold in noodles. Layer in buttered casserole: half the noodle-cheese mixture, all the sirloin tips and remaining half noodle-cheese mixture. Sprinkle with Buttered Breadcrumbs. Bake, uncovered, 20 minutes. Makes 4 servings.

All-In-One Dinner

For a quick meal, always have these ingredients on hand.

1/4 cup (1/2 stick) butter, melted
1/2 cup crushed corn flakes
1 pkg. au gratin potato mix
2 cups boiling water

1 (1-lb.) can salmon, drained,
   boned and skinned
1 (10-oz.) pkg. frozen peas, thawed
1 cup (1/2 pint) cottage cheese

Preheat oven to 400°F (204°C). Toss melted butter with crushed corn flakes; set aside. In a large bowl, blend remaining ingredients and spoon into a 1-1/2-quart casserole. Sprinkle with buttered corn flake crumbs. Bake 35 minutes. Makes 4 to 6 servings.

Noodles Romanoff

The perfect accompaniment for prime rib. You'll enjoy making it.

1 (8-oz.) pkg. wide egg noodles
Water, lightly salted
1 tablespoon butter or oil
1/4 medium onion, finely chopped
2 tablespoons butter
2 tablespoons flour
1/2 teaspoon dry mustard
3/4 teaspoon salt
Dash cayenne pepper

1 cup milk
1/2 teaspoon Worcestershire sauce
Dash Tabasco® sauce
1/4 cup grated sharp Cheddar cheese
1 cup (1/2 pint) dairy sour cream,
   room temperature
1 cup (1/2 pint) small curd cottage cheese
1/4 cup crushed croutons or
   Buttered Breadcrumbs, page 120

Cook noodles in lightly salted water according to package directions, adding 1 tablespoon butter or oil to water; drain. Preheat oven to 350°F (177°C). Butter a 2-quart casserole; set aside. Over medium heat, sauté onion in butter until transparent. Stir in flour, dry mustard, salt and cayenne pepper. Cook 1 minute. Add milk all at once, stirring constantly until sauce thickens. Add Worcestershire sauce, Tabasco® sauce and Cheddar cheese; stir until cheese melts. Empty sour cream and cottage cheese into a large bowl. Gradually add sauce, stirring constantly. Fold noodles into sauce, spoon into buttered casserole and sprinkle with croutons or Buttered Breadcrumbs, page 120. Bake 15 minutes. Makes 6 to 8 servings.

Four ounces of dry noodles makes 2 to 3 hearty or 4 moderate servings.

Secret Treasure Potato Casserole

Only you will know the unique flavor comes from instant mashed potatoes.

Dry instant mashed potatoes,
   for 8 servings
Water
2 cups (1 pint) small curd cottage cheese
1/2 cup dairy sour cream
1 egg, slightly beaten

2 tablespoons grated onion
1-1/2 teaspoons salt
1/4 teaspoon white pepper
2 tablespoons butter, melted
1/2 cup toasted sliced almonds

Preheat oven to 350°F (177°C). Prepare potatoes with water according to package directions *except* omit any salt, butter or milk. Blend in cottage cheese, sour cream, egg, onion, salt and pepper. Spoon into a 13" x 9" x 2" baking dish. Level surface and brush with melted butter. Bake 30 minutes. Lightly brown under broiler, if desired. Sprinkle with toasted almonds. Makes 10 to 12 servings.

Noodle Ring

No last-minute worries about sticky noodles.

4 oz. medium egg noodles
Water, lightly salted
1 tablespoon butter or oil
1-1/2 cups soft breadcrumbs,
   (3 slices bread)
2 tablespoons butter
2 eggs
3/4 cup cottage cheese
1 cup (1/2 pint) dairy sour cream,
   room temperature

3 tablespoons minced green onion
2 tablespoons minced green pepper
2 tablespoons minced pimiento
1 tablespoon minced parsley
1/2 teaspoon Worcestershire sauce
1 teaspoon salt
Dash pepper
Dash garlic powder

Preheat oven to 350°F (177°C). Generously butter a 1-1/2-quart ring mold; set aside. Cook noodles in lightly salted water according to package directions, adding 1 tablespoon butter or oil to water; drain. Sauté breadcrumbs in butter until golden. Press crumbs firmly on bottom and sides of buttered ring mold. Beat eggs in a large bowl. Blend in remaining ingredients. Fold in noodles and pour into mold. Bake 30 minutes and unmold *immediately*. Loosen edge with knife and invert onto warmed serving plate. Makes 4 to 6 servings.

Variation

Fill center of ring with peas or creamed meat, chicken or seafood. Garnish with parsley.

Green And Gold Casserole

Serve this colorful casserole as a vegetable or meatless main dish.

1 lb. fresh zucchini, sliced
Boiling water, lightly salted
1/2 cup Buttered Breadcrumbs,
    page 120
1 (1-lb.) can whole kernel corn
1-1/2 cups small curd cottage cheese
2 tablespoons dairy sour cream

2 tablespoons flour
3/4 teaspoon salt
Dash pepper
2 dashes Tabasco® sauce
2 eggs
1 to 2 tablespoons diced green chilies
1/2 cup grated Cheddar cheese

Preheat oven to 350°F (177°C). Butter a 1-quart casserole; set aside. Cook zucchini in boiling salted water until just tender; drain. Prepare Buttered Breadcrumbs, page 120. Drain corn. In mixer bowl or blender jar, combine cottage cheese, sour cream, flour, salt, pepper, Tabasco® sauce and eggs; beat or blend until smooth. Fold in zucchini, corn and chilies. Pour into buttered casserole. Top with Cheddar cheese and Buttered Breadcrumbs. Bake 45 minutes. Makes 4 main dish servings or 6 protein-rich vegetable servings.

Vegetable Bake

"Planned-over" vegetables are the basis for this meatless casserole.

1 (3-oz.) pkg. cream cheese,
    room temperature
1 cup (1/2 pint) cottage cheese
2 teaspoons lemon juice
1 teaspoon salt
1/2 teaspoon paprika

1/4 teaspoon marjoram
2 eggs, beaten
1/2 cup soft breadcrumbs,
    (1 slice bread)
1 tablespoon minced onion
2 cups cooked vegetables

Preheat oven to 350°F (177°C). Butter a 1-quart casserole; set aside. In a large bowl, blend cream cheese until smooth. Mix in remaining ingredients except cooked vegetables. Fold in vegetables and spoon into buttered casserole. Bake 20 to 25 minutes. Serve immediately. Makes 4 main dish servings or 6 protein-rich vegetable servings.

Variation

Substitute 1 (10-oz.) package frozen vegetables, cooked and drained, for 2 cups cooked vegetables.

Italian-Style Eggplant

An exciting and delicious way to serve eggplant to your family.

1/4 cup Buttered Breadcrumbs,
   page 120
1 small eggplant (about 1 lb.)
Salt and pepper to taste

6 tablespoons (3/4 stick) butter
1 (8-oz.) can tomato sauce
1/2 cup grated Swiss cheese
1 cup (1/2 pint) cottage cheese

Preheat oven to 325°F (163°C). Prepare Buttered Breadcrumbs, page 120. Peel eggplant and cut into 1/2-inch slices. Season with salt and pepper. Sauté half the eggplant in half the butter until lightly browned on both sides. Repeat with remaining butter and eggplant. In an 11" x 7" x 2" baking dish, layer in order, half the following: eggplant, tomato sauce, Swiss cheese and cottage cheese. Repeat layers. Top with Buttered Breadcrumbs. Bake 30 minutes or until hot and bubbly. Makes 6 servings.

It takes 2-2/3 quarts of milk to make 1 pint of creamed style cottage cheese.

Breads & Butters

Not long ago a family wouldn't have considered sitting down to a meal without a plate of bread on the table. The bread went on right along with the salt and the pepper—even if the menu already included potatoes, rice, and pasta! But times and eating habits do change. Between the calorie counters, the carbohydrate calculators and the rebels against supersoft and overwhipped bread, we have come close to cutting a major source of important nutrients out of our diet.

It certainly isn't necessary, or even desirable, to have bread, pasta and potatoes all in the same meal. But, diet or no diet, every meal should include at least one bread or cereal food. Bread isn't a frill food. Breads and cereal foods are one of the basic four food groups. They provide B vitamins and iron necessary to a balanced diet. Nutritionally, it is better to control weight by eating all foods in moderation, than to restrict the amount of bread in your diet.

Plan bread as part of the total balanced meal, and select it carefully to enhance the entrée. Until the late eighteenth century breads were, for the most part, leavened with yeast. At that time a chemical was discovered in America that eventually evolved to baking soda and baking powder as we know them today. Out of this discovery came a whole new repertoire of uniquely American breads. Each area developed its own favorites to go with available meats and vegetables: brown bread to go with baked beans; biscuits for fried chicken; corn bread with ham. With such a heritage, it's not difficult to find just the right bread to fit any menu.

After you have selected the right bread, make it absolutely irresistible by serving it hot, right out of the oven. Don't hesitate to bake up generous batches. Just serve what is to be eaten at one meal and freeze the rest. Reheat it for a later meal. Breads freeze beautifully and can be thawed and refrozen without damage.

Make the act of selecting and baking the right bread worthwhile by using a really good recipe—choose one from this section. Start with Fabulous Biscuits, page 113, if you're a novice, and graduate to the buttermilk and sour cream versions. Most of the bread recipes in this book are made with baking soda and buttermilk or sour cream. This means delicious flavor and moist, tender texture. It also means that little or no baking powder is used. Many people can detect a difference in flavor when bread is baked with baking powder. Give the final touch of glorious enjoyment by serving these delicious breads with real butter. After all, when you can't let yourself eat all you want, shouldn't every bite be the very best?

MUFFINS

A muffin is one of the easiest quick breads there is to make. Take advantage of its simplicity by adding your own special touches. Fold raisins, chopped dates, chopped nuts, diced prunes or grated citrus peel into the finished batter. Don't complicate things by mixing the batter too much. The muffins will only get tough.

YEAST BREADS

Baking yeast breads is usually reserved for leisurely chilly days when everyone is around to enjoy the aroma of the dough while it rises and bakes. The delicious fragrance is second only to the flavor and texture of the generously buttered bread right out of the oven.

If you're a first-timer at making yeast breads, you'll want to know:

How to Soften Yeast—Dry yeast is soaked in warm water to reactivate it. If the water is too hot, the yeast will be destroyed. Sprinkle the dry yeast over warm water (about 110°F, 43°C) and let stand for five minutes. Before adding it to the flour, stir gently to moisten dry particles remaining on top.

Providing Warmth for Rising Dough—The heat from the pilot in a gas oven makes a good temperature for yeast growth. Another good place is the top of a refrigerator or freezer that vents at the back. To use an electric oven, turn on for two minutes and turn off; wait five minutes before putting dough in oven.

BUTTER

The delightful and satisfying flavor of real butter makes almost any food taste better. Cakes and breads made with butter have a special flavor and texture. And, of course, as a spread for coffeecakes, pancakes, breads and crackers, it stands alone.

Such a treasured food deserves the best of care. Like other dairy foods, butter should be kept cold and covered to protect it from oxidation and drying. Careful wrapping or covering also seals out other flavors in the refrigerator. Butter eagerly assumes most flavors—whether you want it to or not.

Many refrigerators have a warmer compartment for storing butter at spreading consistency. This is a convenience, but it is important to store only as much butter in this area as will be used in a day or two. The warmer temperature speeds up flavor change and dries the butter. Butter in its wrapper keeps in the coldest part of the refrigerator for several weeks. For longer storage, wrap the original package with foil and freeze for up to six months. It will stay in perfect condition. Sweet (unsalted) butter should be used within a week or two or frozen for longer storage.

CLARIFIED OR DRAWN BUTTER

The common complaint about frying in butter is that it burns. It is possible to have the wonderful flavor of butter in fried foods without this problem. Clarified butter is the answer. Clarified butter is also known as *drawn butter* or in the Orient as *ghee.*

Butter is 80.5% fat. The remainder is milk, and, in the case of salted butter, salt. It is the protein in the milk that browns when the water evaporates.

If the milky residue is removed, the butterfat can be used for frying and sautéing without burning.

Once you have used clarified butter for frying, you'll find many more uses for it. You'll discover it coats vegetables better than unclarified butter. Serve it hot with artichokes or lobster. Most of all, you will love it for cooking eggs and for sautéing vegetables, seafood and chicken. You won't want to be without it.

Here's how to make clarified butter:

1. Salted or unsalted butter can be clarified. Salt is removed in clarification.

2. Any amount of butter can be clarified at one time.

3. Melt butter in heavy pan over low heat. Butter separates into milky portion on the bottom and oily portion on the top.

4. Cook butter until liquid from milky portion boils off. Clear yellow oil and white fluffs of protein and salt remain. Remove from heat before browning starts.

5. Pour through a fine strainer or 4 layers of cheesecloth into a glass or pottery jar that can be sealed.

6. Refrigerate, covered, until ready to use. It will keep several weeks. For longer storage, freeze.

Browned Butter for Noodles—Melt clarified butter in a saucepan. Heat until it browns slightly. Toss with freshly cooked noodles. Keeps noodles from sticking and imparts a special flavor.

To Butter Hot Vegetables—Drain cooked vegetables thoroughly. Save juices for soups or sauces if you like. Add clarified butter to vegetables. Return to heat to evaporate excess moisture and melt butter. Hold lid on pan and toss vegetables in melted butter. Season and serve.

Save butter wrappers to butter casseroles and baking pans.

Clockwise from top left: Sour Cream Muffins, Crusty Cheese Bread, Butter Balls, Boston Brown Bread, on following page

Fabulous Biscuits

A great way to use whipping cream that's just a little less than fresh.

2 cups biscuit mix
   (do not overmeasure)

1 cup (1/2 pint) whipping cream

Preheat oven to 450°F (232°C). Combine biscuit mix and cream in a medium bowl. Mix just until dough holds together. Turn onto floured board and knead lightly until smooth and elastic, about 10 strokes. Roll out to 1/2-inch thickness. Cut into 2-inch or smaller biscuits. Bake on ungreased baking sheet 10 minutes. Makes 16 two-inch biscuits.

Buttermilk Biscuits

Famous for their fast disappearing act.

2 cups sifted flour
2 teaspoons sugar
2-1/2 teaspoons baking powder
1/2 teaspoon salt

1/4 teaspoon baking soda
2/3 to 3/4 cup buttermilk
5 tablespoons butter, melted

Preheat oven to 450°F (232°C). Sift and measure flour. Sift again into mixing bowl with sugar, baking powder, salt and baking soda. Make a well in center of dry ingredients. Pour in buttermilk and melted butter. Stir with fork *only* until dry ingredients are moistened and dough follows fork around bowl. Turn dough onto lightly floured board and knead gently about 10 strokes. Roll out or pat to 1/2-inch thickness. Using a 2-inch biscuit cutter, cut biscuits without twisting cutter. Bake on ungreased baking sheet 10 to 12 minutes. Makes 14 two-inch biscuits.

Soft-As-A-Cloud Sour Cream Biscuits

The name speaks for itself.

1 cup sifted flour
2 teaspoons baking powder
1 teaspoon sugar
1/4 teaspoon baking soda

1/4 teaspoon salt
1/2 cup dairy sour cream
1/4 cup half-and-half

Preheat oven to 450°F (232°C). Sift and measure flour; sift again with baking powder, sugar, baking soda and salt into a medium bowl. In a small bowl, blend sour cream and half-and-half. Make a well in center of dry ingredients. Pour in sour cream mixture and stir just until dough follows fork around bowl. If too dry, add more half-and-half. Turn dough onto lightly floured board and knead gently 10 to 12 strokes. Roll out or pat dough to 1/2-inch thickness. Using a 2-inch biscuit cutter, cut biscuits without twisting cutter. Bake on ungreased baking sheet 10 minutes. Makes 8 or 9 two-inch biscuits.

Fluffy Buttermilk Muffins

Molasses gives special color and flavor.

2 cups sifted flour
1 teaspoon baking powder
1/2 teaspoon baking soda
1/2 teaspoon salt
2 tablespoons sugar

1 egg
1/2 cup buttermilk
1/2 cup light molasses
2 tablespoons butter, melted

Preheat oven to 400°F (204°C). Butter a 12-cup muffin pan or line with paper baking cups. Sift and measure flour. Sift again with baking powder, baking soda, salt and sugar. Beat egg in a medium bowl. Blend in buttermilk and molasses. Add dry ingredients and melted butter all at once, stirring just until moistened. Fill each cup 2/3 full in prepared muffin pan. Bake 25 minutes. Makes 12 medium muffins.

Sour Cream Muffins

A basic muffin to go with any meal.

2 cups sifted flour
1/3 cup sugar
1 teaspoon baking powder
1/2 teaspoon baking soda
1/2 teaspoon salt

1 egg
1 cup (1/2 pint) dairy sour cream
1/4 cup milk
2 tablespoons butter, melted

Preheat oven to 400°F (204°C). Butter a 12-cup muffin pan or line with paper baking cups. Sift and measure flour. Sift again with sugar, baking powder, baking soda and salt. Beat egg in medium bowl. Blend in sour cream and milk. Add dry ingredients and melted butter all at once, stirring just until moistened. Fill each cup 2/3 full in prepared muffin pan. Bake 15 to 20 minutes. Makes 12 medium muffins.

To make your own whipped butter, leave butter at room temperature until it's slightly softened. Beat with an electric mixer on high speed until very light in color and nearly doubled in volume. Spoon into a serving bowl and serve, or refrigerate until serving time.

Buttermilk Bran Muffins

These are good for you, but you'll make them because they're delicious!

1 egg
3/4 cup buttermilk
1/3 cup light molasses
2 cups whole bran
2/3 cup sifted flour
1/3 cup sugar

1 teaspoon baking powder
1/2 teaspoon baking soda
1/2 teaspoon salt
1/8 to 1/4 teaspoon allspice
1/3 cup raisins
1/4 cup (1/2 stick) butter, melted

Preheat oven to 400°F (204°C). Butter a 12-cup muffin pan or line with paper baking cups. Beat egg in a medium bowl. Blend in buttermilk and molasses. Stir in bran and let stand 3 to 5 minutes. Sift and measure flour. Sift again with sugar, baking powder, baking soda, salt and allspice. Stir in raisins. Stir melted butter into bran mixture. Add dry ingredients all at once, mixing just until moistened Fill each cup 2/3 full in prepared muffin pan. Bake 20 to 25 minutes. Makes 12 medium muffins.

Buttermilk Corn Bread

This corn bread is special because it doesn't fall apart!

2 eggs
1/4 cup sugar
1 cup sifted flour
2/3 cup cornmeal
2 teaspoons baking powder

1/4 teaspoon baking soda
3/4 teaspoon salt
1 cup buttermilk
1/4 cup butter, melted

Preheat oven to 400°F (204°C). Butter and flour an 8" x 8" x 2" baking dish. Beat eggs in a large bowl. Add sugar and mix well. Sift and measure flour. Sift again with cornmeal, baking powder, baking soda and salt. Add dry ingredients alternately with buttermilk to egg-sugar mixture. Stir in melted butter and pour into prepared baking dish. Bake about 25 minutes or until a toothpick inserted in the center comes out dry. Makes 8 to 12 servings.

Variations

Yogurt Corn Bread: Increase baking soda to 1/2 teaspoon. Substitute 1 (8-oz.) carton plain yogurt for buttermilk.
Spider Corn Bread: Double recipe and bake for 30 minutes in preheated, buttered, 10-inch cast-iron fry pan.
Corn Sticks: Bake for 18 minutes in well-buttered, cast-iron corn-stick pans. Makes 12 corn sticks.

Note

For a good crust, corn bread must be baked in a glass, cast-iron or dark-metal pan.

Boston Brown Bread

A "must" with baked beans and cole slaw since the days of the Pilgrims.

1 cup sifted white flour
1 cup sifted whole wheat flour
2 tablespoons sugar
1/2 teaspoon baking soda
3/4 teaspoon salt

3/4 cup raisins
1 egg
1 cup light or dark molasses
3/4 cup buttermilk

Preheat oven to 350°F (177°C). Butter and flour a 9" x 5" x 2-3/4" loaf pan. Sift and measure white and whole wheat flour. Sift again with sugar, baking soda and salt. Toss raisins in flour. Beat egg in a large bowl. Blend in molasses and buttermilk. Add dry ingredients all at once and blend well. Pour into prepared loaf pan. Bake 1 hour or until a toothpick inserted in crusty portion of center comes out clean. Makes 1 loaf.

Banana Nut Bread

A great way to use those overripe bananas.

2-1/4 cups sifted flour
3/4 teaspoon baking soda
1/2 teaspoon salt
1/4 cup (1/2 stick) butter,
   room temperature
3/4 cup sugar

2 eggs
3/4 cup mashed, very ripe banana
   (2 to 3 medium bananas)
1/2 cup dairy sour cream
1/2 cup finely chopped walnuts

Preheat oven to 350°F (177°C). Butter and flour a 9" x 5" x 2-3/4" loaf pan. Sift and measure flour; sift again with baking soda and salt. In a large bowl, cream butter and sugar until light and fluffy. Beat in eggs. Add sifted dry ingredients alternately with banana and sour cream, mixing just until blended. Stir in nuts and pour into prepared loaf pan. Bake 1 hour or until a toothpick inserted in crusty portion of center comes out clean. Remove from pan; cool on rack. Makes 1 loaf.

Before measuring honey, molasses or syrup, butter the measuring cup. You'll get every drop.

Yeast Crescents

Wonderful flavor! Make Yeast Crescent dough into any yeast roll shape or into Old-Fashioned Cinnamon Rolls, page 22.

1 pkg. active dry yeast
1/4 cup warm water
   (110°F, 43°C)
4 cups sifted flour
1 teaspoon salt
1/4 cup sugar

1/2 cup (1 stick) butter,
   room temperature
2 eggs, slightly beaten
3/4 cup dairy sour cream
3/4 teaspoon vanilla

Sprinkle yeast over warm water; let stand 5 minutes. Stir gently to moisten dry particles remaining on top. Sift and measure flour. Sift again with salt and sugar into a large bowl. With electric mixer, cut butter into dry ingredients until mixture resembles fine crumbs. Stir in yeast, eggs, sour cream and vanilla to make a smooth dough. Shape into a ball. Wrap in plastic wrap and refrigerate at least 3 hours or overnight. Divide dough in quarters. On a well-floured board, roll 1 quarter into a 12-inch circle; cut in 8 equal wedges. Roll each wedge starting at the wide end; curve into a crescent shape. Place with point on bottom on ungreased baking sheet. Repeat with remaining dough. Set pan in a warm place. Let rolls rise until doubled in size. Preheat oven to 375°F (191°C). Bake 12 to 15 minutes or until golden brown. Makes 32 crescent rolls.

Crusty Cheese Bread

Crusty, chewy and full of protein.

1 pkg. active dry yeast
1/4 cup warm water
   (110°F, 43°C)
1 cup (1/2 pint) small curd cottage cheese,
   room temperature
1 tablespoon sugar

1-1/2 teaspoons salt
1 egg
2-1/4 to 2-1/2 cups unsifted flour
1 tablespoon butter,
   room temperature

Sprinkle yeast over warm water. Let stand 5 minutes. Stir gently to moisten dry particles remaining on top. With electric mixer, blend softened yeast with cottage cheese, sugar, salt and egg. Add flour in 1/2 cup portions to form stiff dough. Beat well, by hand, after each addition. Cover dough and let rise in a warm place until doubled in size, about 1 hour. Butter a 1-1/2-quart casserole. Stir down dough and turn into buttered casserole. Let rise 30 to 40 minutes longer or until almost doubled in size. Preheat oven to 350°F (177°C). Bake 40 to 50 minutes or until golden brown. Brush crust with butter and serve. Makes 1 loaf.

Variation

Cheese-Onion Bread: Add 1 tablespoon grated onion and 2 tablespoons toasted sesame seeds before adding flour. Mix in 1 cup grated sharp Cheddar cheese when stirring down dough.

Herbed Tomato-Cheese Bread

Delicious with steaks, chops or hamburger patties. Wrap leftovers in foil and refrigerate. It reheats beautifully.

Sour Cream Topping, see below
2/3 cup milk
2 cups biscuit mix

3 medium tomatoes, peeled and
   sliced 1/4-in. thick
Paprika

Sour Cream Topping:
1 medium onion, minced
2 tablespoons butter
3/4 cup dairy sour cream
1/3 cup mayonnaise
4 oz. grated Cheddar cheese
   (about 1 cup)

3/4 teaspoon salt
1/4 teaspoon pepper
1/4 teaspoon leaf oregano
Pinch sage

Preheat oven to 400°F (204°C). Butter a 13" x 9" x 2" baking dish. Prepare Sour Cream Topping. Stir milk into biscuit mix to make a soft dough. Turn dough onto well-floured board and knead lightly 10 to 12 strokes. Pat dough over bottom of buttered baking dish, pushing dough up sides of dish to form a shallow rim. Arrange tomato slices over dough. Spoon on Sour Cream Topping and sprinkle with paprika. Bake 20 to 25 minutes. Let stand about 10 minutes before cutting. Makes 12 servings.

Sour Cream Topping:
Sauté onion in butter until tender. Blend with remaining topping ingredients. Set aside.

Variation

Italian Onion-Cream Bread: When making topping, reduce salt to 1/2 teaspoon; omit Cheddar cheese, oregano and sage. Add 3 tablespoons minced pimiento, 2 tablespoons shredded Parmesan cheese, 1-1/2 teaspoons minced parsley and 1/8 teaspoon basil. Omit tomatoes.

To soften butter quickly, fill a bowl with boiling water. Empty the bowl and invert it over the butter dish. Butter will be spreading soft in minutes.

1. After kneading dough 10 to 12 strokes, pat out over the bottom of the baking dish and push dough up the sides of the dish to form a shallow rim.

2. Place a layer of tomato slices over the dough.

How To Make Herbed Tomato-Cheese Bread

3. Spoon a layer of Sour Cream Topping over the tomato layer. Sprinkle with paprika and bake.

4. Let stand about 10 minutes to cool before cutting.

Cottage Pizza Bread

Bubbly and crisp on the outside, moist and delicious on the inside.

1 (1-lb.) loaf frozen
  ready-to-bake yeast bread
1 egg
1 cup (1/2 pint) cottage cheese
2 tablespoons grated Parmesan cheese
1/2 teaspoon basil

1/2 teaspoon oregano
1/4 teaspoon garlic salt
1/4 teaspoon pepper
1 (6-oz.) can pizza topping
1/2 cup grated mozzarella cheese

Butter a 13" x 9" x 2" baking dish. Thaw bread and divide in half. Stretch half to fit buttered baking dish. Press into place, forming slight rim. In small bowl, beat egg and blend in cottage cheese, Parmesan cheese, basil, oregano, garlic salt and pepper. Spread evenly over dough. Stretch remaining half of dough to fit baking dish. Place over filling and press edges to seal. Let rise until doubled in volume, about 1 hour. Preheat oven to 350°F (177°C). Spread pizza topping evenly over bread. Sprinkle with mozzarella cheese. Bake 30 minutes. Let stand 5 minutes. Cut in squares and serve. Makes 9 to 12 servings.

Buttered Breadcrumbs

Very handy to have around.

1 slice bread (not thin slice)
1 tablespoon butter

1 tablespoon minced parsley,
  if desired

Tear bread into pieces and drop into a blender jar. Blend until crumbly. If blender isn't available, tear bread into small bits with fingers. Melt butter in a fry pan over medium heat. Toss crumbs in butter until lightly browned. Remove from heat and add parsley, if desired. Breadcrumbs can be frozen in an airtight container. Makes 1/2 cup buttered crumbs.

Variations

Parmesan Crumbs: Add 1 to 2 tablespoons shredded Parmesan cheese.
Herbed Crumbs: Add 1/2 teaspoon oregano, sage, basil or marjoram.

Note

Double or triple the recipe, if desired. For best results, crumble only 1 slice of bread at a time in blender.

Italian Butter

Especially good on zucchini, green beans, chicken, veal and bread.

1/2 cup (1 stick) butter, room temperature
2 teaspoons lemon juice

1 tablespoon basil
1/2 teaspoon oregano
1/2 teaspoon garlic salt

Combine butter and seasonings; beat until light and fluffy. Makes just over 1/2 cup.

Blue Cheese Butter

A tasty blend to top hamburger patties, steak, bread and canapés.

1/2 cup (1 stick) butter, room temperature
1-1/2 oz. blue cheese

2 teaspoons dry sherry
1 tablespoon minced parsley
1/2 teaspoon garlic salt

Combine butter and seasonings; beat until light and fluffy. Makes about 1-1/4 cups.

Parmesan Butter

Adds a gourmet touch to French bread, zucchini, peas and pasta.

1/2 cup (1 stick) butter, room temperature
2 teaspoons grated Parmesan cheese

1-1/2 teaspoons basil
1-1/2 teaspoons marjoram
1/4 teaspoon salt

Combine butter and seasonings; beat until light and fluffy. Makes just over 1/2 cup.

Lemon Butter

Brings baked or broiled fish, broccoli and spinach to perfection.

1/2 cup (1 stick) butter, room temperature
1 tablespoon lemon juice

1/4 teaspoon grated lemon peel
1/4 teaspoon garlic salt
1/8 teaspoon pepper

Combine butter and seasonings; beat until light and fluffy. Makes about 1/2 cup.

Herb Butter

Delightful on mushrooms, zucchini, chicken and bread.

1/2 cup (1 stick) butter,
   room temperature
2 teaspoons minced parsley

1 tablespoon minced pimiento
1/4 teaspoon oregano
1/4 teaspoon salt

Combine butter and seasonings; beat until light and fluffy. Makes just over 1/2 cup.

Garlic Butter

This is a subtle version because the garlic is parboiled.

2 to 4 cloves garlic
1/2 cup (1 stick) butter,
   room temperature

1/4 teaspoon salt
1 tablespoon minced parsley

Peel garlic and drop into boiling water for 30 seconds. Drain and crush. Blend all ingredients well and refrigerate. Makes just over 1/2 cup.

Horseradish Butter

Gives roast beef and hamburger patties a devilish touch.

1/2 cup (1 stick) butter,
   room temperature

2 tablespoons horseradish
1/4 teaspoon garlic salt

Combine butter and seasonings; beat until light and fluffy. Makes just over 1/2 cup.

Butter Balls

Use a butter ball paddle set to give a perfect dinner this special touch.

1 stick butter
Kettle of boiling water

Ice water
Small bowl ice water

Cut cold butter in half lengthwise. Cut each half in half lengthwise again, forming 4 long butter sticks. Cut each stick into 4 equal cubes. Pour boiling water over ridged face of butter paddle and plunge into ice water. Repeat for second paddle. The scalding process kills any mold growths. Place cold butter cube between ridged faces of paddles and rotate paddles against each other until butter cube forms a ball. Drop butter ball into small bowl of ice water just until set. Refrigerate in airtight container, or freeze for longer storage. Makes 16 balls, 1-1/2 teaspoons each.

Cheesecakes & Cheese Pies

Finding a clear definition of "cheesecake" and "cheese pie" is very difficult. It depends on where you are, how much liberty you are willing to take with the classic recipes and how imaginative you wish to be. The origins are buried in history. The first cheesecakes may have been made by the ancient Greeks. They were mentioned in a Greek cookbook dated 250 A.D. There were so many versions on the Greek island of Samos that it came to be known as The Cheesecake Island.

To many, cheesecake is the light, dry German variety made with cottage cheese. Another favorite is the moist, solid variety made with cream cheese. Cheese pies are almost universally made from cream cheese and may or may not be baked. There are other variations in both cheesecakes and cheese pies. The only consistent difference between them seems to be in the pan that is used. A cheese pie is baked in a pie plate and usually makes from 8 to 10 servings. A cheesecake is baked in a straight-sided, round cake pan and is usually large enough and rich enough to serve 16 to 20. An investment in a 9-inch springform pan will be worthwhile not only for cheesecakes, but for many other recipes,

too. The big advantage of this pan is that the removable sides make it possible to unmold a dessert without turning it upside down.

Baked cheesecakes and cheese pies are actually custards. The delicate egg mixtures should be baked at low temperatures just long enough for them to set. Overbaking or too-high heat causes them to puff and brown too much during baking and shrink too much on cooling. As with any custard, they will water-off or weep if overbaked. When cooled, these cheesecakes and cheese pies will become level, leaving room for a sour cream topping and a glaze.

Cheesecakes and cheese pies should be thoroughly chilled before cutting and refrigerated to protect the delicate egg custards from spoilage.

There is no need to get into a rut with your favorite cheesecake or cheese pie. You can have infinite variety by adding and changing glazes and garnishes. The fruit glazes, pages 129 to 132, and Chocolate Sour Cream Topping, page 131, are flavor and color touches to glamorize your first cheesecake or give new interest to your favorite cheese pie.

A glaze can be as simple as a can of prepared pie filling or warmed fruit preserves spread over the top of a cheesecake. A ring of well-drained fresh or canned fruit is a beautiful and easy garnish.

Instant Cheese Pie

1 Graham Cracker Crumb Crust,
  page 156
1 (8-oz.) pkg. cream cheese,
  room temperature
1-1/3 cups half-and-half

1 (3-1/4-oz.) pkg. instant lemon or
  vanilla pudding mix
1/2 cup strawberry or raspberry jelly
  or Apricot-Peach Glaze, page 129

Prepare Graham Cracker Crumb Crust, page 156. Set aside. Blend cream cheese until smooth; gradually beat in half-and-half until creamy. Add pudding mix and beat until smooth. Pour into crust. Chill until set. Melt jelly over low heat or prepare Apricot-Peach Glaze, page 129. Pour over chilled pie. Makes 8 servings.

Grasshopper Cream Cheese Pie

Specta

Chocolate Crumb Crust, see below
4 (3-oz.) pkgs. cream cheese,
  room temperature
2/3 cup sugar
2 eggs

1/4 cup green crème de menthe
2 teaspoons white crème de cacao
Chocolate Sour Cream Topping,
  page 131

Chocolate Crumb Crust:
1/4 cup (1/2 stick) butter, melted
1-1/4 cups chocolate cookie crumbs

Preheat oven to 300°F (149°C). Prepare Chocolate Crumb Crust. Set aside. In a large bowl, beat cream cheese until smooth. Blend in sugar, eggs, crème de menthe and crème de cacao. Pour into crust. Bake 40 minutes; cool. Prepare Chocolate Sour Cream Topping, page 131. Spread over surface of cooled pie. Refrigerate at least 5 hours before serving. Makes 8 to 10 servings.

Chocolate Crumb Crust:
Combine crust ingredients. Press onto bottom and sides of a 9-inch glass pie plate.

Clockwise from top center: No-Bake Cheesecake, Cream Cheese Pie, Instant Cheese Pie with Apricot-Peach Glaze, Grasshopper Cream Cheese Pie, Traditional Cheesecake with Raspberry Glaze (variation of Strawberry Glaze), on following pages

Cream Cheese Pie

Your favorite and ours! Make several at once and store in the freezer.

Graham Cracker Crumb Crust, see below
4 (3-oz.) pkgs. cream cheese,
   room temperature
3/4 cup sugar
2 eggs
2 teaspoons vanilla

1 teaspoon lemon juice
1 teaspoon grated lemon peel
Sour Cream Topping, see below
Apricot-Peach Glaze, page 129,
   if desired

Graham Cracker Crumb Crust:
1/4 cup (1/2 stick) butter, melted
1/4 cup sugar

1-1/2 cups graham cracker crumbs
   (about 18 crackers)

Sour Cream Topping:
1 cup (1/2 pint) dairy sour cream,
   room temperature

1/4 cup sugar
1 teaspoon vanilla

Preheat oven to 300°F (149°C). Prepare Graham Cracker Crumb Crust. In a large bowl, beat cream cheese until smooth. Add sugar, eggs, vanilla, lemon juice and lemon peel; beat until blended. Pour into crust. Bake 40 minutes or until center is no longer wet. The filling may crack around the edge but it should not brown. Remove from oven and cool 10 minutes. Prepare Sour Cream Topping. Spread evenly over entire surface of filling. Return to oven 5 minutes. Cool to room temperature and refrigerate at least 5 hours before serving. Top with Apricot-Peach Glaze, page 129, if desired. For freezing, omit glaze and place layer of plastic wrap directly over Sour Cream Topping. Wrap in heavy aluminum foil. Freeze. To thaw, let stand at room temperature about 3 hours. Makes 8 to 10 servings.

Graham Cracker Crumb Crust:
Blend crust ingredients. Press onto bottom and sides of a 9-inch glass pie plate. Bake at 300°F (149°C) 10 minutes.

Sour Cream Topping:
Blend topping ingredients together.

Variation

Cream Cheesecake: Substitute a 9-inch springform pan for pie plate. Prepare crust as directed. Prepare double recipe of filling. Pour into crust and bake 1 hour 15 minutes or until set. To make topping, increase sour cream to 1-1/2 cups and sugar to 1/3 cup. Proceed according to recipe directions. Makes 16 to 20 servings. For a less flavorful, less sweet cheesecake crust, use the Zwieback Crumb Crust from the Traditional Cheesecake recipe, page 129.

Traditional Cheesecake

Appreciate the subtle flavor of the cheese!

Zwieback Crumb Crust, see below
4 eggs, separated
1/2 teaspoon salt
2 tablespoons lemon juice
1 teaspoon vanilla
1 teaspoon almond extract

1 cup sugar
2/3 cup sifted flour
1-1/2 teaspoons grated lemon peel
2 cups (1 pint) cottage cheese
1 cup (1/2 pint) dairy sour cream

Zwieback Crumb Crust:
1/4 cup (1/2 stick) butter, melted
1 (6-oz.) pkg. zwieback crumbs
    (1-1/2 cups)

1-1/2 teaspoons cinnamon

Preheat oven to 300°F (149°C). Prepare Zwieback Crumb Crust; set aside. In a medium bowl, beat egg yolks until light. Blend in salt, lemon juice, vanilla, almond extract, sugar, flour and lemon peel. Empty cottage cheese into a large bowl. Add small amount of egg yolk mixture. Beat on high speed until curd is broken and nearly smooth. Add remaining egg yolk mixture and sour cream; beat until blended. Beat egg whites until stiff but not dry. Fold into cheese mixture. Pour into crust. Bake 1 hour. Refrigerate 5 hours before serving. Makes 12 to 16 servings.

Zwieback Crumb Crust:
Butter and flour a 9-inch springform pan. Blend crust ingredients; press onto sides and bottom of pan. Tilt pan to press crumbs onto sides.

Variations

If desired, reserve up to 1/4 cup Zwieback Crumb Crust mixture for cheesecake garnish. After the cake has baked 30 minutes, sprinkle crumbs over top and return to oven for remaining 30 minutes.
Hoop Cheesecake: Increase salt to 1 teaspoon. Substitute 2 (8-oz.) packages hoop or pot cheese for cottage cheese.

Apricot-Peach Glaze

A perfect complement for cheesecake.

1 (16-oz.) can apricot or peach halves
3 tablespoons sugar
1 tablespoon cornstarch

1 teaspoon lemon juice
Yellow and red food coloring

Drain fruit; reserve 3/4 cup syrup. In a small saucepan, blend sugar and cornstarch to remove lumps. Blend in reserved syrup. Cook over medium heat until thickened and clear. Remove from heat. Stir in lemon juice and food coloring. Place wax paper directly on top of hot glaze; refrigerate until cool. Arrange fruit halves, cut-side down, in a ring over surface of chilled cheesecake or cheese pie. Spoon cooled glaze over. Makes glaze for 1 nine-inch cheesecake or cheese pie.

No-Bake Cheesecake

It's easy to serve this cheesecake from an elegant serving platter—just remove the sides of the springform pan.

2 envelopes unflavored gelatin
3/4 cup sugar
1/4 teaspoon salt
2 eggs, separated
1 cup milk
1 tablespoon lemon juice

1 teaspoon grated lemon peel
1 teaspoon vanilla
Spicy Graham Cracker Crust, see below
1/4 cup sugar
1 cup (1/2 pint) whipping cream
3 cups (1-1/2 pints) cottage cheese

Spicy Graham Cracker Crust:
3 tablespoons butter, melted
2 tablespoons sugar
1 cup (12 crackers) graham cracker crumbs

1/2 teaspoon cinnamon
1/2 teaspoon nutmeg

Mix gelatin, 3/4 cup sugar and salt in top of double boiler. Add egg yolks and milk. Beat until well blended. Cook over boiling water, stirring constantly, until gelatin is dissolved. Remove from heat. Stir in lemon juice, lemon peel and vanilla. Refrigerate, stirring occasionally until mixture mounds slightly when dropped from a spoon. While mixture is chilling, prepare Spicy Graham Cracker Crust, set aside. Beat egg whites until frothy. Gradually add 1/4 cup sugar; continue beating until stiff and glossy. Set aside. Whip cream until stiff. Set aside. In a large bowl, beat cottage cheese with electric mixer on high speed until curd breaks. Blend in thickened gelatin mixture. Fold in whipped cream and then beaten egg whites. Pour into crust. Sprinkle with reserved crumbs. Refrigerate about 4 hours or until firm. Makes 10 to 12 servings.

Spicy Graham Cracker Crust:
Blend crust ingredients; reserve 2 tablespoons crumb mixture. Press remaining crumbs onto bottom of a 9-inch springform pan.

Variation

Elegant Cheesecake Ring: Press crust mixture onto bottom and partway up side of a large bundt pan. Prepare 1-1/2 times the filling. Pour into crust and chill until set. Unmold carefully.

Cranberry Glaze

A special glaze to brighten your fall and winter.

3 tablespoons sugar
1 tablespoon cornstarch

1 (1-lb.) can whole cranberry sauce
1/2 teaspoon grated lemon peel

In a stainless steel, glass or enamel saucepan, blend sugar and cornstarch to remove lumps. Gradually blend in cranberry sauce and lemon peel. Cook, stirring constantly until thickened and clear. Refrigerate. When cooled, spread over chilled cheesecake or cheese pie and refrigerate. Makes glaze for 1 nine-inch cheesecake or cheese pie.

Cherries Jubilee Glaze

For extra-special compliments, serve over Traditional Cheesecake, page 129.

1 (1-lb.) can dark sweet pitted cherries
2 tablespoons sugar
5 cloves
1 cinnamon stick
Peel of 1/2 lemon
   (removed with vegetable peeler)

Water, if necessary
1 tablespoon cornstarch
2 tablespoons kirsch liqueur,
   if desired

Drain syrup from cherries into a saucepan. Add sugar, cloves, cinnamon stick and lemon peel. Simmer, covered, 15 minutes. Strain off cloves, cinnamon and lemon peel. The syrup remaining should measure about 2/3 cup. Add water or reduce as necessary. Remove about 2 tablespoons syrup. Cool and blend thoroughly with cornstarch. Add slowly to hot syrup, stirring constantly until mixture boils and becomes clear and thickens. For real "jubilee" flavor, warm kirsch liqueur in ladle over candle or burner. Tip ladle into flame to ignite. When flame dies, add liqueur to sauce. Fold in drained cherries and cool. Spread over chilled cheesecake. Refrigerate until set. Makes glaze for 1 nine- or ten-inch cheesecake or cheese pie.

Chocolate Sour Cream Topping

Chocolate lovers prefer this to plain sour cream topping.

4 oz. semisweet or milk chocolate
1/2 cup dairy sour cream,
   room temperature

Melt chocolate over hot water or on very low heat. When melted, remove from heat and blend in sour cream. Spread over surface of cooled cheesecake or cheese pie. Refrigerate until firm. *Do not bake!* Makes topping for 1 nine-inch cheesecake or cheese pie.

Strawberry Glaze

A fabulous topping for your favorite cheesecake or cheese pie.

1 (10-oz.) pkg. frozen strawberries, thawed
1 tablespoon cornstarch
1/4 cup sugar
Dash salt

1/2 teaspoon lemon juice
1/2 teaspoon vanilla
1 to 2 drops red food coloring

Combine strawberries, cornstarch, sugar and salt in a saucepan; blend. Cook until clear and thickened. Remove from heat. Stir in remaining ingredients. Place wax paper directly on top of hot glaze; refrigerate. When cool, spread over chilled cheesecake or cheese pie. Refrigerate until set. Makes glaze for 1 nine-inch cheesecake or cheese pie.

Variations

Raspberry Glaze: Substitute 1 (10-oz.) package frozen raspberries for strawberries. Before cooling, press through fine strainer or cheesecloth to remove seeds. Omit food coloring.
Pineapple Glaze: Substitute 1 (8-1/2-oz.) can crushed pineapple for strawberries; drain. Reserve pineapple. Cook drained syrup with cornstarch, sugar and salt. Fold in pineapple after syrup cools. Use yellow food coloring.

Cakes & Frostings

One of the first cooking projects most children want to try is baking a cake. There is something deeply satisfying about hearing your family rave over the cake you baked—whether you are 8, 18 or 80. With so many mixes available today, it is not difficult to bake a very satisfactory cake. But the Mmmmmmms and Ahhhhhhs will be even more fervent with the greater moistness, better flavor and better keeping qualities of a homemade cake made with real butter and buttermilk, sour cream or yogurt. Find out by baking some of the cakes in this section.

These cakes are especially delicious for several reasons. To start with, they are made with butter. This immediately suggests delightful flavor. But that's not all. Butter makes cakes more moist and rich tasting, too. This is because it doesn't contain emulsifiers. Emulsifiers are added to the vegetable shortenings used in many cake mixes and recipes because they allow more air to be whipped into the batters. This greater volume of air and greater dispersion of the fat detract from the moistness of the cake. Even though a cake made with butter may actually have less fat, it will have a richer taste and texture.

Another reason that these cakes are better is that they are made with cultured dairy products. The characteristic flavor, aroma and texture of cakes and breads made with sour cream, buttermilk and yogurt are well known and appreciated. In addition to this, the fact that recipes made with cultured dairy products contain little or no baking powder further enhances this flavor. Are you aware that baking powder has a flavor? Some describe it as metallic, others as bitter or burning. Notice the difference when you use baking soda and cultured dairy products. There is no off-flavor to cover the subtle flavors of the other ingredients.

You can enjoy this advantage in any standard cake recipe you now use. Convert it to buttermilk or yogurt by following the method in this section. If you already have an old-fashioned recipe calling for sour milk, just use buttermilk. No other chang-

es are necessary. Sour milk recipes come from the days when milk soured naturally because it wasn't pasteurized. Another point about old-fashioned recipes—many of them call for the baking soda to be stirred into the buttermilk to dissolve it. This procedure is all right, but because baking soda is ground finer now and dissolves readily, it's usually sifted with the flour.

The finishing touch you put on these cakes is another reason why they are going to be better. Try Creamy Butter-Cheese Frosting, page 143, or Easiest Chocolate Frosting, page 142. Or how about Whipped Cream Topping, page 144? Bake cakes in different flavors and frost them to match Start with the recipes as they are given here, then branch out and create your own variations. Your cakes will be constantly in demand!

CONVERTING CAKES TO BUTTERMILK, YOGURT OR SOUR CREAM

A cake recipe is really a formula. It combines ingredients to achieve a particular rising power and level of acidity so that the finished cake will be light, moist and delicately browned. If a batter is too acid, the cake will shrink and fall, taste doughy and never brown properly. If a batter has too much soda, the cake will be dry, crumbly, grayish in color and have a soapy taste. To arrive at a good formula, the acid ingredients must be balanced by baking soda or, to a lesser degree, egg whites. Although most foods are on the acid side, the level is not high enough to affect the results. Only the highly acid foods, such as yogurt, buttermilk, sour cream, citrus juices, honey, molasses, brown sugar and cream of tartar need to be balanced. By adding soda to recipes containing these ingredients, a proper acid level can be achieved and a good amount of rising power can be obtained.

The easiest way to get a properly balanced cake is, of course, to use a tested recipe like the ones in this book. But it is possible to take a promising standard plain milk or water cake and convert it to an even better flavored buttermilk or yogurt cake. This is done simply by adding soda to balance the acid of these ingredients and subtracting baking powder.

A rough rule is to decrease the baking powder by twice the amount of soda you are adding.

If a recipe calls for 1 cup of milk or water you may:

Substitute 1 cup of buttermilk, add 1/2 teaspoon baking soda and subtract 1 teaspoon baking powder if present.

Substitute 1 cup of plain yogurt, add 1 teaspoon baking soda and subtract 2 teaspoons baking powder.

If a recipe calls for 1 cup of buttermilk you may:

Substitute 1 cup of plain yogurt, add 1/2 teaspoon baking soda and subtract 1 teaspoon baking powder if present.

Substitute 1/2 cup of plain yogurt and 1/2 cup water. Do not change the baking soda or baking powder quantities.

Substituting sour cream for plain milk or water is more complicated because sour cream is both higher in fat and lower in liquid than these products. The substitute can be made, but a little trial and error may be necessary. Here is a rule to guide you.

If a recipe calls for 1 cup of plain milk or water you can:

Substitute 1 cup sour cream, add 2 or 3 tablespoons milk or water, add 1/2 teaspoon baking soda and subtract 1 teaspoon baking powder. It may be necessary to subtract 2 or 3 tablespoons of fat from recipe.

GENERAL RULES FOR CAKE BAKING

1. Have all ingredients at room temperature— eggs, butter, buttermilk, sour cream. Sugar and baking soda dissolve better and faster.

2. Measure accurately—especially acid ingredients and soda. See page 181 for instructions on measuring dairy foods. If substitutions are necessary, follow rules to the letter.

3. Butter and flour the baking pans on the inside bottom only, except where indicated otherwise. Use butter wrappers to rub butter on pans.

4. Preheat oven well in advance and do not open oven door until last third of baking time.

5. Do not overbake cakes. Overbaking causes drying. A cake is fully baked when it shows one of the following signs: The edges begin to pull away from the pan, or the surface springs back when lightly tapped with finger, or a toothpick inserted in the center comes out dry—except in the case of fruit pulp cakes.

WHIPPED CREAM

Few dessert toppings are as simple to make as whipped cream. See Whipped Cream Topping, page 144. A few tips will help guarantee your success every time.

1. A day or two (or longer) age on cream thickens it and improves its whipping qualities.

2. The cream, bowl and beaters should be thoroughly chilled before beating.

3. Use fine granulated sugar, if available.

4. The more sugar added to whipped cream, the less firm it will whip. Add as little sugar as possible to get the flavor you want. For greatest stability, add the sugar gradually after whipping has begun.

5. Whip cream in a deep, narrow bowl to prevent splattering and to speed whipping.

6. One cup of whipping cream yields approximately 2 cups of whipped cream.

Basic Buttermilk Cake

Being basic doesn't keep this cake from being great!

2-1/4 cups sifted cake flour
3/4 teaspoon baking powder
3/4 teaspoon baking soda
1/4 teaspoon salt
1/2 cup (1 stick) butter,
   room temperature

1-1/2 cups sugar
2 eggs
1 teaspoon vanilla
1 cup buttermilk
Your favorite frosting,
   pages 142 to 144

Preheat oven to 375°F (191°C). Line 2 nine-inch, round cake pans with wax paper. Sift and measure flour; sift again with baking powder, baking soda and salt. Cream butter and sugar in a large bowl. Beat in eggs, 1 at a time. Add vanilla and beat until light and fluffy. Add dry ingredients in 3 portions, alternating with buttermilk; beat well after each addition. When all ingredients have been added, beat at medium speed 1 minute. Pour into prepared pans . Bake 20 to 25 minutes or until a toothpick inserted in center comes out dry. Cool on racks 15 minutes. Remove from pans and cool completely before frosting. Frost with any variation of Creamy Butter-Cheese Frosting, page 143, Superb Chocolate Frosting, page 142, or Easiest Chocolate Frosting, page 142. Makes 12 to 16 servings.

Variations

Extra-Rich Buttermilk Cake: Increase butter to 3/4 cup (1-1/2 sticks).
Buttermilk Chocolate Cake: Reduce sifted flour to 2 cups. Omit baking powder and increase baking soda to 1 teaspoon. Either granulated or light-brown sugar may be used. Add 2 ounces baking chocolate, melted, to butter-sugar mixture.
Gold Cake: Substitute 6 egg yolks for 2 whole eggs.
Spice Cake: Sift 1 teaspoon cinnamon, 1/2 teaspoon cloves, 1/4 teaspoon nutmeg with dry ingredients. Substitute light-brown sugar for half the granulated sugar. Frost with the Panocha variation of Creamy Butter-Cheese Frosting, page 143.
Sheet Cake: Bake in a 13" x 9" x 2" baking pan about 30 minutes.

Light-brown sugar and dark-brown sugar give very different results in cakes. Dark-brown sugar makes a dryer, less sweet cake.

Deluxe Sour Cream Cake

A heavenly cake with very special variations.

2 cups sifted cake flour
3/4 teaspoon baking powder
1/2 teaspoon baking soda
1/4 teaspoon salt
1/2 cup (1 stick) butter,
   room temperature

1-1/2 cups sugar
2 eggs
1 teaspoon vanilla
1 cup (1/2 pint) dairy sour cream,
   room temperature
Frosting

Preheat oven to 375°F (191°C). Line 2 nine-inch, round cake pans with wax paper. Sift and measure flour; sift again with baking powder, baking soda and salt. Cream butter and sugar in a large bowl. Beat in eggs, 1 at a time. Add vanilla and beat until fluffy and light in color. Add sifted dry ingredients in 3 portions, alternating with sour cream. When all ingredients have been added, beat on medium speed 1 minute. Pour batter into prepared pans. Bake about 25 minutes or until a toothpick inserted in center comes out dry. Cool on racks 15 minutes. Remove from pans and cool completely before frosting. Makes 12 to 16 servings.

Variations

Deluxe Sour Cream Chocolate Cake: Add 2 ounces melted baking chocolate to butter-sugar mixture. Omit baking powder and increase baking soda to 3/4 teaspoon.

Deluxe Date Cake: Substitute light-brown sugar for half the granulated sugar. Sift 1/8 teaspoon allspice with dry ingredients. Fold 3/4 cup chopped dates and 1/2 cup finely chopped walnuts into finished batter.

Deluxe Pineapple Cake: Stir well-drained contents of 1 (8-3/4-oz.) can crushed pineapple into finished batter.

Fiftieth Anniversary Cake: Substitute light-brown sugar for half the granulated sugar. Beat 2 tablespoons grated orange peel into finished batter and fold in 3/4 cup chopped pecans. Bake in buttered and floured 9-inch tube pan at 350°F (177°C) 45 minutes or until toothpick inserted in cake comes out dry. Before cooling and removing cake from pan, poke with holes at 1/2-inch intervals. Dissolve 1/4 cup sugar in 1/4 cup orange juice and, if desired, 2 or 3 tablespoons Cointreau®. Spoon over cake. Cool completely before removing from pan. Wrap carefully in foil or plastic wrap and store at least 24 hours before cutting.

If you are baking a cake in a glass baking dish instead of a specified metal pan, reduce the oven temperature by 25°F (14°C).

1. Substitute light-brown sugar for half the sugar in the basic recipe. Grate orange peel to make 2 tablespoons and chop pecans to make 3/4 cup.

2. Fold orange peel and pecans into the finished batter.

How To Make Fiftieth Anniversary Cake

3. Bake in a buttered and floured 9-inch tube pan 45 minutes or until a toothpick inserted in cake comes out dry. Remove from oven and, with a toothpick, poke holes at 1/2-inch intervals. Spoon the mixture of sugar, orange juice and Cointreau®, if desired, over cake.

4. Cool cake completely before removing from pan. Wrap in plastic wrap or foil. Store at least 24 hours before cutting.

Scrumptious Yellow Cake

This recipe proves that yogurt is great for cakes.

2-1/2 cups sifted cake flour
1 teaspoon baking soda
1/2 teaspoon baking powder
1/2 teaspoon salt
3/4 cup (1-1/2 sticks) butter,
    room temperature

1 cup sugar
2 eggs
1-1/2 teaspoons vanilla
1 (8-oz.) carton plain yogurt
Citrus Frosting variation of
    Creamy Butter-Cheese Frosting, page 143

Preheat oven to 350°F (177°C). Line 2 nine-inch, round cake pans with wax paper. Sift and measure flour; sift again with baking soda, baking powder and salt. Cream butter and sugar in a large bowl. Add eggs, 1 at a time; beat well after each addition. Add vanilla and beat until light and fluffy. Add dry ingredients in 3 portions alternating with yogurt. When all ingredients have been added, beat on medium speed 1 minute. Pour into prepared cake pans. Bake 25 to 30 minutes or until a toothpick inserted in center comes out dry. Cool on racks 15 minutes. Remove from pans and cool completely before frosting. Frost with Citrus Frosting variation of Creamy Butter-Cheese Frosting, page 143. Makes 12 to 16 servings.

Gingerbread

What could be more natural than gingerbread made with buttermilk.

2-1/2 cups sifted flour
1 teaspoon baking powder
1-1/2 teaspoons baking soda
1 teaspoon ginger
2 teaspoons cinnamon
1/2 cup (1 stick) butter,
    room temperature
3/4 cup light-brown sugar,
    firmly packed

2 eggs
3/4 cup light molasses
1 cup buttermilk
Whipped Creme Fraîche, page 168, or
    Whipped Cream Topping, page 144,
    or sour cream, sweetened with
    brown sugar

Preheat oven to 350°F (177°C). Butter and flour a 13" x 9" x 2" cake pan. Sift and measure flour; sift again with baking powder, baking soda, ginger and cinnamon. Cream butter and brown sugar in a large bowl. Beat in eggs, 1 at a time, mixing well after each addition. Blend in molasses. Add dry ingredients in 3 portions alternating with buttermilk; beat well after each addition. Pour into prepared pan. Bake 35 to 40 minutes or until a toothpick inserted in center comes out dry. Serve warm or cooled with Whipped Creme Fraîche, page 168, Whipped-Cream Topping, page 144, or sour cream sweetened with brown sugar. Makes 16 to 20 servings.

Aunt Vada's Best Banana Cake

Use bananas so ripe they're about to pour out of their skins.

2-1/2 cups sifted cake flour
1-3/4 cups sugar
2-1/4 teaspoons baking powder
3/4 teaspoon baking soda
1 teaspoon salt
3/4 cup (1-1/2 sticks) butter,
   room temperature
1-1/4 cups mashed, very ripe banana
   (about 3 medium)

2/3 cup buttermilk
2 eggs
2/3 cup finely chopped walnuts
Creamy Butter-Cheese Frosting or the
   Banana Butter-Cheese Frosting
   variation, page 143

Preheat oven to 350°F (177°C). Line 2 nine-inch, round cake pans with wax paper. Sift and measure flour, sift again into large bowl with sugar, baking powder, baking soda and salt. Add butter, banana and 1/3 cup buttermilk; beat 2 minutes. Add remaining buttermilk and eggs; beat 2 minutes. Fold in walnuts. Pour into prepared pans. Bake 30 to 35 minutes or until a toothpick inserted in center comes out dry. Cool on racks 15 minutes. Remove from pans and cool completely before frosting. Frost with Creamy Butter-Cheese Frosting or Banana Butter-Cheese Frosting variation, page 143. Makes 12 to 16 servings.

Variation

Banana Sheet Cake: Bake in a 13" x 9" x 2" buttered and floured baking pan at 350°F (177°C) 40 minutes.

Delectable Chocolate Cake

An old-fashioned cake with a new yogurt twist.

2 oz. unsweetened baking chocolate
2 eggs, separated
1/2 cup sugar
1-3/4 cups sifted cake flour
1-1/2 teaspoons baking soda

3/4 teaspoon salt
1 cup sugar
1/3 cup cooking oil
1 (8-oz.) carton plain yogurt
1/3 cup milk

Preheat oven to 350°F (177°C). Line 2 nine-inch, round cake pans with wax paper. Melt chocolate in a double boiler. Beat egg whites until frothy. Gradually add 1/2 cup sugar, beating constantly. until stiff and glossy. Set aside. Sift and measure flour; sift again into a large bowl with baking soda, salt and 1 cup sugar. Add oil and about half the yogurt; beat 1 minute. Add remaining yogurt, milk, egg yolks and melted chocolate; beat 1 minute. Fold in beaten egg whites. Pour into prepared pans. Bake 25 to 30 minutes or until a toothpick inserted in center comes out dry. Cool on racks 15 minutes. Remove from pans and cool completely before frosting. Makes 12 to 16 servings.

Prune Cake

Moist and delicious.

1-1/2 cups sifted flour
1 teaspoon baking soda
1/4 teaspoon salt
1/2 teaspoon cinnamon
1/2 teaspoon nutmeg
1/2 teaspoon allspice
1/4 teaspoon ground cloves
1/2 cup (1 stick) butter,
  room temperature

1-1/2 cups sugar
2 eggs
2/3 cup prune pulp from chopped,
  cooked, pitted prunes
2/3 cup buttermilk
1/3 cup chopped walnuts
Creamy Butter-Cheese Frosting,
  page 143

Preheat oven to 350°F (177°C). Line 2 eight-inch, round cake pans with wax paper. Sift and measure flour; sift again with baking soda, salt, cinnamon, nutmeg, allspice and cloves. Cream butter and sugar in a large bowl. Beat in eggs, 1 at a time, mixing well after each addition. Blend in prune pulp. Add dry ingredients in 3 portions, alternating with buttermilk; beat well after each addition. Stir in nuts. Pour into pans. Bake 30 to 35 minutes or until a toothpick inserted in center comes out dry. Cool on racks 15 minutes. Remove from pans and cool completely before frosting. Frost with Creamy Butter-Cheese Frosting, page 143. Makes 12 to 16 servings.

Variation

Prune Sheet Cake: Bake in 13" x 9" x 2" baking pan 45 to 50 minutes.

Old-Fashioned Devil's Food Cake

This is the cake you remember from your childhood.

3 oz. unsweetened baking chocolate
2-1/4 cups sifted cake flour
2 teaspoons baking soda
1/2 teaspoon salt
1/2 cup (1 stick) butter,
  room temperature

1 (1-lb.) box or 2-1/3 cups
  light-brown sugar, firmly packed
3 eggs
2 teaspoons vanilla
3/4 cup buttermilk
3/4 cup boiling water

Preheat oven to 350°F (191°C). Line 2 nine-inch, round cake pans with wax paper. Melt chocolate in a double boiler. Sift and measure flour; sift again with baking soda and salt. Cream butter and brown sugar in a large bowl. Add eggs, 1 at a time, beating well after each addition. Add vanilla and melted chocolate; beat until light and fluffy. Add dry ingredients in 3 portions, alternating with buttermilk; mix well after each addition. Blend in boiling water. Pour into prepared pans. Batter will be very thin. Bake 25 to 30 minutes or until a toothpick inserted in center comes out dry. Cool on racks 15 minutes. Remove from pans and cool completely before frosting. Makes 12 to 16 servings.

Superb Chocolate Frosting

Smooth and creamy. Sour cream takes the edge off the sweetness.

1 (6-oz.) pkg. semisweet chocolate morsels
1/2 cup dairy sour cream
1 teaspoon vanilla

1/4 teaspoon salt
2-1/2 cups powdered sugar

Melt chocolate morsels over hot water or on very low heat. Remove from heat. Blend in sour cream, vanilla and salt. Gradually beat in powdered sugar until smooth. If too soft to spread, refrigerate briefly. Makes filling and frosting for 2 eight- or nine-inch layers.

Saucy Angel Frosting

Easy and delicious whipped cream frosting. Especially good for angel food cake.

1 cup (1/2 pint) whipping cream
2 tablespoons sugar
1 teaspoon vanilla

1 (8-oz.) carton pineapple
   fruit-blended yogurt

Pour cream into a small mixer bowl; refrigerate bowl and beaters until well-chilled. Whip cream until frothy. Gradually add sugar and continue beating until stiff. Add vanilla and yogurt; fold until well-blended. Split angel food cake. Fill and frost; refrigerate. Serve within 2 hours. Makes filling and frosting for 1 small loaf angel food cake.

Variations

Substitute cherry, boysenberry, orange or lime fruit-blended yogurt for pineapple.
24-Hour Saucy Angel Frosting: Soften 1 teaspoon unflavored gelatin in 2 tablespoons water in a heat-proof cup. Place cup in pan of simmering water until gelatin dissolves. Cool. As soon as sugar is added to cream, drizzle in dissolved gelatin. Continue beating until stiff. Proceed according to recipe directions. Frosting will hold well 24 hours in refrigerator.

Easiest Chocolate Frosting

Absolutely the easiest chocolate frosting ever, and not too sweet.

10 to 12 oz. semisweet or
   milk chocolate

2 cups (1 pint) dairy sour cream,
   room temperature

Melt chocolate over boiling water or on very low heat. Stir until smooth. Remove from heat and blend in sour cream. If too soft to spread, refrigerate briefly. Makes filling and frosting for 2 nine-inch layers.

Creamy Butter-Cheese Frosting

Perfect basic frosting. Try your own variations.

1 (3-oz.) pkg. cream cheese,
  room temperature
1/4 cup (1/2 stick) butter,
  room temperature

2 tablespoons milk
1 teaspoon vanilla
1/8 teaspoon salt
1 (1-lb.) box powdered sugar

Beat cream cheese and butter until fluffy. Blend in milk, vanilla and salt. Gradually add powdered sugar. Beat until smooth and creamy. Makes filling and frosting for 2 or 3 nine-inch layers.

Variations

Chocolate Butter-Cheese Frosting: Beat 2 ounces unsweetened chocolate, melted, into finished frosting. Add milk or cream as necessary.

Orange Butter-Cheese Frosting: Substitute 3 tablespoons frozen orange juice concentrate for milk.

Banana Butter-Cheese Frosting: Substitute 1/2 teaspoon banana extract for 1/2 teaspoon of the vanilla.

Maraschino Butter-Cheese Frosting: Substitute 2 tablespoons maraschino cherry juice for milk. Stir in 3 tablespoons minced maraschino cherries. Add red food coloring.

Citrus Frosting: Add 1-1/2 teaspoons grated orange, lime, grapefruit or lemon peel to finished frosting.

Panocha Frosting: Omit 1/2 cup of the powdered sugar. Heat 1/2 cup brown sugar, firmly packed, with butter and milk until sugar melts; cool. Beat in cream cheese and remaining ingredients.

Coconut Butter-Cheese Frosting: Toast 1 cup or 1 (3-1/2-oz.) can flaked coconut. Crumble half and stir into finished frosting. Garnish with remaining half.

Whipped Chocolate-Cheese Frosting

Especially for angel food or sponge cakes.

1 (6-oz.) pkg. semisweet chocolate morsels
1 cup (1/2 pint) whipping cream
1 (3-oz.) pkg. cream cheese,
  room temperature
1 tablespoon half-and-half

1/8 teaspoon salt
3/4 cup light-brown sugar,
  firmly packed
1 teaspoon vanilla

Melt chocolate morsels over boiling water or on very low heat. Smooth melted chocolate with rubber scraper and cool to room temperature. Whip cream until stiff; refrigerate. Beat cream cheese, half-and-half or milk and salt until blended. Gradually add brown sugar and beat until smooth. Blend in vanilla and melted chocolate. Refrigerate until mixture mounds when dropped from a spoon. Fold in whipped cream. If too soft to spread, refrigerate briefly. Makes frosting for 1 ten-inch angel food, chiffon or sponge cake.

Variation

Whipped Butterscotch-Cheese Frosting: Substitute butterscotch morsels for chocolate morsels. Add 2 tablespoons water to melted butterscotch; blend well. Increase salt to 1/4 teaspoon.

Whipped Cream Topping

No topping tastes as good as real whipped cream. Try one of our colorful variations.

1 cup (1/2 pint) whipping cream
Dash salt
1/2 teaspoon vanilla, peppermint, almond or
    other flavor extract

1 to 2 tablespoons sugar
Food coloring, if desired

Combine cream, salt and vanilla or flavor extract in a small bowl. Refrigerate bowl and beaters until well chilled. Beat cream until frothy. Gradually add sugar and continue beating until stiff. Add a few drops food coloring, if desired. Refrigerate. Will maintain consistency 2 or 3 hours. Makes 2 cups.

Variations

Whipped Cream Frosting: Double recipe to frost 1 ten-inch angel food cake. Soften 1 teaspoon unflavored gelatin in 2 tablespoons water in a heat-proof cup. Place cup in pan of simmering water until gelatin dissolves. Cool. As soon as sugar is added to cream, drizzle in dissolved gelatin. Continue beating until stiff. Frosting will hold well 24 hours in refrigerator.

Cinnamon Whipped Cream: Substitute brown sugar for granulated sugar. Add 1/2 teaspoon ground cinnamon.

Cinnamon Red-Hot Whipped Cream: Omit sugar and vanilla. Boil 1/4 cup red cinnamon candies in 1/4 cup water until dissolved; continue boiling until thickened. Cool and add to cream before whipping.

Chocolate Whipped Cream: Use 1 tablespoon sugar only. Add 1/4 cup instant hot chocolate powder.

Mocha Whipped Cream: Add 1 teaspoon instant coffee to chocolate variation.

Crème de Menthe Whipped Cream: Fold 2 tablespoons crème de menthe into finished topping.

Pies & Pastries

Baking a great pie is one of the most convincing ways to display ingenuity and talent in the kitchen. There is no question about it, pie baking is a test of skill—not just one skill, but many skills. After all, a pie is not a simple creation. It is a crust, a filling, perhaps a topping, and a lot of coordination. Pies are baked or unbaked. There are custard pies, cream pies, chiffon pies, gelled pies, fruit pies, double-crust pies, lattice-topped pies, deep-dish pies and tarts. Each variety demands its own special techniques. Great pie bakers may be born—but more than likely they are developed out of good training, lots of experience, more than a fragment of experimentation and, of course, a lot of recipes with potential for greatness.

Here are original recipes to let you display your skill. As you first scan them you may think they compose a simple collection of favored classic pies. Investigate more closely, eye the ingredients, follow the procedure and you'll see that somewhere in each is locked a surprise element. There may be a hidden layer of delightfully flavored cream cheese, or some fruit-blended yogurt giving zing to a cream pie. Maybe the surprise is a background of sour cream rounding out the flavor of a fruit pie. These recipes are unique in that they open up new interest and variation for the most experienced pie baker. But many are still simple enough so the novice can enjoy success on a first try.

It's usually the pie crust that makes the new baker uneasy. With the many pre-baked crusts, ready-to-bake frozen crusts and ready-to-roll pie-crust mixes, it's possible to bake a pie without all the problems of crust-making. The main idea is to enjoy the fabulous fillings . If you're ready to try your hand at a pie crust from scratch, there are recipes for standard pastry and crumb crusts at the end of this section. For new flavor enjoyment, try Cream Cheese Pastry, page 154, or Cottage Cheese Pastry, page 156.

Tucked in among the pie recipes, page 154, is a recipe for Cream Puffs—elegant, delicious, impressive cream puffs! Here is the answer for the new cook who doesn't have the experience or equipment to bake a pie. Cream puffs are so simple to make and they can hold an unlimited number of luscious things—including most of the cream pie-fillings in this section.

In these pages there are many delightful recipes to help you please and impress your eager following.

To prevent soggy crusts on custard or baked fruit pies, prepare the bottom crust and pierce it repeatedly with fork tines. Bake 8 minutes in a preheated 425° F (218° C) oven. Remove from oven, brush with beaten egg and bake 2 more minutes. Fill the crust and bake at about 350° F (177° C) until done.

Buttermilk Custard Pie

You'll try this delicious dessert and wonder why you've been neglecting custard pies.

1/3 cup butter, room temperature
1 cup sugar
3 eggs, separated
3 tablespoons flour
1/4 teaspoon salt

1 teaspoon lemon juice
1/2 teaspoon grated lemon peel
1-1/2 cups buttermilk
1 unbaked Standard Pastry Crust,
   page 157

Preheat oven to 450°F (232°C). In a large bowl, cream butter and sugar until light. Beat in egg yolks. Add flour, salt, lemon juice and peel; beat until well-blended. Blend in buttermilk. Beat egg whites until stiff but not dry. Fold into custard. Pour into Standard Pastry Crust, page 157. Bake 10 minutes. Reduce oven temperature to 350°F (177°C) and bake 40 minutes longer. Cool. Makes 6 to 8 servings.

French Apple Pie

This is apple pie with the "à la mode" built in. Delicious!

1 egg
1 cup (1/2 pint) dairy sour cream,
   room temperature
3/4 cup sugar
2 tablespoons flour
1/4 teaspoon vanilla
Dash salt

2-1/4 cups finely chopped, peeled
   cooking apples (2 to 3 apples)
1/4 teaspoon grated lemon peel
1 unbaked Standard Pastry Crust,
   page 157
Crumb Topping, see below

Crumb Topping:
1/4 cup (1/2 stick) butter,
   room temperature
1/2 cup sugar

1/3 cup flour
3/4 teaspoon cinnamon

Preheat oven to 450°F (232°C). Beat egg in a large bowl; blend in sour cream, sugar, flour, vanilla and salt. Fold in apple and lemon peel. Pour into Standard Pastry Crust, page 157, and bake 10 minutes. Reduce oven temperature to 350°F(177°C) and bake 30 minutes longer or until crust is golden brown. While pie is baking, prepare Crumb Topping. Sprinkle topping over pie and bake 15 minutes longer. Serve warm or cool. Makes 6 to 8 servings.

Crumb Topping:
Cut butter into sugar, flour and cinnamon. Electric mixer can be used.

Clockwise from top center: Peaches & Cream Pie, Strawberry Surprise Pie, Cool Lemon Pie, French Apple Pie, Orange Parfait Pie (variation of Strawberry Parfait Pie), Buttermilk Custard Pie, Luscious Cherry-Cheese Pie

Lime-Divine Pie

A favorite of ours. Try it on a warm day.

1 (3-oz.) pkg. lime gelatin
1 cup boiling water
1 (8-oz.) pkg. cream cheese,
   room temperature
1 (8-oz.) carton lime
   fruit-blended yogurt

1 prebaked Standard Pastry Crust,
   page 157, or 1 Graham Cracker Crumb
   Crust, page 156
1 recipe Whipped Cream Topping,
   page 144
Chocolate curls for garnish

Dissolve gelatin in boiling water. Cool to room temperature. In a large bowl, beat cream cheese until smooth. Gradually blend in yogurt. Add gelatin slowly, beating until smooth. Pour into pre-baked Standard Pastry Crust, page 157, or Graham Cracker Crumb Crust, page 156. Chill until firm. Frost with Whipped Cream Topping, page 144. Garnish with chocolate curls. Makes 6 to 8 servings.

Variations

Fruit-Flavored Divine Pie: Substitute boysenberry, cherry, strawberry or orange fruit-blended yogurt and a matching flavored gelatin for the lime flavor. Use raspberry gelatin with boysenberry yogurt.

Creamy Lime-Divine Pie: For a softer, more tangy pie at about 40 calories less per serving, substitute 1 cup (1/2 pint) sour cream for cream cheese.

Peaches & Cream Pie

Canned peaches make this an easy year-round pie.

1 (1-lb.) can sliced peaches
1 (1-lb. 13-oz.) can sliced peaches
1 cup (1/2 pint) dairy sour cream,
   room temperature
1/2 cup sugar
2 tablespoons flour

1/2 teaspoon grated lemon peel
1/2 teaspoon vanilla
1/4 teaspoon almond extract
1/8 teaspoon salt
1 unbaked Standard Pastry Crust for
   Double-Crust Pie, page 157

Preheat oven to 450°F (232°C). Drain both cans of peaches thoroughly in colander. Blend remaining ingredients except pie crust. Fold in well-drained peach slices. Pour into bottom of Standard Pastry Crust for Double-Crust Pie, page 157. Cover with top crust and seal edges carefully; crimp edges and cut design in center. Bake 10 minutes. Reduce oven temperature to 350°F (177°C) and bake 30 minutes longer. Serve warm or cool. Makes 6 to 8 servings.

Cool Lemon Pie

It's beautiful and delicious.

1 (3-1/2-oz.) pkg. lemon pudding
   and pie-filling mix
3/4 cup sugar
1/4 cup water
3 egg yolks
1 cup boiling water
1 cup (1/2 pint) dairy sour cream
2 tablespoons lemon juice

1 teaspoon grated lemon peel
1 prebaked Standard Pastry Crust,
   page 157
1 recipe Whipped Cream Topping,
   page 144
1/4 to 1/2 cup chopped nuts or
   several pieces sugared lemon peel

In a stainless steel, glass or enamel saucepan, combine pudding mix with sugar and 1/4 cup water. Blend in egg yolks. Add 1 cup boiling water and cook, stirring constantly until mixture thickens and first bubbles appear. Cool slightly at room temperature. Pudding will stiffen if cooled too much. Empty sour cream into a small mixer bowl and put in freezer with beaters until *very* cold. Beat 4 to 5 minutes on high speed until doubled in volume; see page 158 for hints on whipping sour cream. Stir lemon juice and lemon peel into warm pudding. Fold in whipped sour cream. Pour into prebaked Standard Pastry Crust, page 157, and refrigerate 4 to 5 hours. Garnish with Whipped Cream Topping, page 144, and chopped nuts or sugared lemon peel. Makes 6 to 8 servings.

Variations

Substitute 1 Graham Cracker Crumb Crust, page 156, 1 Cream Cheese Pastry, page 154, or 6 to 8 tart shells for Standard Pastry Crust.

Cottage Cheese Custard Pie

Even desserts can boost protein counts—especially this one.

1 unbaked Standard Pastry Crust,
   page 157
2 cups (1 pint) cottage cheese
3 eggs

3/4 cup sugar
2 tablespoons flour
Juice and grated peel of 1 lemon

Preheat oven to 450°F (232°C). Bake pastry crust 6 minutes; cool. Reduce oven temperature to 350°F (177°C). In a large bowl, beat cottage cheese to a smooth curd. Add eggs, sugar, flour, lemon juice and peel; beat until well-blended. Or, put all ingredients in blender jar and blend until smooth. Pour into Standard Pastry Crust, page 157. Bake 50 to 60 minutes or until a knife inserted in pie just off center comes out clean. Cool 1 hour before serving. Makes 6 servings.

Really Raisin Pie

For hearty appetites.

1-1/2 cups seedless raisins
Water
1 egg
1 cup (1/2 pint) dairy sour cream,
  room temperature
1 cup light-brown sugar,
  firmly packed
3 tablespoons flour

2 teaspoons champagne vinegar or
  distilled vinegar
1 teaspoon cinnamon
1/4 teaspoon nutmeg
1/4 teaspoon salt
1 unbaked Standard Pastry Crust for
  Double-Crust Pie, page 157

Preheat oven to 450°F (232°C). Place raisins in a saucepan with water to cover. Cover and simmer 5 minutes or until raisins have plumped; drain. Beat egg in a medium bowl. Blend in remaining ingredients except pie crust. Fold in drained raisins. Pour into bottom of Standard Pastry Crust for Double-Crust Pie, page 157. Top with pastry or lattice pastry strips and seal edges carefully. Crimp edges and cut design in center of plain top crust. Bake 10 minutes. Reduce oven temperature to 350°F (177°C) and bake 25 minutes longer. Serve warm for fullest flavor. Makes 6 to 8 servings.

Chocolate-Marshmallow Pie

A great chocolate pie!

1 (4-oz.) bar German sweet chocolate
2 cups miniature marshmallows
2 tablespoons sugar
Dash salt
1/2 cup milk
1 (8-oz.) pkg. cream cheese,
  room temperature

1 cup (1/2 pint) whipping cream
1/4 teaspoon vanilla
1 prebaked Standard Pastry Crust,
  page 157
1 recipe Whipped Cream Topping,
  page 144, if desired

Melt chocolate and marshmallows with sugar, salt and milk in top of double boiler. In a large bowl, beat cream cheese until smooth. Gradually add melted chocolate mixture, blending well. Refrigerate until cool. Whip cream with vanilla. Fold into cooled chocolate mixture. Refrigerate until mixture mounds when dropped from a spoon. Spoon into prebaked Standard Pastry Crust, page 157, and shape into decorative swirls. Refrigerate until set. Garnish with Whipped Cream Topping, page 144, if desired, and serve. Makes 6 to 8 servings.

Strawberry Surprise Pie

Glazed fresh strawberries on a snowy layer of cream cheese.

Strawberry Glaze, see below
1 (8-oz.) pkg. cream cheese,
   room temperature
1/3 cup sugar
2 tablespoons half-and-half
1 tablespoon lemon juice
1/2 teaspoon grated lemon peel

1 cooled, prebaked Standard Pastry
   Crust, page 157, or
   8 individual tart shells
1-1/2 pints fresh strawberries,
   washed and stemmed
1/2 recipe Whipped Creme Fraîche,
   page 168

Strawberry Glaze:
1/2 pint fresh strawberries,
   washed and stemmed
3/4 cup water
1/2 cup sugar

1 tablespoon cornstarch
1 teaspoon unflavored gelatin
Red food coloring

Prepare Strawberry Glaze; set aside. In a medium bowl, beat cream cheese with sugar, half-and-half, lemon juice and lemon peel until light and fluffy. Spread in cooled prebaked Standard Pastry Crust, page 157, or tart shells. Arrange strawberries, stem-end down, over cream cheese layer. Pour cooled glaze over all. Refrigerate 3 to 4 hours. Serve garnished with a dollop of Whipped Creme Fraîche, page 168. Makes 8 servings.

Strawberry Glaze:

In a medium saucepan, crush strawberries with potato masher. Add water and sugar. Simmer 5 minutes. Press through strainer to remove pulp. Cool. Blend cornstarch and gelatin with 1/4 cup cooled strawberry juice to remove lumps. Add to remaining strawberry juice. Cook over medium heat, stirring constantly just until thickened and clear. Add food coloring as desired. Cool to room temperature.

Variation

Red, White and Wow Cherry Pie: Omit glaze, strawberries and Whipped Creme Fraîche. Spoon contents of 1 (1-lb. 5-oz.) can cherry pie filling over cream cheese filling in crust.

Shiny aluminum foil pans reflect heat and cause soggy crusts. Place pie or tart shells on a dark cookie sheet for baking. Better yet, use a glass or dull-metal pie pan to start with.

Tropical Banana Cream Pie

So easy you won't mind making it over and over!

1 (3-3/4-oz.) pkg. instant vanilla
   pudding mix
1 cup (1/2 pint) dairy sour cream
3/4 cup half-and-half
1 Graham Cracker Crumb Crust,
   page 156, or 1 prebaked
   Standard Pastry Crust, page 157

3 to 4 bananas
1 recipe Whipped-Cream Topping,
   page 144

Combine instant pudding mix, sour cream and half-and-half; mix according to package directions. Pour about 1/3 of the pudding into Graham Cracker Crumb Crust, page 156, or prebaked Standard Pastry Crust, page 157. Arrange cut or whole bananas over. Cover with remaining pudding. Chill until firm. Garnish with Whipped Cream Topping, page 144, and serve. Makes 6 to 8 servings.

Variation

Coconut Cream Pie: Substitute 1 (3-1/2-oz.) can flaked coconut for bananas. Fold all but 1/4 cup coconut into pudding. Toast reserved coconut, if desired, and sprinkle over Whipped Cream Topping.

Strawberry Parfait Pie

Parfait with pizzazz—also low in calories.

1 (3-oz.) pkg. strawberry gelatin
1 cup boiling water
1 pint fresh strawberries
2 (8-oz.) cartons strawberry
   fruit-blended yogurt

1 prebaked Standard Pastry Crust,
   page 157, or 1 Graham Cracker
   Crumb Crust, page 156
1 recipe Whipped Cream Topping,
   page 144, if desired

Dissolve gelatin in boiling water. Cool to room temperature. Wash and stem strawberries. Reserve 6 berries for garnish; slice remaining berries. Gradually blend cooled gelatin into yogurt. Chill until mixture mounds when dropped from a spoon. Fold in sliced strawberries. Spoon into prebaked Standard Pastry Crust, page 157, or Graham Cracker Crumb Crust, page 156. Chill until set. Garnish with whole strawberries and Whipped Cream Topping, page 144, if desired. Makes 6 servings.

Variations

Fruit-Flavored Parfait Pie: Omit strawberries. Substitute boysenberry, lemon, lime or orange fruit-blended yogurt and a matching flavored gelatin for the strawberry flavor. Use raspberry gelatin with boysenberry yogurt. Fold well-drained mandarin orange segments into orange variation.

Luscious Cherry-Cheese Pie

A beautiful pie—and so easy!

1 (3-oz.) pkg. cherry flavored gelatin
3/4 cup boiling water
Chocolate Snap Crust, see below

1 cup (1/2 pint) cottage cheese
1 cup (1/2 pint) whipping cream
1/2 can (1-lb. 5-oz. size) cherry pie filling

Chocolate Snap Crust:
2 (2-3/4-oz.) boxes chocolate snaps
2 tablespoons butter, melted

Preheat oven to 425°F (218°C). Dissolve gelatin in boiling water; cool. Prepare Chocolate Snap Crust; set aside. Combine cooled gelatin with cottage cheese in blender jar. Blend on low speed until smooth. Refrigerate until slightly thickened. Whip cream until stiff. Fold into cheese-gelatin mixture. Refrigerate until mixture mounds when dropped from a spoon. Spread canned pie filling into crust. Fill with whipped mixture and shape into decorative swirls. Refrigerate until firm. Makes 8 servings.

Chocolate Snap Crust:
Reserve 16 snaps; crush remaining snaps and mix with melted butter. Press onto bottom of a 9-inch pie plate. Arrange reserved snaps around side. Bake 5 minutes; cool.

Boysenberry Cream Puffs

Absolutely delicious—and not too sweet.

2 cups (1 pint) whipping cream
1/4 teaspoon salt
1/2 teaspoon vanilla
1/4 cup sugar

2 (8-oz.) cartons boysenberry
    fruit-blended yogurt
1 recipe Cream Puffs, page 154
Powdered sugar

Combine cream, salt and vanilla in a medium mixer bowl. Refrigerate bowl and beaters until well chilled. Beat cream until frothy. Gradually add sugar and continue beating until stiff. Fold in yogurt. Spoon mixture into Cream Puffs, page 154. Refrigerate until serving time. Sift powdered sugar over puffs before serving. Makes 12 large puffs.

Variations

Fruited Cream Puffs: Substitute lime, orange, pineapple or strawberry fruit-blended yogurt for boysenberry.

Cream Puffs

Cream puffs are also wonderful holders for seafood or chicken salads.

1 cup water
1/2 teaspoon salt
1/2 cup (1 stick) butter

1 cup sifted flour
4 eggs, room temperature

Preheat oven to 425°F (218°C). Bring water to boil with salt and butter. As soon as butter melts and a full boil begins, add flour all at once and stir rapidly. Remove from heat as soon as mixture holds together and looks like cornmeal mush. Add eggs, one at a time, beating well after each addition. Drop by tablespoonfuls onto cookie sheet. Allow for expansion. Bake 20 minutes. Reduce heat to 325°F (163°C) and bake 20 minutes longer or until golden and crisp. Remove from oven. Make slit in each puff or cut off tops to allow steam to escape. Cool on racks and fill. Makes 12 large puffs.

Variation

Appetizer or Tea Puffs: Drop by half teaspoonfuls onto cookie sheet. Bake at 400°F (204°C) for about 15 minutes. Makes about 60 puffs.

Cream Puff Fillings

Whipped Cream: Fill puffs with 2 recipes Whipped Cream Topping, page 144.
Banana or Coconut: Fill puffs with 2 recipes Tropical Banana Cream Pie filling, page 152.
Chocolate-Marshmallow: Fill puffs with 1 recipe Chocolate-Marshmallow Pie filling, page 150.
Lemon: Fill puffs with 1 recipe Cool Lemon Pie filling, page 149.
Ice Cream: Fill puffs with any flavor ice cream.

Cream Cheese Pastry

Excellent for pies and sweet or savory tarts. See Petite Pâtes, page 29.

1/2 cup (1 stick) butter
1 (3-oz.) pkg. cream cheese,
  room temperature

1-1/4 cups sifted flour
1/4 teaspoon salt

In a large bowl, blend butter and cream cheese with electric mixer. Add flour and salt, all at once; beat on low speed, just until mixture leaves sides of bowl and forms a ball. Turn dough onto well-floured board and roll to an 11-inch circle. Roll onto rolling pin or fold in quarters. Place carefully over a 9-inch pie plate. Do not stretch pastry dough as this causes shrinkage during baking. Trim pastry 1/2 inch from pie-plate rim. Moisten underside of overhanging pastry. Fold edge over and press together. Crimp edge of crust. Pierce sides and bottom of pastry with a fork. Refrigerate 1 hour. Bake in preheated 450°F (232°C) oven 8 minutes or until golden. Makes pastry for 1 nine-inch pie.

1. As soon as the mixture resembles cornmeal mush, remove from heat. Add the eggs one at a time and beat well after each addition.

2. Drop mixture by tablespoonfuls on unbuttered cookie sheet. Leave space for expansion during cooking.

How To Make Cream Puffs

3. After baking, remove puffs from the oven and slit or cut off tops to let steam escape. Cool on racks.

4. Fill puffs, replace top and sprinkle with powdered sugar, if desired.

Cottage Cheese Pastry

Special flavor and extra protein!

1-1/2 cups sifted flour
1/8 teaspoon salt
1/2 cup (1 stick) butter,
   room temperature

1/4 cup cottage cheese

Combine all ingredients in mixer bowl. Beat on low speed just until dough leaves sides of bowl and forms a ball. Turn dough onto wax paper. Press into a ball and flatten on a lightly floured board. Roll out to an 11-inch circle. Roll onto rolling pin or fold in quarters. Place carefully over a 9-inch pie plate. Do not stretch pastry dough as this causes shrinkage during baking. Trim pastry 1/2-inch from pie plate rim. Moisten underside of overhanging pastry. Fold edge over and press together. Crimp edge of crust. Chill 3 hours. Preheat oven to 450°F (232°C). Bake 10 to 12 minutes or until golden. Makes pastry for 1 nine-inch crust.

Graham Cracker Crumb Crust

A great crust for a beginner.

1-1/2 cups graham cracker crumbs
   (18 crackers)

1/4 cup sugar
1/4 cup (1/2 stick) butter, melted

Preheat oven to 375°F (191°C). Blend graham cracker crumbs, sugar and melted butter. Distribute evenly over bottom and sides of a 9-inch pie plate with fork. Press into place. For perfectly shaped crust, press an 8-inch pie plate onto crumbs, sliding it against sides to pack and smooth. Form rim by pressing side of finger between 2 pie plate rims. Proceed around pie. Edges of crumb crusts formed this way do not burn as readily. Bake 8 minutes. Cool on rack before filling. Makes 1 nine-inch crust.

Standard 9-inch pie pans vary tremendously in the amount of filling they'll hold. If your pans are large, you may want to prepare 1-1/2 times the filling, with gelled pies in particular, to fill the crusts generously. The crusts available in supermarkets are particularly small.

Standard Pastry Crust

This classic pastry gives you an option to use butter.

1/2 cup shortening or 1/4 cup
   shortening and 1/4 cup (1/2 stick) butter
1-1/2 cups sifted flour

3/4 teaspoon salt
3 to 4 tablespoons ice water

Using pastry blender or 2 knives, cut shortening into flour and salt in a large bowl. Mixture should look like coarse meal. Sprinkle ice water over mixture, 1 tablespoon at a time, tossing rapidly with a fork. Dough should clump together. Add more water only if mixture is still *very* dry and crumbly. Turn dough onto wax paper. Press together into a ball and flatten on lightly floured board. Roll out to an 11-inch circle. Roll onto rolling pin or fold in quarters. Place carefully over a 9-inch pie plate. Do not stretch dough, as this causes shrinkage. Trim pastry 1/2-inch from rim of pie plate. Patch pastry with excess pieces. Moisten surfaces to be joined and press together. Moisten underside of overhanging pastry. Fold edge over and press together. Crimp edge of crust. To make prebaked pastry crust, pierce sides and bottom of crust with a fork about every inch. Bake in preheated 450°F (232°C) oven 10 to 12 minutes or until golden. Cool on rack. Makes 1 nine-inch pastry crust.

Variation

Pastry for Double-Crust Pie: Use 2/3 cup shortening, 2 cups sifted flour, 1 teaspoon salt and 4 to 6 tablespoons water.

Ready-made crusts and some homemade crusts have thin edges that burn easily. As soon as the edges are fully cooked and browned, wrap a strip of aluminum foil around them and continue baking.

More Desserts

The dessert that follows a beautiful meal is somewhat like the finale of a sensitive play. It should complete and clarify the meaning of the entire production. The appetizer sets the stage. The central message revolves around the entrée. The vegetables, pastas, breads and garnishes support and complement it. Dessert closes the performance. If it's too rich and heavy, it overwhelms the theme. If the dessert is too mundane, it's anti-climactic. The dessert that ends a beautiful meal must be light and simple, yet glamorous and dramatic.

In this section you'll find light and airy production numbers that great hotel chefs choose to conclude sumptuous banquets. If you think these desserts--Charlotte Russe, page 163, Berry Bavarian, page 166, and Lemon Cheese Soufflé, page 166--need a chef's skill to prepare, read the recipes. They take no special skills, and can be prepared in advance.

Few desserts are as glamorous as fruit. The jewel colors and natural shapes of fruit are beautiful simplicity. The glamour comes from the garnish of a soft creamy sauce—such as Whipped Sour Cream Topping, page 168. Expect more than a murmur of appreciation when your guests discover that sour cream is a marvelous flavor complement to fruit.

A chilled frozen dessert provides a refreshing ending for a filling dinner. The very special frozen desserts such as Bali Hai Ice Cream, page 170, and Orange Freeze, page 173, have a surprise quality that comes from their uniquely delicious flavor.

Your guests will shower compliments on you when you make the final act of your next dinner a dessert that lets them remember the enjoyment of the entire production. But remember one thing. They'll be expecting you to top your performance next time.

WHIPPING SOUR CREAM

Sour cream brings out the full flavor of fresh, frozen or canned fruit. See Whipped Sour Cream Topping, page 168. But first, here are some tips to help you get perfect results.

1. One cup of dairy sour cream makes 1-3/4 to 2-1/2 cups whipped sour cream.

2. Sour cream whips best if it is *very* cold.

3. It takes 4 to 5 minutes to whip sour cream. This is considerably longer than sweet cream. If it takes longer than 5 minutes, the cream probably is not cold enough. Rechill and whip again.

4. Sour cream whips to soft peaks. It will never become very stiff or turn to butter—no matter how long it's whipped.

5. Whipped sour cream can be whipped again—several times if necessary. Chill completely each time and whip as before.

FROZEN DESSERTS

Pull out that neglected ice cream freezer and have some simple old-fashioned fun making homemade ice cream or sherbet. If you don't have a mechanical freezer, use the freezer section of your refrigerator.

Fast freezing is the most important factor in making smooth-textured ice cream. Follow your mechanical freezer instructions for icing and salting to give the best freezing conditions. If you use the freezer section of your refrigerator set it on the coldest setting and place the freezing tray in the coldest spot. Even under the best circumstances home freezers cannot begin to match the sub-zero temperatures used to freeze ice creams commercially. Homemade ice cream recipes attempt to compensate for this by requiring you to beat them as they freeze. This happens automatically in mechanical ice cream freezers. If you are freezing ice cream in the freezer section of a refrigerator, you must beat partially frozen ice cream to a mush two or three times during the freezing process. This will keep the ice crystals small and the texture creamy. Ingredients like gelatin, egg white, cream and fruit pulp also promote creaminess.

Ice creams and sherbets will not keep forever—particularly the homemade ones. Eat them as soon as they're made—that's the fun of it!

Strawberries Juliet

Our version of Strawberries Romanoff is easier and lower in calories.

2 pints fresh strawberries, washed and stemmed
1/4 cup sugar
1 tablespoon lemon juice
1 tablespoon Cointreau® liqueur,
   if desired

1 pint vanilla ice cream
1 (8-oz.) carton strawberry
   fruit-blended yogurt

Reserve 8 strawberries for garnish. Halve remaining berries and mix with sugar, lemon juice and Cointreau®, if desired. Refrigerate. At serving time, spoon halved strawberries into 8 sherbert glasses. Beat ice cream until soft. Fold in yogurt for marbled effect. Spoon sauce over berries immediately and garnish with whole strawberries. Makes 8 servings.

Ambrosia

Because ambrosia is the food of Greek gods, it must have a very special aroma and flavor.

2 medium oranges,
   peeled and sectioned
1 pint fresh strawberries, washed,
   stemmed and halved
1 (15-3/4-oz.) can pineapple chunks or
   1/2 small fresh pineapple, chunked

Orange Cream Topping, see below
1 large banana, sliced
1/2 cup toasted coconut

Orange Cream Topping:
3/4 cup dairy sour cream
2 tablespoons light-brown sugar

3/4 teaspoon grated orange peel
Dash salt

Prepare oranges, strawberries and pineapple; refrigerate. Prepare Orange Cream Topping. At serving time, slice banana and add to fruit. Alternate layers of fruit with coconut and Orange Cream Topping in 6 four-ounce parfait glasses. Makes 6 servings.

Orange Cream Topping:
Combine topping ingredients in a small mixer bowl. Place with beaters in freezer until well-chilled. Whip topping mixture until doubled in volume, about 5 minutes. Refrigerate.

Fresh Strawberries with Whipped Sour Cream Topping, on following pages

Chocolate-Rum Mousse

The French word mousse *actually means* froth. *This dessert mousse is light enough to follow a big dinner.*

1 cup (1/2 pint) dairy sour cream
1 cup (1/2 pint) whipping cream
1-1/2 teaspoons unflavored gelatin
2 tablespoons water
2 tablespoons milk
1/4 cup light-brown sugar,
   firmly packed

1/8 teaspoon salt
1 (6-oz.) pkg. chocolate morsels
1 teaspoon rum extract
1/2 teaspoon vanilla
2 egg whites

In a large bowl, combine sour cream and whipping cream; refrigerate. Soften gelatin in water in a heat-proof cup. Place cup in a pan of simmering water until gelatin is dissolved. Heat milk with half the brown sugar and all the salt in top of double boiler until sugar dissolves. Add chocolate morsels and continue heating until melted. Remove from heat. Blend in rum extract, vanilla and dissolved gelatin. Beat egg whites until frothy. Gradually add remaining sugar, beating until stiff but not dry. Stir about 1/4 of the beaten egg whites into chocolate mixture until blended. Fold in remaining egg whites. Without cleaning beaters, whip the cream mixture until stiff. Add chocolate mixture and fold until well blended. Spoon into a 1-quart serving dish or 8 individual sherbet dishes. Chill until set. Makes 8 half-cup servings.

Variations

Chocolate Charlotte: Line a 9-inch springform pan with split lady fingers, cut-side in. Fill with a double recipe of Chocolate-Rum Mousse. Makes 16 servings.
Chocolate Soufflé: Fasten a 2-1/2-inch-wide sturdy foil collar around a 6-cup soufflé dish. Fill with a double recipe of Chocolate-Rum Mousse. When set, remove foil collar. Makes 16 servings.
Chocolate-Rum Mousse Pie: Fill a 9-inch prebaked pastry crust with 1 recipe Chocolate-Rum Mousse. Makes 8 servings. For individual servings, spoon Chocolate-Rum Mousse into puff pastry, cream puff or tart shells.

Coconut-Boysenberry Mousse

A light frozen dessert. Try it with orange yogurt.

1 cup (3-1/2-oz. can) coconut, toasted
1 cup (1/2 pint) whipping cream
1 egg white
2 tablespoons sugar

1/4 teaspoon vanilla
1 (8-oz.) carton boysenberry
   fruit-blended yogurt

To toast coconut, preheat oven to 350°F (177°C). Spread coconut evenly over a shallow pan. Bake, stirring often, 8 to 12 minutes or until golden. Turn freezer control to coldest setting. Combine whipping cream, egg white, sugar and vanilla in a bowl and beat until stiff. Fold in yogurt and toasted coconut. Reserve some coconut for garnish. Spoon into an ice tray; freeze until firm. Makes 4 to 6 servings.

Charlotte Russe

Charlotte Russe is a Bavarian cream in a lady-finger-lined mold. Very special.

11 or 12 lady fingers,
   split lengthwise
4 eggs, separated
2 cups milk
2 envelopes unflavored gelatin
1/2 cup sugar

1/4 teaspoon salt
1/2 teaspoon vanilla
1/4 cup fresh lemon juice
1 tablespoon grated lemon peel
2 cups (1 pint) dairy sour cream
1/4 cup sugar

Line sides of a 9-inch springform pan with split lady fingers, cut-side in. Beat egg yolks and milk in top of a double boiler. Blend in gelatin, 1/2 cup sugar and salt. Cook over boiling water, stirring constantly until custard coats a metal spoon. Remove from heat. Stir in vanilla, lemon juice and lemon peel. Let stand at room temperature. Empty sour cream into a large mixer bowl. Place with beaters in freezer to chill. Beat egg whites until frothy. Gradually add 1/4 cup sugar, beating until stiff and glossy. Without cleaning beaters, whip chilled sour cream until doubled in volume, about 5 minutes. Combine egg whites, whipped sour cream and custard; fold until well-blended. Pour into lady-finger-lined pan. Refrigerate until set. Remove sides from pan and serve. Makes 12 to 14 servings.

Strawberry-Yogurt Shimmy

Not only for calorie watchers. Try it with other yogurt and gelatin flavors.

1 (3-oz.) pkg. strawberry gelatin
3/4 cup boiling water
3/4 cup ice water

1 (8-oz.) carton strawberry
   fruit-blended yogurt
Dairy sour cream for topping

Dissolve gelatin in boiling water. Add ice water and chill to consistency of unbeaten egg white. Whip thickened gelatin until fluffy. Fold in yogurt until blended. Refrigerate until set. Spoon into dessert dishes; top with sour cream. Makes 4 to 6 servings.

Confetti Cream Cake

A spectacular dessert. Choose other gelatin flavors to match your party color scheme.

1 (3-oz.) pkg. *each* orange,
   lime and strawberry gelatin
5-1/4 cups boiling water
Crumb Crust, see below
1 (3-oz.) pkg. lemon gelatin
1/4 cup sugar

1 cup boiling water
1 cup (1/2 pint) whipping cream
1 (8-oz.) pkg. cream cheese,
   room temperature
1-1/2 recipes Whipped Cream Topping,
   page 144

Crumb Crust:
1 cup graham cracker crumbs
   (12 crackers)

1 tablespoon sugar
2 tablespoons butter, melted

Prepare "confetti" by dissolving each package of orange, lime and strawberry gelatin in 1-3/4 cups boiling water. Pour each gelatin mixture into a shallow pan and chill until set. Cut in small cubes. Prepare Crumb Crust; set aside. Dissolve lemon gelatin and sugar in 1 cup boiling water. Cool to room temperature. Whip cream until stiff; refrigerate. In a large bowl, beat cream cheese until smooth. Gradually beat in cooled lemon gelatin. Fold in whipped cream; blend well. Using a spatula, scoop "confetti" into cream cheese mixture. Gently fold together and pour into springform pan. Refrigerate several hours until set. Prepare Whipped Cream Topping, page 144. Remove sides from springform pan and frost cake with topping. Refrigerate until serving time. Frosting will hold several hours. Makes 16 servings.

Crumb Crust:
Combine crust ingredients and press onto bottom of a 9-inch springform pan.

Note
To hold frosted cake for 24 hours, add 1 teaspoon unflavored gelatin, softened in 2 tablespoons water, to topping according to directions for Whipped Cream Frosting, page 144.

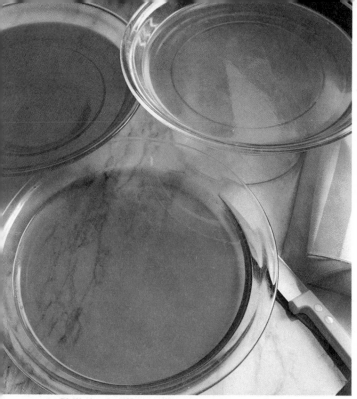

1. Chill the 3 different flavored gelatins in 3 pie plates or shallow pans. When set, cut in small cubes.

2. Combine the crust ingredients and press into the bottom of a springform pan.

How To Make Confetti Cream Cake

3. With a spatula, gently fold the gelatin cubes into the cream cheese mixture. Pour into the springform pan. Refrigerate until cake is set.

4. Remove sides from the pan. Frost the cakes with Whipped Cream Topping. Refrigerate until ready to serve.

Berry Bavarian

This recipe strays from the traditional but only to lower the calories a bit.

1 (10-oz.) pkg. frozen raspberries, thawed
2 teaspoons unflavored gelatin
2 tablespoons water
1 cup half-and-half

1/2 cup sugar
2 teaspoons lemon juice
1 cup (1/2 pint) dairy sour cream

Drain raspberries; reserve syrup. Soften gelatin in water. In top of double boiler, combine half-and-half, sugar and softened gelatin. Heat, stirring constantly just until sugar and gelatin have dissolved. Add 2 tablespoons reserved raspberry syrup. Cool to room temperature. Press raspberries through strainer to remove seeds. Stir lemon juice into purée. Spoon sour cream into a small mixer bowl. Place with beaters in freezer until ice crystals begin to form around outside of sour cream. Remove from freezer and beat on high speed 4 to 5 minutes or until doubled in volume. Fold with raspberry purée into cooled half-and-half mixture. Pour into a 1-quart mold. Refrigerate until set. Unmold to serve. Makes 6 to 8 servings.

Variation

Strawberry Bavarian: Substitute frozen strawberries for raspberries. Decrease sugar to 1/3 cup.

Lemon Cheese Soufflé

This mock soufflé is an elegant light dessert that can double as a glamorous molded salad.

2 envelopes unflavored gelatin
1/3 cup water
1 (3-1/2- or 4-oz.) pkg. lemon
   pudding and pie-filling mix
   (not instant)
2 cups milk
1/4 cup sugar

2 eggs, separated
2 tablespoons lemon juice
1 teaspoon grated lemon peel
2 cups (1 pint) small curd cottage cheese
1/3 cup chopped pecans
1 cup (1/2 pint) dairy sour cream

Fasten a 2-1/2-inch-wide aluminum foil collar around top of a 1-quart soufflé dish. Soften gelatin in water in a cup. Cook pudding mix with milk according to package directions. Stir in softened gelatin and sugar until dissolved. Beat egg yolks in a large bowl. Gradually add hot pudding, lemon juice and peel, stirring constantly. Cover surface of pudding with wax paper and cool to room temperature. Do not refrigerate or gelatin will set. When thoroughly cooled, blend in cottage cheese and pecans. Spoon sour cream into a small bowl. Place with beaters in freezer to chill. Beat egg whites until stiff but not dry. Without cleaning beaters, whip chilled sour cream on high speed 4 to 5 minutes or until doubled in volume. Fold into egg whites. Fold whipped mixture into pudding and pour into soufflé dish. Refrigerate until set. Makes 8 to 10 servings.

Boysenberry Torte

Not really a torte, but it has the ingredients, the beauty and the delicious flavor.

1 (8-1/2-oz.) pkg. chocolate wafers,
   crushed (about 2 cups)
2 tablespoons melted butter,
   if desired
1/2 cup (1 stick) butter,
   room temperature
2 cups powdered sugar
2 eggs

1 teaspoon grated lemon peel
1 (2-1/8-oz.) pkg. chopped pecans
   (1/2 cup)
2 cups (1 pint) whipping cream
1/4 cup granulated sugar
2 (8-oz.) cartons boysenberry
   fruit-blended yogurt

Reserve 1/2 cup crushed wafers. Press remaining crushed wafers onto bottom of a 9-inch square or an 11" x 7" x 2" baking dish. For a firmer crust, blend crumbs with 2 tablespoons melted butter. Cream 1/2 cup butter with powdered sugar. Add eggs, 1 at a time, beating until smooth and creamy. Stir in lemon peel. Drop creamed mixture by tablespoonfuls onto crushed wafers. Spread carefully to prevent mixing with crumbs. Sprinkle pecans over creamed mixture. Pour cream in a small bowl. Refrigerate with beaters until well-chilled. Whip cream until frothy. Gradually add granulated sugar and beat until stiff. Fold in yogurt. Spread mixture evenly over nuts. Sprinkle with reserved crushed wafers and refrigerate 1 to 2 hours. Cut in squares to serve. Makes 9 to 12 servings.

Variation

For a cool look, substitute lime yogurt for boysenberry.

Coeur à la Crème

Fresh cheeses and cream in a heart-shaped mold surrounded by chunks of colorful fresh fruit.

1 (8-oz.) pkg. cream cheese,
   room temperature
2 cups (1 pint) small curd cottage cheese

1/4 cup whipping cream
Fresh cut fruit: strawberries,
   peaches, pears, pineapple, apples

Blend cream cheese. Beat in cottage cheese until smooth. Whip cream until stiff. Fold into cheese mixture. Line a large strainer or coeur à la crème mold with 3 layers of cheesecloth. Fill with cheese mixture. Cover with cheesecloth and a flat plate that fits inside the strainer or mold to press down on the cheese mixture. Place a heavy object on top. Support strainer or mold on rim of a large deep bowl. Refrigerate and drain at least 12 hours. To serve, invert strainer or mold onto serving platter; remove cheesecloth. Surround with cut fruit. Makes 6 to 8 servings.

Variation

Pashka: Add 1/3 cup sugar and 1/2 teaspoon vanilla with cheeses. Fold in 1 cup chopped candied or dried fruit and 1/2 cup blanched slivered almonds before pressing into mold. Serve garnished with candied fruit and nuts. Pashka is a traditional Russian Orthodox Easter dessert. It is molded in a pyramid shape and decorated in Easter motifs.

Quick Peach Brûlée

Sounds French—but you won't find it in a French cookbook because it's a famous Creole recipe.

1 (1-lb. 13-oz.) can peach halves,
   well-drained
2 cups (1 pint) dairy sour cream,
   room temperature
1 tablespoon granulated sugar

1/2 teaspoon grated orange or
   lemon peel
3/4 cup light-brown sugar,
   firmly packed

Arrange peach halves in a 9-inch glass pie plate. Blend sour cream, granulated sugar and orange or lemon peel. Spread over fruit. Just before serving, sprinkle brown sugar evenly over sour cream layer, completely covering the entire surface. Broil 3 inches from broiler 1 to 3 minutes or until sugar melts. Serve *immediately* or surface will become very liquid. Makes 6 to 8 servings.

Whipped Sour Cream Topping

Perfect for fruit and lower in calories than whipped cream.

1 cup (1/2 pint) dairy sour cream
2 tablespoons sugar

Dash salt
1/2 teaspoon vanilla

Combine all ingredients in a small mixer bowl. Place bowl and beaters in freezer. When ice crystals begin to form around outside of sour cream, remove from freezer and beat on high speed 4 to 5 minutes or until doubled in volume. The sour cream will thin at first. Makes about 2 cups.

Whipped Crème Fraîche

A beautiful blend of whipped cream and sour cream—the best of both.

1/2 cup dairy sour cream
1/2 cup whipping cream
2 tablespoons sugar

1/2 teaspoon vanilla
Dash salt

Combine sour cream and whipping cream in a small mixer bowl. Refrigerate with beaters until well chilled. Beat creams until frothy. Gradually add sugar, vanilla and salt, beating until quite stiff. Refrigerate until serving time. Will maintain consistency 1 to 2 hours. Makes about 2 cups.

Variation

Orange Creme Fraîche: Add 1 tablespoon orange juice, 1 teaspoon lemon juice and 1/2 teaspoon grated orange peel.

Cottage Cheese Fluff

Delicious and chock-full of protein. Try it on peaches, pineapple, berries, pears or grapes.

1 cup (1/2 pint) dairy sour cream
1/4 cup sugar
1/2 teaspoon lemon juice

1/8 teaspoon cinnamon
1 cup (1/2 pint) small curd
  cottage cheese ·

Combine sour cream, sugar, lemon juice and cinnamon in a small mixer bowl. Place with beaters in freezer until *very* cold. Beat sour cream mixture until thick and doubled in volume, about 5 minutes. Fold in cottage cheese and refrigerate. Will maintain consistency several hours. Makes about 2-1/2 cups topping.

Variations

Cherry-Fluff Parfait: Add 1/2 teaspoon nutmeg to topping. Alternate with 1 (1-lb. 5-oz.) can cherry pie filling and 1 cup graham cracker crumbs (12 crackers) in 8 parfait glasses.

Hindu-Fluff Parfait: Omit cinnamon and lemon juice; add 1/4 teaspoon each almond extract, lemon extract and ground cardamom. Spoon into dessert glasses. Add drained peach halves and additional topping. Garnish with toasted slivered almonds.

Lemon-Buttermilk Ice Cream

Easy and delicious in your mechanical ice cream freezer.

1 envelope unflavored gelatin
1/4 cup water
3 cups buttermilk
2 cups (1 pint) whipping cream
1 (6-oz.) can frozen lemonade concentrate,
  thawed

3/4 cup sugar
2 tablespoons vanilla
1-1/2 teaspoons grated lemon peel
1/4 teaspoon salt
10 drops yellow food coloring

Soften gelatin in water in a heat-proof cup. Place cup in a pan of simmering water until gelatin is dissolved. Blend in remaining ingredients; stir in dissolved gelatin. Pour into ice cream freezer container. Let can revolve a few minutes to dissolve sugar before adding ice. Add ice and salt to freezer. Complete freezing process following equipment instructions. Makes 2-1/2 quarts ice cream.

Bali Hai Ice Cream

Every taste reminds you of your own special island.

1 egg, separated
1 (6-oz.) can frozen lemonade concentrate,
    thawed
1/2 cup sugar
2 tablespoons lemon juice
2 cups (1 pint) dairy sour cream
2 ripe medium papayas, mashed
    (about 1-1/2 cups)

2 small bananas, peeled and mashed
Food coloring, if desired
Toasted shredded coconut,
    for garnish
Chopped macadamia nuts,
    for garnish

Turn freezer control to coldest setting. In a large bowl, beat egg yolk. Blend in lemonade concentrate, sugar and lemon juice. Blend in sour cream and fruit. Beat egg white until soft peaks form. Fold into sour cream mixture. Pour into a 9-inch square baking dish or 2 ice trays and freeze. When ice crystals begin to form, turn into a large bowl and beat with electric mixer to consistency of soft mush. Return to dish or trays and freeze. Repeat 2 or 3 times for best texture. If ice cream seems pale, add food coloring. Garnish with toasted shredded coconut or chopped macadamia nuts. Makes 1-1/2 quarts ice cream.

Peach Ice Cream

Peaches and sour cream blend for old-fashioned goodness.

1 egg
1 cup (1/2 pint) dairy sour cream
1 cup (1/2 pint) whipping cream
1 cup sugar

2 tablespoons lemon juice
1/2 teaspoon vanilla
2 cups diced fresh peaches
    (about 4 or 5 medium)

Turn freezer control to coldest setting. Beat egg in a large bowl. Blend in remaining ingredients. Pour into a 9-inch square baking dish or 2 ice trays and freeze. When ice crystals begin to form, turn into a large bowl and beat with electric mixer to consistency of soft mush. Return to dish or trays and freeze. Repeat 2 or 3 times for best texture. Makes 6 to 8 servings.

Note

This may also be made in a mechanical ice cream freezer. Fill freezer container with ice cream mixture and freeze according to freezer instructions.

Cool Orange Sherbet

Refreshing and different served in hollowed-out orange cups.

1-1/2 teaspoons unflavored gelatin
2 tablespoons water
2-1/2 cups buttermilk
1/2 cup sugar
1 (6-oz.) can frozen orange juice concentrate

2 tablespoons lemon juice
1 egg, separated
5 drops yellow food coloring
1 drop red food coloring

Turn freezer control to coldest setting. Soften gelatin in water in a heat-proof cup. Place cup in a pan of simmering water until gelatin is dissolved. Strain buttermilk to remove butter particles. Blend with sugar, juice concentrate, lemon juice, egg yolk and food coloring. Stir in dissolved gelatin. Beat egg white until soft peaks form. Fold into buttermilk mixture. Pour into a 9-inch square baking dish or 2 ice trays and freeze. When ice crystals begin to form, turn into a large bowl. Beat with electric mixer to consistency of soft mush. Return to dish or trays and freeze. Repeat 2 or 3 times for best texture. Makes 6 to 8 servings.

Lime Sherbet

Cool and refreshing nourishment.

1 (3-oz.) pkg. lime gelatin
2/3 cup sugar
1 cup boiling water

2 cups buttermilk
1 tablespoon lemon juice
1 teaspoon grated lemon peel

Turn freezer control to coldest setting. In a large bowl, combine gelatin, sugar and boiling water. Stir to dissolve. Cool to room temperature. Strain buttermilk to remove butter particles. Blend buttermilk, lemon juice and lemon peel into gelatin mixture. Pour into a 9-inch square baking dish or 2 ice trays and freeze. When ice crystals begin to form, turn into a large bowl. Beat with electric mixer to consistency of soft mush. Return to dish or trays and freeze. Repeat 2 or 3 times for best texture. Makes 6 to 8 servings.

Buttermilk-Pineapple Sherbet

We get requests for this over and over again.

1 (8-3/4-oz.) can crushed pineapple	1 egg, separated
1/2 cup sugar	1 tablespoon lemon juice
1/4 teaspoon salt	2-1/2 cups buttermilk
1 teaspoon unflavored gelatin	

Turn freezer control to coldest setting. Drain pineapple; reserve syrup. Combine reserved syrup, sugar, salt and gelatin in a saucepan. Heat until sugar and gelatin are completely dissolved. Cool. Beat egg yolk in a large bowl. Blend in cooled syrup, lemon juice and buttermilk. Fold in drained pineapple. Beat egg white until soft peaks form. Fold into pineapple mixture. Pour into a 9-inch square baking dish or 2 ice trays and freeze. When ice crystals begin to form, turn into a large bowl and beat with electric mixer to consistency of soft mush. Return to dish or trays and freeze. Repeat 2 or 3 times for best texture. Makes 6 to 8 servings.

Orange Freeze

A dessert treat with a minimum of calories.

1/2 cup orange juice	1/4 teaspoon salt
1/4 cup honey	1 tablespoon lemon juice
1 (8-oz.) carton orange fruit-blended yogurt	2 egg whites

Turn freezer control to coldest setting. Blend orange juice with honey. Add yogurt, salt and lemon juice. Mix thoroughly. Pour into an ice tray; freeze until nearly firm. When orange mixture is nearly frozen, beat egg whites until stiff but not dry. Turn frozen mixture into a large bowl. Beat to consistency of soft mush. Fold in beaten egg whites. Return to ice tray and freeze. Makes 4 to 6 servings.

Move sherbet trays from freezer to refrigerator section 15 minutes before serving.

Frosted Lemon Cookies

A tender, lemony, mouth-watering cookie.

2 cups sifted flour
1/2 teaspoon baking soda
1/2 teaspoon baking powder
1 cup sugar

1/2 cup (1 stick) butter
2 eggs
1/2 cup buttermilk
Lemon Frosting, see below

Lemon Frosting:
2 tablespoons butter
2 cups powdered sugar
3 tablespoons lemon juice

Grated peel of 1/2 lemon
2 to 3 drops yellow food coloring

Preheat oven to 375°F (191°C). Butter cookie sheets. Sift and measure flour. Sift again with baking soda and baking powder. Cream sugar and butter. Beat in eggs 1 at a time. Blend buttermilk into creamed mixture. Add dry ingredients and mix thoroughly. Drop by teaspoonfuls onto buttered cookie sheets. Allow room for expansion. Bake 8 to 10 minutes or until edges are barely browned. Cool on rack. Prepare Lemon Frosting. Frost cooled cookies. Store in airtight containers with wax paper between layers. Makes 4 dozen cookies.

Lemon Frosting:
Combine frosting ingredients and beat until light and creamy.

Vanilla Cream Cheese Cookies

Our favorite buttery crisp cookie. They keep very well in airtight containers.

1 cup (2 sticks) butter
1 (3-oz.) pkg. cream cheese
1 cup sugar

1 egg yolk
2 tablespoons vanilla
2-1/2 cups sifted cake flour

Cream butter, cream cheese and sugar. Blend in egg yolk and vanilla. Mix in flour. Form dough into a log 1-1/2 inches in diameter and roll in wax paper. Refrigerate at least 2 hours. Preheat oven to 325°F (163°C). Cut log into 1/4-inch slices. Bake 25 minutes or until edges are golden. Cool on rack. Makes 5 dozen cookies.

Variations

Sparkly Cream Cheese Cookies: Press colored sugar crystals into rounds before baking.
Chocolate-Dip Cream Cheese Cookies: Dip rims of cooled baked cookies in melted chocolate morsels.

Marbled Brownies

It's hard to tell who enjoys these most—children or adults.

1 (8-oz.) pkg. cream cheese,
   room temperature
1/4 cup sugar
1 egg
1/2 teaspoon vanilla
1 (15-1/2- or 16-oz.) pkg. brownie mix

Water
1 or 2 eggs
1/2 cup chopped nuts, if desired
1 recipe Chocolate Sour Cream
   Topping, page 131

Preheat oven to 350°F (177°C). Butter a 9-inch square baking pan; set aside. Beat cream cheese until smooth. Blend in sugar, 1 egg and vanilla. Prepare cake version of brownie mix with water, eggs and nuts, if desired, according to package directions. Spread half the prepared brownie batter in buttered pan and pour cream cheese mixture over. Top with remaining brownie batter and swirl through cream cheese mixture to create marbled effect. Bake 45 minutes. Cool on rack 2 hours. Frost with Chocolate Sour Cream Topping, page 131. When topping is set, cut in squares and serve. Makes 16 brownies.

Golden Nuggets

Everyone should have some icebox cookie dough in the refrigerator.

3 cups sifted flour
1 teaspoon baking powder
1/4 teaspoon baking soda
1 teaspoon salt
1 cup (2 sticks) butter,
   room temperature
1/2 cup light-brown sugar,
   firmly packed

1 cup granulated sugar
1 teaspoon vanilla
1 tablespoon lemon juice
1/2 cup dairy sour cream
1 (3-1/2-oz.) can flaked coconut

Sift and measure flour. Sift again with baking powder, baking soda and salt. In a large bowl, cream butter, brown sugar and granulated sugar until fluffy. Mix in vanilla and lemon juice. Add dry ingredients alternately with sour cream, mixing just until well blended. Cover and refrigerate at least 2 hours. May be refrigerated for as long as 1 week. Freeze for longer storage. Preheat oven to 400°F (204°C). Shape teaspoonfuls of dough into balls and roll in flaked coconut. Bake on unbuttered cookie sheets 10 to 12 minutes or until golden. Cool on rack. Makes about 6 dozen cookies.

Variation

Nutty Drop Cookies: Stir 1/2 cup chopped nuts into dough with dry ingredients. Omit chilling period. Drop by teaspoonfuls onto unbuttered cookie sheet. Bake 8 to 10 minutes or until edges are golden.

Kipfel

You'll love these tiny nut-filled tarts! For a change, fill them with jam or preserves.

2-1/2 cups sifted flour
1/4 teaspoon salt
1 cup (2 sticks) butter

1 cup (1/2 pint) cottage cheese
Nut Filling, see below

Nut Filling:
1/3 cup milk
2 cups ground walnuts
2/3 cup sugar

1/2 teaspoon vanilla
Dash salt

Sift and measure flour. Combine with salt in a large mixing bowl. Using pastry blender, cut butter into flour until mixture resembles coarse meal. Add cottage cheese and mix until dough holds together. Shape into a ball, wrap in plastic wrap and chill 1 hour. Prepare Nut Filling; set aside. Preheat oven to 425°F (218°C). Butter cookie sheets. On well-floured board, roll dough 1/8-inch thick. Cut into 2-1/2- or 3-inch rounds. Place dab (less than 1 level teaspoon) of filling on center of each round. Moisten edge, fold in half and press to seal. Crimp curved edge and pierce top with fork tines. Bake on unbuttered cookie sheet 10 to 12 minutes or until nicely browned. Cool on rack. Makes about 40 small tarts.

Nut Filling:
Combine all filling ingredients and blend.

Chocolate Cream Cheese Fudge

The "unbeatable" fudge.

1 (3-oz.) pkg. cream cheese
1/4 cup (1/2 stick) butter

1 teaspoon milk
1 (13-oz.) pkg. walnut-fudge frosting mix

Butter an 8- or 9-inch square baking pan. Combine cream cheese, butter and milk in a stainless steel or enamel saucepan. Stir over low heat until melted and well-blended. Remove from heat. Stir in frosting mix. Return to medium heat. Cook, stirring until smooth and glossy. Turn into buttered pan and refrigerate until firm. Cut into squares. Makes about 1 pound fudge.

Pecan Chocolate Log

Children enjoy the stirring, shaping and rolling.

1 (6-oz.) pkg. chocolate morsels
1 (8-oz.) pkg. cream cheese,
   room temperature

1 teaspoon vanilla
1 (1-lb.) box powdered sugar
2 cups minced pecans

Melt chocolate over boiling water or on very low heat. Remove from heat and stir with rubber scraper to smooth. Blend in cream cheese and vanilla. Mixture will become glossy and seem to separate. Blend powdered sugar into chocolate mixture. Electric mixer may be used. Refrigerate until firm. Place half of chocolate mixture on wax paper. Form into a log 1-1/2 inches in diameter. Roll log in pecans. Repeat with remaining half. Wrap in foil or plastic wrap. Refrigerate until firm. Cut in 1/2-inch slices. Store in refrigerator. Makes 2 pounds candy.

Variations

Chocolate Spheres: Shape teaspoonfuls of chilled chocolate mixture into balls. Roll in chopped nuts or grated milk chocolate.
Chocolate Drops: Drop teaspoonfuls of warm chocolate mixture onto wax paper. Top with whole nuts, cherries or dried fruits.
Pecan Butterscotch Log: Substitute butterscotch morsels for chocolate morsels.

If you need a 2-1/2-inch cookie cutter, use an empty deviled ham can or 8-ounce tomato sauce can.

Nutrition & Dairy Foods

The signs of being well-nourished are similar to the signs of good general health: healthy skin, good muscle tone, adequate energy, a good appetite and a positive outlook. The symptoms of bad nutrition could be: susceptibility to illness, aches and pains, poor muscle tone, lack of energy, poor teeth, poor skin, poor hair and fingernails, depression or loss of appetite. One of our most serious and noticeable nutrition problems is caused by overeating.

Good nutrition is important during times of stress. The body needs more nutrients when under emotional or physical hardship: illness, injury, surgery, immobility, extreme physical exertion, exposure to extreme temperatures. Even pregnancy, obesity and growth are forms of physical stress. Any individual may be subject to one or several of these stresses at any one time. The best prevention or preparation for stress is a continually well-nourished body.

WHAT IS GOOD NUTRITION?

The science of nutrition is young. Historically, it's still a new idea that one can become sick from something one didn't eat! Eating a variety of nutritious foods is only the beginning of good nutrition. The body is not truly nourished until the nutrients have been absorbed in the digestive system and actually used in the cells of the body.

Essential nutrients are dependent on each other for greatest efficiency. For example, the absorption and use of iron is greatly improved by the presence of vitamin C, protein, copper and several of the B vitamins. Calcium absorption is improved by the presence of phosphorus, protein, butterfat and vitamins A, C and D (the sunshine vitamin). Therefore, a variety of foods should be eaten at the same time to provide a wide range of nutrients. The vitamins and minerals in a pill taken with a cup of coffee for breakfast are not nearly as effective as the vitamins in foods provided in a well-balanced meal.

HOW TO ACHIEVE GOOD NUTRITION

The easiest way to start preparing a well-balanced meal is to plan it according to the Basic Four Food Groups:

The Milk Group—3 or more glasses daily for children, 4 or more glasses for teenagers, or 2 or more for adults. Whole, lowfat or nonfat milk, butter-milk or yogurt (ice cream can supply part).

Breads and Cereals—4 or more servings daily. Enriched or whole grain breads or cereals.

The Meat Group—2 or more servings daily. Meat, fish, poultry or eggs, cottage cheese or ripe cheese. Dry beans, peas and nuts can serve as alternatives.

Vegetables and Fruits—4 or more servings daily. Include dark green or yellow vegetables and fruits or vegetables with vitamin C.

WHY IS MILK SO IMPORTANT?

Milk supplies more necessary nutrients than any other food. Without milk it would be difficult to get an adequate supply of calcium or riboflavin. Milk supplies protein, phosphorus, vitamin A and thiamine, too.

CALCIUM

Calcium is the most important nutrient milk provides. Although many foods contain small amounts of calcium, milk is the only common food that consumed in normal quantities can provide the recommended daily calcium allowance for children, teenagers and adults. Three-quarters of the calcium in the average diet comes from dairy foods.

The need for calcium in building strong bones and teeth is well known. But muscle and nerve tissues, especially the heart, also need calcium in the fluids surrounding them for smooth passage of nerve impulses and muscle contraction. Calcium is essential for the normal clotting of blood. The body loses calcium daily, especially during emotional upset or with perspiration from physical effort, heat or fever. Calcium is lost whenever the body is immobile or extremely inactive. When not enough calcium is provided in the diet, the body mechanisms withdraw necessary amounts from the bones. Inadequate calcium during the growing years results in slower growth, smaller stature and, possibly, rickets. Later in life, lack of calcium can cause irreversible bone damage or disease.

Milk provides phosphorus in the most workable proportion for helping the body to absorb and use calcium. The butterfat in milk contains vitamin A and an enzyme that also stimulates the absorption of calcium.

PROTEIN

Did you know dairy foods provide generous amounts of protein? A cup of cottage cheese or a quart of milk both provide about 30 grams of protein, over half the recommended daily allowance for an adult woman, and a significant contribution toward the requirements of men and teenagers. And with very few calories!

Most of the protein in milk is casein—a protein unique in milk. All milk protein is easy to digest and is complete, which means it contains some of each of the essential amino acids for body building.

RIBOFLAVIN

More than 50% of the riboflavin in our food supply comes from dairy foods. Riboflavin is water soluble and therefore is not present in the fat portion of milk products. Riboflavin is necessary in the process of converting food to energy. Its presence is revealed by clear skin, bright eyes and general good health.

VITAMIN A

A quart of whole milk provides about half the vitamin A requirement for children, and about a quarter of the requirement for teenagers and adults. Because vitamin A is fat soluble, the products with higher milk fat content contain relatively more. Just one tablespoon of butter provides almost 10% of the adult daily allowance. In milk fat, vitamin A is in "ready-to-use" form. Vitamin A helps prevent infection by maintaining healthy skin and mucous membranes. It also prevents night blindness.

PLANNING MEALS TO INCLUDE DAIRY FOODS

It doesn't matter a great deal whether we drink regular, extra-rich, lowfat or nonfat milk, or buttermilk, chocolate milk or any other beverages made from these milks. Eight ounces of any of these provide about one-third of the daily adult calcium requirement. For those who just won't drink their two to four glasses a day, there are other solutions. A carton of yogurt can be a breakfast, a snack, a sack lunch, a fruit salad dressing or a dessert. Ice cream provides milk nutrients, too.

COOKING FOR COMPLIMENTS
Deep appreciation is expressed to the following people who so generously gave their time to counsel in the writing of this chapter:
Dr. Zoe Anderson, Home Economics Department—Foods and Nutrition, San Diego State College.
Dr. George Briggs, Chairman, Department of Nutritional Sciences, University of California—Berkeley.
Mrs. Marie Harrington, Home Advisor—Nutrition, University of California, Agricultural Extension Service.
Home Economists of the California Dairy Council, Los Angeles.

How Dairy Foods Are Made

These are the basic procedures in getting dairy products ready for the consumer:

Separation—of the cream from the nonfat portion of the milk is the first step in the processing of milk. Cream is lighter than nonfat milk and therefore can be separated from it in a centrifuge. The cream and nonfat milk must be separated to standardize the fat content of each product.

Standardization—is the process of blending cream, whole milk and nonfat milk in various combinations to arrive at an exact fat content for the finished product. The fat contents of dairy products are set by law and have much to do with the texture, flavor and the cost of the finished products.

Fortification—is the process of adding nutrients such as concentrated nonfat milk, vitamins, minerals or other nutrients to a food.

Homogenization—is a process by which the fat particles of the milk are broken into hundreds of smaller particles. Milk or cream is heated to 130°F (54°C) and forced through very small openings, causing the fat particles to shatter. Homogenized milk has several advantages over unhomogenized milk: the flavor is richer, it stays fresh longer, gives more uniform cooking results and is easier to digest.

Not all products are homogenized. Whipping cream would not whip satisfactorily if the fat particles were too small. The cream used for churning butter and buttermilk is not homogenized.

Pasteurization—is a heat treatment to insure freedom from any harmful bacteria present in milk. It is accomplished almost simultaneously with homogenization. Milk is heated to a minimum of 161°F (72°C), held for a period of 15 seconds, then cooled immediately.

CULTURED PRODUCTS

The processing of cultured products and cheeses is more complicated and takes the standardized, pasteurized and homogenized milk through additional stages.

Yogurt, sour cream and buttermilk are cultured dairy products. Cheeses are also cultured, but in a different way.

To manufacture cultured dairy products in the creamery, a culture of selected laboratory-controlled microorganisms is added to warm pasteurized milk or cream and allowed to develop in temperature-controlled rooms. When the right degree of acidity has developed, the product is refrigerated immediately to stop the growth of the "culture."

Specific cultures are chosen for specific products because of the flavor or degree of acidity they will develop. Lowfat yogurt and buttermilk are very similar in fat content, yet acid and flavor differences are great because different cultures are used. Sour cream and buttermilk are made with similar cultures but still do not have the same flavor or texture because of the difference in fat content.

CHEESES

Cheese making is an ancient and fascinating process. Cheeses vary in flavor, color, shape, texture, caloric content and use. This diversity is created by using milks from different animals and with different fat levels. The cultures used and the length of aging are also varied. Cheese can range from moist cottage cheese to chewy mozzarella, hard Parmesan or moldy, soft Camembert.

The recipes in this book call for fresh, unripened cheeses—cottage cheese, hoop cheese and cream cheese. The processes for making each of these cheeses are very similar. Cream cheese is made from cream. Cottage cheese and hoop cheese are made from nonfat milk. Uncreamed cottage cheese and hoop cheese may be the same or nearly the same as the bakers' cheese, pot cheese or farmer cheese.

To make cottage or hoop cheese curd, pasteurized nonfat milk is put into a large vat and warmed to about 76°F (24°C). A laboratory-controlled culture is added and the mix is held at a set temperature until a specific acid level develops and the "custard" is set. The "custard" is cut into small cubes with a wire cheese knife. The spacing of the wires varies with the size of curd desired. The temperature of the vat is raised to approximately 135°F (57°C) to pull the clear yellow whey from the cheese curd. Curds are a concentration of most of the protein in the milk. They are thoroughly washed with clear water and drained.

Salt and cream are mixed with drained cottage cheese curd to make cottage cheese. Lowfat cottage cheese, only partially creamed, is made by mixing salt, concentrated nonfat milk and just a small amount of cream with the nonfat cottage cheese curd.

Hoop cheese is plain large curd cottage cheese pressed together and packaged. Some salt is added in processing.

BUTTERMILK

Buttermilk is normally a byproduct of butter. Anyone who has overbeaten whipped cream has an idea how butter is extracted from cream. As the chilled cream is beaten, the fat globules begin to clump together. Soon the smooth cream separates into light yellow creamy butter and a thin liquid called buttermilk.

BUTTER

Salted butter is generally preferred in the United States for eating. Unsalted or sweet butter is preferred in Europe. Salted butter keeps a bit longer, but sweet butter is wonderful for baking.

FROZEN DESSERTS

Frozen desserts of fine texture and flavor are no accident. Expert formulation, finest quality ingredients and ultrahigh-speed freezing equipment are responsible for quality ice creams, ice milks and sherbets. The primary difference between various types of frozen desserts is their fat content. Products range from sherbets with 1.25% milk fat, to ice cream with as high as 14%. The processing is essentially the same. The liquid ingredient (cream or other liquid), sugar and flavorings are put into huge cylinder freezers. They are whipped together and frozen until the mixture reaches a soft consistency. This soft ice cream is poured into cartons, sealed and moved immediately to the subzero freezing mechanism which freezes it rapidly to preserve the creamy texture.

IMITATION DAIRY PRODUCTS

An imitation dairy product is, by law, a product made from fresh nonfat milk and vegetable fat—like imitation ice milk, imitation sour cream and imitation ice cream. It contains the same amount of protein and calcium as the natural milk product because it is made from milk. Imitation dairy products are not lower in fat and calories than natural dairy products; the amount of fat must be the same, so the calories are about the same, also. The advantage of imitation dairy products is lower cost.

Easy Ways To Measure Dairy Foods

BUTTER

Measure butter while firm. It measures the same when melted.

1 stick butter = 1/2 cup or 8 tablespoons
1/2 stick butter = 1/4 cup or 4 tablespoons
1/4 stick butter = 2 tablespoons
1 pat butter = a 1/4-inch slice of the stick or 1-1/2 teaspoons

SOUR CREAM, COTTAGE CHEESE, YOGURT

Measure in standard measuring spoons or graduated measuring cups, the ones you use for sugar and flour. Level with a straight-edged spatula. It's easy to overmeasure in glass measuring cups because the measuring line is not level with the top of the cup.

Let the carton do the measuring whenever possible:

1 pint cottage cheese or sour cream
  = 2 cups or 16 ounces volume
1/2 pint cottage cheese or sour cream
  = 1 cup or 8 ounces volume

MILK, BUTTERMILK, HALF-AND-HALF, WHIIPPING CREAM

Measure in glass measuring cups and check measurement at eye level. Use buttermilk in old-fashioned recipes calling for sour milk.

1 quart = 4 cups or 32 ounces volume
1 pint = 2 cups or 16 ounces volume
1/2 pint = 1 cup or 8 ounces volume

CREAM CHEESE, HOOP CHEESE

These can usually be measured by cutting.

An 8-ounce package = 1/2 pound or almost 1 cup
Half an 8-ounce package = almost 1/2 cup
A 3-ounce package cream cheese = 6 tablespoons or slightly more than 1/3 cup

Note: 8 ounces by volume is usually the same as, or at least similar to 8 ounces by weight. Exceptions include whipped or aerated products and products high in fat or sugar.

Equipment For Cooking With Dairy Foods

NECESSARY EQUIPMENT

Standard measuring cups & spoons.

Straight-edged spatula.

Enamel, glass, ceramic, stainless steel or non-stick pans—to make white sauces.

Double boiler.

Bain Marie or a chafing dish with a water bath beneath—for cooking and holding sour-cream sauces and other delicacies at gentle low temperatures.

Accurate thermostatically controlled appliances—for holding delicate sauces and for good baking results.

Pyrex, enamel and ceramic casseroles and baking dishes.

Wooden spoons and rubber scrapers—for stirring sauces. Metal spoons rubbing against metal pans, especially aluminum, cause milk and sour cream sauces to gray.

A wire whip—for quick and easy blending.

HELPFUL TO HAVE

Butter paddles—for making butter balls.

Butter molds.

Butter curler.

An ice cream scoop with a thin cutting edge.

A coeur à la crème mold.

CONVERSION TO METRIC MEASURE

WHEN YOU KNOW	SYMBOL	MULTIPLY BY	TO FIND	SYMBOL
teaspoons	tsp	5	milliliters	ml
tablespoons	tbsp	15	milliliters	ml
fluid ounces	fl oz	30	milliliters	ml
cups	c	0.24	liters	l
pints	pt	0.47	liters	l
quarts	qt	0.95	liters	1
ounces	oz	28	grams	g
pounds	lb	0.45	kilograms	kg
Fahrenheit	°F	5/9 (after subtracting 32)	Celsius	C
inches	in	2.54	centimeters	cm
feet	ft	30.5	centimeters	cm

LIQUID MEASURE TO MILLILITERS

1/4 teaspoon	=	1.25 milliliters
1/2 teaspoon	=	2.5 milliliters
3/4 teaspoon	=	3.75 milliliters
1 teaspoon	=	5 milliliters
1-1/4 teaspoons	=	6.25 milliliters
1-1/2 teaspoons	=	7.5 milliliters
1-3/4 teaspoons	=	8.75 milliliters
2 teaspoons	=	10 milliliters
1 tablespoon	=	15 milliliters
2 tablespoons	=	30 milliliters

LIQUID MEASURE TO LITERS

1/4 cup	=	0.06 liters
1/2 cup	=	0.12 liters
3/4 cup	=	0.18 liters
1 cup	=	0.24 liters
1-1/4 cups	=	0.3 liters
1-1/2 cups	=	0.36 liters
2 cups	=	0.48 liters
2-1/2 cups	=	0.6 liters
3 cups	=	0.72 liters
3-1/2 cups	=	0.84 liters
4 cups	=	0.96 liters
4-1/2 cups	=	1.08 liters
5 cups	=	1.2 liters
5-1/2 cups	=	1.32 liters

FAHRENHEIT TO CELSIUS

F	C
200°	93°
225°	107°
250°	121°
275°	135°
300°	149°
325°	163°
350°	177°
375°	191°
400°	204°
425°	218°
450°	232°
475°	246°
500°	260°

Index

A

All-In-One Dinner, 106
Ambrosia, 159
Appetizers, 23-32
Appetizers, Dips & Spreads, 23-39
Apple-Cream Custard Coffeecake, 20
Apricot Peach Glaze, 126-127, 129
Artichokes California-Style, 90-91
Aunt Vada's Best Banana Cake, 139

B

B.L.T.C.C. Sandwich, 41-42
Bacon-Stuffed Mushrooms, 25, 30-31
Baja Shrimp Salad, 65
Baked Potato With Sour Cream, 92
Bali Hai Ice Cream, 170-171
Banana Nut Bread, 116
Basic Buttermilk Cake, 135
Basic Dressing For Fruit Salad, 50
Basic Four Food Groups, 178
Basic Sour Cream Dressing, 48
Basic Sour Cream Sauce, 72
Bean Olé Dip, 33
Beef Stroganoff, 78-79
Berry Bavarian, 166
Berry Buttermilk Nog, 44
Beverages, 40-45
Blue Cheese Butter, 121
Borsch à la Crème, 63
Boston Brown Bread, 112, 116
Boysenberry Cream Puffs, 153
Boysenberry Torte, 167
Braunschweiger Spread, 38
Breads, 110, 112-120, 178
Breads & Butters, 110-123
Breakfast & Brunch, 7-22
Breakfast Rolls, 20-22
Broccoli en Casserole, 94
Butter, 24, 111, 121-123, 133-134,
    179-181
Butter Balls, 112, 122
Buttered Breadcrumbs, 120
Buttermilk, 4, 6, 40-41, 46-47,
    69-70, 110, 133-134, 178-181
Buttermilk Biscuits, 113
Buttermilk Bran Muffins, 115
Buttermilk Coolers, 41-42
Buttermilk Corn Bread, 115
Buttermilk Custard Pie, 146-147
Buttermilk Fried Chicken, 71
Buttermilk Pancakes, 12-13
Buttermilk-Pineapple Sherbet, 173
Buttermilk Waffles, 16

C

Cakes & Frostings, 133-134
Calcutta Dip, 35
California Fruit-Yogurt Mold, 62
California Shrimp Curry, 87
Canapés, 23-24
Can Opener Sour Cream Sauce, 72
Caraway Goulash, 86
Carrot & Raisin Salad, 53
Charlotte Russe, 163
Cheese Apple, 39
Cheese Blintzes, 16
Cheesecakes & Cheese Pies, 124-132
Cheeses, 179-180
Cherries Jubilee Glaze, 131
Cherry-O-Crab Appetizers, 25, 30
Chicken Curry, 82
Chicken Divan, 81
Chicken Paprikash, 84
"Chili" Tomato Soup, 63
Chilimex Casserole, 100-101
Chocolate Cream Cheese Fudge, 176
Chocolate Malt, 43
Chocolate-Marshmallow Pie, 150
Chocolate-Rum Mousse, 162
Chocolate Sour Cream Topping, 131
Clarified Butter, 111
Coconut-Boysenberry Mousse, 162
Coeur à la Crème, 167
Coffeecakes, 17-20
Combination Fruit Salad, 50-51
Confetti Cream Cake, 164-165
Confetti Egg Salad, 67
Conversion To Metric Measure, 182
Cooked Zucchini-Mushroom Salad, 56
Cookies, 174-175
Cool Lemon Pie, 146, 149
Cool Orange Sherbet, 172
Corned Beef Spread, 39
Cottage Cheese, 4, 6-7, 40-41, 46-47,
    69-70, 96, 124, 178, 180-181
Cottage Cheese Main Dishes & Vegetables
    96-109
Cottage Cheese Custard Pie, 149
Cottage Cheese Dip, 34
Cottage Cheese Fluff, 169
Cottage Cheese Pancakes, 14
Cottage Cheese Pastry, 156
Cottage Cheese Sandwich Ideas, 41
Cottage Cheese Soufflé, 15
Cottage Dressing, 49
Cottage Enchiladas, 102
Cottage Hollandaise Sauce, 71
Cottage Meat Loaf, 97
Cottage Pizza Bread, 120
Cottage Quiche, 11
Cottage Scrambled Eggs, 8
Crab & Water Chestnut Dip, 34
Crab Meat Casserole, 99
Cranberry Glaze, 130
Cream Cheese, 6-7, 23-24, 124, 145,
    180-181
Cream Cheese Pastry, 154

Cream Cheese Pie, 126-128
Cream Cheese Tea Sandwiches, 28
Cream Puffs, 153-155
Creamy Butter-Cheese Frosting, 143
Creamy Guacamole Dip, 34
Creamy Roquefort Dressing, 48
Creamy Scrambled Eggs, 8
Crème Vichyssoise Glacé, 63
Crusty Cheese Bread, 112, 117
Cucumbers In Sour Cream, 55
Cultured Products, 133, 179

D

Danish Cheese Balls, 52
Delectable Chocolate Cake, 139
Delightful Yogurt Pancakes, 14
Deluxe Sour Cream Cake, 136-137
Desserts, 70, 124-177
Deviled Ham Spread, 38
Devil's Dip, 32
Dilly Crab Spread, 38
Dips, 24, 32-36
Dried Beef Dip, 35

E

Easiest Chocolate Frosting, 142
Easy Hamburger Wellington, 86
Easy Ways To Measure Dairy Foods, 181
Eggs, 7-11
Emerald & White Vegetable Delight, 93
Equipment For Cooking With Dairy
    Foods, 181

F

Fabulous Biscuits, 113
Fabulous Buttermilk Donuts, 21
Family Pancakes, 12
Farmer's Chop Suey, 54
Festive Avocado Dip, 33
Fiftieth Anniversary Cake, 136-137
Fillet of Sole Gourmet, 84-85
Fluffy Buttermilk Muffins, 114
Freezing Dairy Foods, 6
French Apple Pie, 146-147
French Omelet For One, 9
Fresh Mushroom Salad, 55
Fresh Strawberries With Whipped Sour
    Cream Topping, 160-161
Freshness of Dairy Products, 4, 6
Frosted Lemon Cookies, 174
Frostings, 142-144
Frozen Desserts, 6, 158, 169-173, 180
Frozen Fruit Delight, 53
Fruit Ring Mold With Dressing, 60-61

G

Garlic Butter, 122
Garlic Fried Chicken, 82
General Rules For Cake Baking, 134
Ginger Cheese Balls, 52
Gingerbread, 138
Golden Nuggets, 175
Graham Cracker Crumb Crust, 156
Grasshopper Cream Cheese Pie, 125-127
Green And Gold Casserole, 108

Green Goddess Dressing, 49
Green Chili Dip, 35

H
Ham & Egg Casserole, 11
Hamburger Noodle Bake, 97
Hampshire Cole Slaw, 54
Hampshire Creamed Eggs, 10
Hearty Beef & Corn Casserole, 87
Herb Butter, 122-123
Herbed Tomato-Cheese Bread, 118-119
Horseradish Butter, 122
Horseradish Dip, 35
Horseradish Sauce, 74-75
Hot Chocolate, 41
How Dairy Foods Are Made, 179-180
Hurry-Curry Appetizer Meatballs, 25-26

I
Ice Cream, 6, 158, 169-171, 180
Iced Middle East Cucumber Soup, 58-59, 64
Imitation Dairy Products, 180
Instant Cheese Pie, 125-127
Instant White Sauce, 72
Instant White Sauce Mix, 71
Islander Buttermilk Nog, 45
Italian Butter, 121
Italian-Style Eggplant, 109

K
Kidney Bean Salad, 65
Kipfel, 176

L
Lasagne, 103
Layered Buttermilk Crumb Cake, 17
Layered Perfection Salad, 57
Lemon Butter, 121
Lemon-Buttermilk Frost, 43
Lemon-Buttermilk Ice Cream, 169
Lemon Cheese Soufflé, 166
Lemon-Lime Ring Mold, 57-59
Lemon-Orange Freeze, 44
Lime Sherbet, 172
Lime-Divine Pie, 148
Liverwurst Dip, 36
Lobster Newburg, 81
Luscious Cherry-Cheese Pie, 146, 153

M
Manicotti, 104-105
Marbled Brownies, 175
Mashed Potatoes, 92
Meal-In-A-Pot, 98
Mellow Macaroni-Cheese Bake, 88
Miniature Cornucopias, 25, 32
Molded Citrus-Crunch Salad, 62
Molded Pineapple-Chutney Salad, 56
Molded Salads, 47, 56-62
More Desserts, 158-177
Muffins, 110, 112, 114-115
Mushrooms In Sour Cream Sauce, 27
Mustard Sauce, 73

N
New England Corned Beef Mold, 68

No-Bake Cheesecake, 126-127, 130
Noodle Ring, 107
Noodles Romanoff, 106
Nutty Blue Cheese Spread, 37
Nutrition & Dairy Foods, 178-179

O
Old-Fashioned Cinnamon Rolls, 22
Old-Fashioned Devil's Food Cake, 140
Olive Dip, 36
Omelet Fillings, 9
Open-Sesame Appetizer Meatballs, 26
Orange Buttermilk Nog, 45
Orange Freeze, 173
Orange Parfait Pie, 146, 152
Orange Sauce, 73

P
Pancakes & Waffles, 12-14, 16-17
Parmesan Butter, 121
Pastries, 145-157
Peach Ice Cream, 170
Peaches & Cream Pie, 146, 148
Pecan Chocolate Log, 177
Pecan Dressing, 74
Perky Dill Dip, 32
Petite Pâtes, 25, 29
Pies & Pastries, 145-157
Potatoes, 70, 74, 89-90, 92
Prune Cake, 140-141

Q
Quiche, 7, 11
Quick Bean Dip, 36
Quick Canapés, 24-25
Quick Cheese Danish, 20
Quick Hamburger Stroganoff, 80
Quick Peach Brûlée, 168
Quick Sour Cream Scalloped Potatoes, 74

R
Raspberry Glaze, 126-127, 132
Really Raisin Pie, 150
Red Caviar Dip, 36
Roquefort Cheese Dressing, 48
Roquefort Dip, 33
Roquefort Sauce, 73

S
Salad Dressings, 46-50
Salads, 46-68
Salmon Mousse, 67
Salmon-Cheese Casserole, 102
Saucy Angel Frosting, 142
Savory Clam Puffs, 27
Scrumptious Yellow Cake, 138
Secret Treasure Potato Casserole, 107
Sesame-Cheese Spread, 37
Sherbets, 6, 158, 172-173, 180
Shrimp Stuffed With Nutty Blue Cheese Spread, 25, 37
Simple Sirloin Dish, 104
Singapore Chicken Salad, 68
Snacks, 40-42
Snacks & Beverages, 40-45
Snow-Capped Cranberry Mold, 60
Soft-As-A-Cloud Sour Cream Biscuits, 113 •

Soufflés, 7, 15, 166
Soups, 47, 63-64
Sour Cream, 4, 6-7, 23-24, 46-47, 69-70, 76-77, 110, 133-134, 145, 158, 179-181
Sour Cream Coffeecake Sublime, 18-19
Sour Cream Dressings, 46-50
Sour Cream Main Dishes & Vegetables, 76-95
Sour Cream Muffins, 112, 114
Sour Cream Sauces on Vegetables, 70
Sour Cream Scalloped Potatoes, 90
Sour Cream Waffles, 17
South-Of-The-Border Chili Casserole, 100
Special Touches For Familiar Foods, 69-75
Spinach à la Crème, 93
Spirited Sprouts, 95
Spreads, 37-39
Standard Pastry Crust, 157
Strawberries Juliet, 159
Strawberry Glaze, 132
Strawberry Parfait Pie, 152
Strawberry Surprise Pie, 146, 151
Strawberry-Yogurt Shimmy, 163
Stuffed Baked Potatoes, 89
Stuffed Iceberg Lettuce, 64
Superb Chocolate Frosting, 142
Swedish Meatballs, 83

T
Taking Care Of Dairy Foods, 4-6
Tasty Appetizer Meatballs, 26
Thousand Island Dressing, 49
Three-Way Potato Salad, 66
Tortilla Chip Casserole, 88
Traditional Cheesecake, 126-127, 129
Tropical Banana Cream Pie, 152
Tropical Delight Punch, 45
Tuna Casserole, 98
Tuna-Noodle Casserole, 89
Tuna-Noodle Favorite, 99

V
Vanilla Cream Cheese Cookies, 174
Veal Strips In Herbed Sauce, 80
Vegetable Bake, 108
Very Special Creamed Carrots, 94

W
Waldorf Salad, 52
Whipped Chocolate-Cheese Frosting, 143
Whipped Cream, 134
Whipped Crème Fraîche, 168
Whipped Cream Topping, 144
Whipped Sour Cream Topping, 158, 160-161, 168
Whipping Sour Cream, 158

Y
Yeast Breads, 110, 117
Yeast Crescents, 117
Yogurt, 4, 6, 40, 46-47, 77, 133-134, 145, 179-181
Yogurt Delight, 44

Z
Zucchini With Sour Cream Topping, 95